D1784973

# Appropriating the Middle Ages
# Scholarship, Politics, Fraud

Studies in Medievalism XI

2001

# Studies in Medievalism

## Edited and founded by Leslie J. Workman

# Appropriating the Middle Ages
# Scholarship, Politics, Fraud

Edited by
Tom Shippey
with
Martin Arnold
(Associate Editor)

Studies in Medievalism XI 2001

Cambridge
D. S. Brewer

© Studies in Medievalism 2001

*All Rights Reserved.* Except as permitted under current legislation
no part of this work may be photocopied, stored in a retrieval system,
published, performed in public, adapted, broadcast,
transmitted, recorded or reproduced in any form or by any means,
without the prior permission of the copyright owner

First published 2001
D. S. Brewer, Cambridge


D. S. Brewer is an imprint of Boydell & Brewer Ltd
PO Box 9, Woodbridge, Suffolk IP12 3DF, UK
and of Boydell & Brewer Inc.
PO Box 41026, Rochester, NY 14604–4126, USA
website: http://www.boydell.co.uk

ISBN  0 85991 626 X

ISSN  0738-7614

A catalogue record for this book is available
from the British Library

Library of Congress Cataloging-in-Publication Data
applied for

This publication is printed on acid-free paper

Printed in Great Britain by
Antony Rowe Ltd, Chippenham, Wiltshire

# Studies in Medievalism

| Founding Editor | Leslie J. Workman |
| Editor | Tom Shippey (Saint Louis) |
| Associate Editor | Martin Arnold (Hull) |
| | |
| Corresponding Editors | Geraldine Barnes (Sydney) |
| | Ulrich Müller (Salzburg) |
| | Domenico Pietropaolo (Toronto) |
| | Toshiyuki Takamiya (Keio) |
| | Andrew Wawn (Leeds) |
| | |
| Advisors | Rolf H. Bremmer Jr (Leiden) |
| | Norman F. Cantor (New York) |
| | Alice Chandler (Princeton, New Jersey) |
| | Otto Gründler (Western Michigan) |
| | Paul Szarmach (Western Michigan) |
| | Richard J. Utz (Tübingen, Northern Iowa) |

**Studies in Medievalism** provides an interdisciplinary medium of exchange for scholars in all fields, including the visual and other arts, concerned with any aspect of the post-medieval idea and study of the Middle Ages and the influence, both scholarly and popular, of this study on Western society after 1500.

**Studies in Medievalism** is published by Boydell & Brewer, Ltd., P.O. Box 9, Woodbridge, Suffolk IP12 3DF, UK; Boydell & Brewer, Inc., P.O. Box 41026, Rochester, NY 14604–4126, USA. Orders and inquiries about back issues should be addressed to Boydell & Brewer at the appropriate office.

Submissions and inquiries regarding future volumes should be addressed to the Editor, **Studies in Medievalism**, English Dept., Saint Louis University, 221 N. Grand Blvd., St. Louis, MO 63103, USA, tel. 314–977–7196, fax 314–977–1514, e-mail <shippey@slu.edu>. Contributors should submit the original manuscript and one copy with an abstract: unsolicited manuscripts should be accompanied by a stamped self-addressed envelope. When a manuscript is accepted for publication, copy on an IBM-compatible disk will be required.

## Acknowledgments

The Editors make grateful acknowledgment for technical and other assistance to Saint Louis University and Hull University.

The device on the title page comes from the title page of **Des Knaben Wunderhorn: Alte deutsche Lieder,** edited by L. Achim von Arnim and Clemens Brentano (Heidelberg and Frankfurt, 1806).

The epigraph is from an unpublished paper by Lord Acton written about 1859, printed in Herbert Butterfield, **Man On His Past** (Cambridge University Press, 1955), 212.

# Studies in Medievalism

Volume XI 2001

Two great principles divide the world, and contend for the mastery, antiquity and the middle ages. These are the two civilizations that have preceded us, the two elements of which ours is composed. All political as well as religious questions reduce themselves practically to this. This is the great dualism that runs through our society.

Lord Acton

# Editorial Note

The last two issues of *Studies in Medievalism* have been devoted to the theme of "Medievalism in the Academy," and this topic continues to figure in the present volume – always, however, with a difference. Richard Utz's study of F.J. Furnivall points out that for all the respect paid to him by British and American scholars, and the genuine affection felt for him by German-speaking scholars, the latter group steadily and consistently refused to grant him, as it were, professional status as a "philologist." There has been more than one academy, and the nineteenth-century fissure between British and German ideas of the university – with the American academy between them, but tending more to the latter – has remained in existence in medieval studies up to the present. In a related way Geraldine Barnes's study of the American discovery of Old Norse – one of a series of works now appearing from Australia on the reception of Norse – does indeed consider the role of the academy, but notes also how this affected and was affected by much broader concerns of nationalism and self-image.

The two contributions by scholars from the Netherlands, Sophie van Romburgh on Franciscus Junius's entry into the field of Old English studies and Rolf H. Bremmer Jr on Junius as a Chaucer scholar, meanwhile take us back to a period when there was, in the modern sense, no academy: though having said that, it must immediately be conceded that the scholarship of such precursors of the modern university as Junius and his circle is highly impressive in any terms, and perhaps especially so when one considers their many other duties and activities. Betsy Bowden's study of the illustrations of the Canterbury prigrimage by William Blake and Thomas Stothard also contains a slight element of irony. Hardly any artist, perhaps, is better placed in modern academic standing than Blake, whose illustration has indeed been selected as a logo by the New Chaucer Society. Yet in his own time he faced competition on equal terms from artists who have received no such later validation; while he and his competitors, as Bowden shows, were also liable to be appreciated and understood in a way till now almost literally a closed book to the modern academic world, which is, entirely literally, pedestrian when not automotive.

Some contributions to issue XI, however, take us outside the academy. Werner Wunderlich's detailed study of the reworking of a

Mozart opera for a particular social event shows how music could be brought together with Merovingian history in the service of Bavarian politics; and shows also, with its extensive reference to musical medievalism, how frequently and powerfully the medieval world being rediscovered in the nineteenth century by historians and philologists was used in order to legitimise dynasties, to make political statements, to gain by no means transient political advantage. The suggestions sometimes heard that medieval studies (and medievalism) need to *acquire* contemporary relevance fail to notice how often and how much they have already had it. A similar point is made by Judith Johnston's study of the origin and reception of Lady Charlotte Guest's translation of *The Mabinogion*, a work still making its impact in popular culture, but one which is ambiguous both in its intention and its results. Should it have been left as the private property of its language group? Or was its "appropriation" by Victorian England (and since then of course by the Anglophone academy) an enrichment? The question arises for many works, with many different fates, from the *Grimms' Fairy Tales*, now universally known, to Lönnrot's immensely successful but still relatively nationalistically restricted reconstruction of the *Kalevala*.

Two final contributions remind us that medievalism also has a financial dimension. Without this it would not have been worthwhile for the "Spanish Forger" studied by John B. Friedman to create and sell his considerable *oeuvre*, one further example of which is detailed here, with implications as to the likely provenance of the forger himself. Stephen Watson further considers the whole phenomenon of the medieval as a tourist attraction, one of the most familiar and significant ways in which the medieval world is encountered by most people – but, of course, a way entirely outside the control of the academy and (perhaps as a result) too often felt to be beneath the dignity of its members. However, those who do not like the way in which the medieval is sold and packaged are obliged, in a democracy, to make their case and seek to persuade their fellows – as, to return to the beginning of this note, Furnivall did so engagingly and enthusiastically (if not philologically).

In a previous editorial note, to issue IX, it was remarked that medievalism ought to be seen as "inclusive of any and all previous attempts at rewriting and/or rethinking the medieval past," and I would like wholeheartedly to endorse this opinion, adding only the words "or re-imaging," so as to take in visual as well as literary media. There is no contribution in issue XI which addresses popular, commercial, or mass-cultural forms of medievalism, but these will be welcome in future issues as in past ones; as will entirely academic studies of the kind or kinds mentioned above.

After all, it could be said that there is no completely un-scholarly medievalism left in the world. Even the most unashamedly mass-cultural "Robin Hood" serial on TV will be found to derive from some scholarly edition of the past, albeit at twentieth-hand, while even the naivest viewing of a castle ruin is likely to be affected by some memory of teaching at school, however badly understood or dimly remembered. Nor are scholars as unaffected by early enthusiasms as they may feel obliged to pretend. Nor, finally, can any practising pedagogue in the medieval field in the present day afford to neglect any bait for his or her hook (though we should certainly try to provide better ones). Studies on both popular and academic topics will continue to be welcome for *Studies in Medievalism*, as indeed will studies of the many negotiations between them.

*Tom Shippey*
*Saint Louis University*
*August 2000*

While this volume was in press, all those connected with *Studies in Medievalism* were saddened to hear of the death, on April 1st 2001, of Leslie Workman, founding editor of the series, and main proponent, for many years, of medievalism as an academic field. His achievement has already been recognised in the volume *Medievalism in the Modern World: Essays in Honour of Leslie Workman* (Turnhout, 1998), edited by Richard Utz and Tom Shippey. We hope to commemorate Leslie further with sessions at future conferences, and a memorial issue of *Studies in Medievalism*.

# Why Francis Junius (1591–1677) Became an Anglo-Saxonist, or, the Study of Old English for the Elevation of Dutch[1]

## Sophie van Romburgh

The name of Francis Junius (1591–1677) is inextricably connected with the study of Old English, and his achievements have been lauded by historians of the discipline, yet his incentives for undertaking it in the first place have hardly been assessed.[2] An appreciation of his motivations appears to be of considerable value, however, because they reveal how Junius turned to the northern languages of the early Middle Ages, notably Old English, to elevate his mother tongue Dutch. They place his Germanic studies in a new perspective, and uncover a hitherto unrecognised connection between Old English studies and Dutch lexicography in the seventeenth century. In order to discover what induced Junius to involve himself with Old English, we should return to the early years of his studies, well before he made the *editio princeps* of the so-called Cædmon manuscript and of the Gothic Gospels, or acquired the expertise which was to qualify him as the greatest seventeenth-century philologist of the Germanic languages.[3] In this respect it should be borne in mind that Junius began to devote himself to the study of the Germanic languages only in his mid-fifties, after having spent a working life as a tutor and having examined classical art in his hours of study at the splendid London court of Thomas Howard, second Earl of Arundel. Old English was one of the languages Junius devoted himself to earliest, but it was not the beginning of his studies. Recently, Breuker has suggested in an excellent article that "Junius may. . . have studied Anglo-Saxon in 1649 in order to write a Dutch etymological dictionary."[4] Evidence in Junius's publications, his manuscript notes as well as his correspondence have now allowed me not only to confirm Breuker's assumption, but also to deduce that the compilation of an etymological dictionary of his mother tongue Dutch was Junius's very first Germanic project and his reason for undertaking the study of Old English – and of Frisian and Old Norse.

In the following I have tried to unfold my reconstruction. For ease of reference, I first present a summary of aspects of Junius's life prior to his involvement in the Germanic languages. Then I discuss the character of the Dutch etymological dictionary and the contextual factors which seem to have inspired Junius to undertake the writing of it. Finally, I assess the reasons why Junius turned to Old English for the purpose of the dictionary, and the place it received in it.

### Junius's life until the mid-1640s

Throughout his life, Junius moved in the upper circles of scholars, dignitaries, prelates and artists in both the Low Countries and England.[5] He was the son of Joanna (d.1591), the daughter of the Antwerp nobleman Simon l'Hermite, and Franciscus Junius (1545–1602), the French nobleman and Protestant theologian who was renowned for his philological work on the Bible and accepted the chair of Theology at Leiden University in 1592. Junius was first educated at the Latin School of his brother-in-law, the eminent Dutch humanist Gerardus Vossius (1577–1649), and studied artes and presumably Theology at Leiden from 1608, in the days of such philologists as Bonaventura Vulcanius (1538–1614) and Joseph Scaliger (1540–1609) in the tradition of the so-called Leiden Philological School.[6] His education made him thoroughly acquainted with the study of languages and the principles of etymology. For his future Germanic studies he could consequently revert to the methods acquired during his student days.

Junius began his career as a minister in 1617, but because of his refusal to take sides in the crisis dividing the Dutch Reformed Church, he resigned the ministry two years later. In 1622, after having stayed as a private man in Paris and London, he entered the service of the Earl Marshal of England, Thomas Howard (1585–1646), second Earl of Arundel, the art collector and connoisseur. During the next twenty-four years, Junius was a tutor to several members of the family, mostly at the family's magnificent London court. At the same time, he spent his leisure scouring classical literature in Arundel's library for references to the visual arts. These endeavours resulted in an unprecedented theory on the perception of art in classical antiquity, De Pictura veterum (1637), and a comprehensive encyclopaedia of classical artists and artefacts, published posthumously as *Catalogus artificum* (1694). In the later 1630s, he prepared English and Dutch translations of his art theory, titled *The Painting of the Ancients* (1638) and *De Schilder-konst der Oude* (1641) respectively.[7] They reveal a favourable attitude towards the northern vernaculars from a humanist steeped in the classics, and thus may have prepared the way for Junius's ensuing Germanic studies, as indicated below. Presumably no earlier than 1639, Junius became Arundel's librarian. Still in his patron's service, now as tutor to Aubrey de Vere (1626–1703), twentieth Earl of Oxford, he moved with his pupil to the Low Countries in the spring of 1642. He remained there for most of the next thirty-three years, but also made repeated stays of longer and shorter duration in England, including one in the years 1647/8 to 1651. It is to some two or three years after his return to the Low Countries that his earliest notes on Germanic languages can be traced back.

*The beginning of Junius's northern studies, including Old English*

While continuing to add occasionally to his art-historical projects, Junius began to involve himself with the study of his mother tongue, Old English and other Germanic languages during the first few years which he spent in the Low Countries again, that is, in the mid-1640s. Recently, Breuker has reconstructed on the basis of direct and indirect references that in the early 1640s Junius was still occupied with his tutorship and his art-historical projects – the *Catalogus artificum* and an enlarged edition of his art theory – while he displayed an acquaintance with various Germanic languages, Old English among them, in the later 1640s.[8] The assumption that Junius did not study the Germanic languages prior to the mid-1640s is supported by a lack of any references to such studies. In his commendable study on the Old Germanic studies of Junius's friend Jan van Vliet (1622–1666), Dekker has demonstrated that Junius did not include the Germanic material from Arundel's library in his studies at all, "since neither the Old High German nor the Old English glosses in the Arundel manuscripts (now British Library, MSS Arundel 293, 514, and 60, 155 respectively) occur among Junius' transcripts."[9] Especially note-worthy in this respect is the fact that Junius failed to collate MS Arundel 60 in his own copy of John Spelman's 1640 edition of the Old English Psalter (now Bodleian Library, MS Junius 33), notwithstanding his usual predilection for making collations.[10] Furthermore, Junius did not refer to Henry Spelman's *Archaeologus* (1626), an antiquarian encyclopaedia of legal terminology, in *De Pictura* and its translations, but did do so in his notes for the enlarged second edition, which suggests that he had only examined Spelman's book after having finished the first edition and the translations.[11] Finally, Junius did not share the particular interest of the circle of English Anglo-Saxonists in the Anglo-Saxon church or law.[12] Although these scholars might have introduced Junius to Old English, his interest was so overwhelmingly directed to the language, and this not even in order to publish an Old English dictionary, that his incentive for studying it may more likely be found elsewhere.[13]

Breuker came close to the motives of Junius's Germanic studies with his observation that "[t]o the earliest datable work belongs an etymological dictionary of Dutch."[14] A glimpse of such a dictionary can be found in two entries, on Dutch *vriend* "friend" and *vyand* "foe," which include Old English, Frisian, English and Greek and date from 1648–49.[15] These entries led Breuker to assume that "Junius may. . . have studied Anglo-Saxon in 1649 in order to write a Dutch etymological dictionary," as noted above. Further evidence for the onetime existence of such a dictionary Breuker found in Junius's reference to an entry *evangelie* "gospel" from "Etymologicum nostrum Teutonicum," in an alphabetical list of entries of Dutch monosyllabic words purportedly truncated from the initial letters of Greek words, and in a reference to such a dictionary by Junius's friend Johannes Fredericus Gronovius (1611–1671), to which I will return below.[16] In addition, Dekker has taken Junius's inclusion of notes on Dutch *bren* from "loose leaves containing Dutch etymologies" in the entry BERN in his English etymological dictionary *Etymologicum Anglicanum* (1743) as "further evidence that Junius had worked on a similar project for the Dutch language."[17]

Thanks to the many details of Junius's life which have come to light during my research for the edition of his correspondence, I have now been able to unravel that the very first project in Junius's Germanic studies was precisely the compilation of an etymological dictionary of Dutch, carrying the (working) title "Etymologicum Teutonicum," and that his motivations for doing so were founded in a desire to elevate his mother tongue. My reconstruction has led me to conclude that Junius's research for this dictionary formed the true stimulus to study Old English and such other Germanic languages as Frisian, Old Norse and Gothic. Thus, at least initially, Junius conceived his study of Old English as embedded in a larger programme – his search for the ancestry and origin of Dutch. In turn, Junius's lexicographical examinations of the ancient stages of his mother tongue can be seen to agree with contemporary endeavours in the Low Countries to advance and standardise the vernacular, as part of a more general trend towards the construction of a Dutch national or ethnic self. Junius's search for a Dutch identity thus inspired him to turn to the early Middle Ages and make his first strides in Old English studies. In what follows, I will first consider the information available on the dictionary itself, and attempt to unfold my reconstruction next.

*Junius's etymological dictionary of Dutch*[18]

Junius's "Etymologicum Teutonicum" appears to have been an ambitious undertaking. In May 1650, writing from London, Junius informed his nephew Franciscus Junius F.N. (1624–1678) in Amsterdam that

> I am now wholly applying myself to submitting to the press at the first possible opportunity an etymological dictionary, in which I have brought back several thousands of Dutch words to their Greek origins, having mostly sought the reasoning for the origins from ancient documents in the Franco-Celtic, Anglo-Saxon and Gothic languages.[19]

A year and a half later, when he returned with his treasure to Holland, his friends were impressed. Gronovius, for instance, reported in October 1651 that "Francis Junius . . . has a lexicon ready on the origins of our mother tongue, in which there is much excellent information from ancient Anglo-Saxon documents."[20] The next month, Gronovius also congratulated Junius in person on his "splendid work on Anglo-Saxon, or indeed on the origins of almost all vernacular languages in Europe today."[21] It is, incidentally, relevant to note that Junius seems to have used the term Teutonic to refer to the Dutch language, including Frisian and its earlier stages.[22]

The historian of Germanic linguistics, however, will look in vain for Junius's "Etymologicum Teutonicum." Notwithstanding its existence in manuscript in 1651, it was already dispersed into loose notes, presumably by Junius's own doing, in the mid-1650s. Initially, Junius probably had to postpone its printing due to pecuniary problems, since he had been expecting an outstanding stipend from the Arundel family for years and even was compelled to proceed against them in the mid- and later 1650s.[23] One of the reasons that Junius in 1655 claimed to need the money, for instance, was for him "to have Anglo-Saxonike, Runike, & Gothike letters cutt & cast," for "hee had by eight or tenn yeeres studie made some observations which were readie for the press."[24] In expectation of his stipend, he directed his attention to other projects and, when he gained access to Franconian manuscripts and the Gothic Gospels in 1654, came to study the Germanic languages of the early Middle Ages from a comparative perspective instead of deriving his etymologies from Greek, as Breuker has reconstructed.[25] In the course of a few years, Junius may have considered his previous work outdated by his wider resources of early medieval Germanic data and a new method.[26] In whatever way the sheets of the manuscript dictionary had diffused, he seems not to have regretted it. He only rarely used excerpts from the "Etymologicum" in his subsequent studies, and when he did, his brief introductions to quotations from it add to the impression that he had become displeased with it.[27]

Together with the above descriptions of the manuscript, the entries of the "Etymologicum Teutonicum" which Junius quoted in his published and unpublished work offer insight into its structure, much as its exact appearance obviously remains a matter of conjecture. I have recovered a dozen (parts of) such entries in all of Junius's published work and another two from a browse of MS Junius 116c to date, in addition to the aforementioned notes on *vriend, vyand* and *bren*, the reference to *evangelie* and the entries of Dutch monosyllabic words truncated from the first letters of Greek words.[28] Junius usually introduced the excerpts from the "Etymologicum" which he included in his other work with such phrases as "meanwhile, it will not trouble me to copy from my dispersed shreds of Netherlandic etymologies to this entry what occurred to me on this word [i.e. Dutch *kokeloer*] many years ago."[29] The etymologies themselves usually go back to Greek, illustrated by means of comparative evidence in contemporary languages, such as German, English, Frisian, Welsh, French, Spanish, and Danish, or quotations from Latin classical authors. The early medieval Germanic languages used in the retrieved etymologies are predominantly Old English, to a less extent Old Norse (or "Cimbric," as Junius called it, or Gothic, with which he still confused it), and sporadically Old High German (or "Franconian"). The following excerpt from the entry CHIRRE in Junius's English etymological dictionary, *Etymologicum Anglicanum*, may serve as an example of the nature and structure of the entries in the "Etymologicum Teutonicum:"

> I had already noted down my humble conjecture about everything in the Netherlandic Etymologicum, which it does not trouble me to add here in order to gratify those who like to appreciate a variety of conjectures: *karien, korien, koerien* "to wail like a turtle-dove or a pigeon." See what Kiliaan has on this word.[30] The Anglo-Saxons used *ceorian* for it; Runic **kur** is

"murmur, suppression of the voice;" finally, Danish *kæremæl* is "complaint." All these seem to have a great affinity with the word γαϱύειν, which is found with Pindar used in Doric for γηϱύειν "to sing, speak, sound". . .[31]

As we shall see below, Old English figures quite prominently in the retrieved excerpts from the "Etymologicum Teutonicum." Before considering the place of Old English in the dictionary, however, I will first discuss Junius's motivation to contribute to the elevation of Dutch by writing an etymological dictionary.

*The incentives and context for Junius's Dutch etymological dictionary*

Since Junius never seems to have explicitly formulated the purpose and aims of his Germanic studies, they must be assembled from his various writings composed before, during but also well after the early years of these studies, and be interpreted against the broader context of contemporary trends. His most comprehensive recollection of the incentives for his Germanic studies is the first section of his dedicatory letter to the Swedish Chancellor Count Magnus Gabriel de la Gardie (1622–1686) prefixed to his edition of the Gothic Gospels in 1665.[32] Junius opened this letter with a praise of Dutch, or "Teutonic." What is more, he expressed his admiration for the Gothic Gospels in terms of their usefulness for his search for the origin of Dutch. This is remarkable, for the Swedish Chancellor surely shared Junius's interest in Gothic, but by no means necessarily so his enthusiasm over the splendour of "Teutonic." Seen in this light, Junius's description of the motivation for his Germanic studies gains weight:

> Such a great splendour overflowed the ancient Teutonic language everywhere, that foreigners of great name in our century willingly granted it the primacy. . .; and, as I was intent on this fame of the most excellent language, it therefore also seemed disgraceful to me, besides others, not to know the earliest root, lineage and earliest childhood of the noble language, and not to know through which courses it proceeded to a loftiness which is also recognised by other peoples.[33]

The course of the argument, to which I will return below, is that despite his varied endeavours to find the origin of the language via "Theotiscan," or Old High German, and Old English, his searches had only received a true push forward upon his receipt of the Gothic Gospels in 1654. For our purposes, however, the principal point of this recollection is that Junius claimed to have directed his attention to the study of Germanic languages out of a desire to retrieve the origin and history of his mother tongue Dutch. Thus, he was led to approach the Middle Ages for the use he could make of the early northern vernaculars for the elevation of Dutch.

Such a motivation is supported by Joannes Graevius (1632–1703) in his "Vita" of Junius. Although he indicated that Junius's study of Old English was prior to his examinations of other older Germanic languages, Graevius did not suggest that it was either the beginning or the aim of Junius's studies. Instead, he recounted that Junius studied Old English in order to be better equipped for his work on the origins of Dutch and English:

> when having come across many ancient Anglo-Saxon books in England, he [i.e. Junius] began to cultivate that language, and when he realised that it was very useful for the illustration of Netherlandic, which was his vernacular, German and English, and for the examination of their genuine origins, he put much effort and toil into learning it thoroughly. Later he added to this a knowledge of all ancient northern languages, Gothic, Frankish, Icelandic, Cimbric – which is also called Runic – Frisian, as well as Welsh. . .[34]

The illustration of Netherlandic Junius undertook to do in his "Etymologicum Teutonicum;" that of English in what became the *Etymologicum Anglicanum*; but that of contemporary German Junius never took in hand, as far as is known.

The pride Junius took in his mother tongue and his actual contribution to its splendour by way of compiling the "Etymologicum Teutonicum" are explained by several contextual factors, factors which seem to have stimulated Junius's transition from the study of the visual arts of classical antiquity to preparing a Dutch etymological dictionary.

For the purposes of this paper, Junius's English and Dutch translations of his Latin art theory are relevant in at least two respects. Firstly, they reveal that he was equally well at home in Dutch as in English, notwithstanding his previous inexperience in writing or composing expository prose in either of them; after all, his education, studies and correspondence had always been conducted in Latin, except for the Dutch sermons he must have preached during his brief ministry.[35]

Secondly, and more importantly, they reveal that Junius considered the status and quality of the vernaculars sufficiently high to express scholarly topics and bear the voices of the classics. In the Renaissance, such had already been accepted by Englishmen as regards their own mother tongue. There were accordingly quite a number of English translations of the classics to serve Junius as example.[36] In the Low Countries, on the other hand, the vernacular had begun to gain prestige in this respect somewhat later than in England.[37] Far fewer translations of classical texts had consequently yet been prepared in Dutch.[38] The acceptance of the vernacular in England, as well as encouragements by the Dutch authors Johan van Heemskerck (1597–1656) and Jan de Brune (1616–1649), a nephew of Junius, both of whom came to see him in London in the mid- and later 1630s, may well have inspired his decision to translate his art theory into Dutch – which he actually undertook to do earlier than the English one, although he finished and published it later. However, Junius was compelled to enrich his mother tongue in order to make it suit the topic of his book. It was exactly his successful embellishment of Dutch which was praised by his nephew Jan in the introduction to the translation.[39] I postulate that Junius's searches for the proper style and the proper vocabulary for his translations and the need to enrich especially his mother tongue made him all the more aware of the similarities and differences of contemporary English and Dutch, and thus formed one of the triggers which led him to study Dutch a few years later.

*De Schilder-konst* was indeed characteristic of the discourse on the standardisation of the vernacular in the Low Countries at the time. All sorts of encouragements for the use, embellishment and purification of Dutch were being expressed in treatises and in meetings of dignitaries and authors.[40] To begin with, the official Dutch translation of the Bible, the *Statenvertaling*, had appeared only in 1637. In the elite circles in which Junius and his brother-in-law Vossius used to move were authors who contributed to the standardisation of Dutch by selecting the dialect of the Holland towns as the prestigious form of the language in which to write their literature, and by discussing the nature of the vernacular at the same time. During Junius's absence in England, they had significantly increased the status of their mother tongue. To restrict myself to Junius's immediate circle of acquaintances and relatives, among them was one of the greatest seventeenth-century Dutch poets and playwrights, Joost van den Vondel (1587–1679), who had furnished an epigram for Junius's portrait that adorned *De Schilder-konst* and composed a laudatory poem on Junius in 1644. In his nephew Jan de Brune, Junius found another promoter of the vernacular, as even appears from Jan's aforementioned introduction to *De*

*Schilder-konst.* Furthermore, Jan's uncle Johan de Brune (1588–1658), the brother of Junius's brother-in-law, had demonstrated the glory of Dutch in a collection of proverbs in 1636, and was still to voice his concern over the purity of the language in the late 1660s.[41] Johan van Heemskerck, who had published the Dutch pastoral *Batavische Arcadia* in 1637, may serve as a final example.

Interest in Dutch was concerned not only with its standardisation, but also with its purity and the growing influx of especially French words in the speech of young people, who thus tried to appear fashionable and intellectual.[42] The use of French loanwords was so obvious that Dutch authors in Junius's circle both ridiculed this affected form of the language in their literature and searched for an unspoiled, pure form of Dutch at the same time.[43] Junius agreed with those who condemned or mocked the corruption of the vernacular. In a letter to the German philosopher Johann Clauberg (1622–1665), who was preparing etymological observations himself, he voiced his conviction in topical fashion, by saying that the cause of the unwanted eloquence spoiling the vernacular was the fact that

> the ambitious youths, returned to their fatherland from abroad, are preposterously striving after a reputation of unusual fluency with peasants and the uncultivated ears of commoners by means of an unashamed rattling and pompous style of words adopted from fake Latin languages.[44]

By the fake Latin languages he meant the Romance languages, French and Italian in particular, as appears from another reference to them in a letter to his friend, the antiquary Sir William Dugdale (1605–1686). In it, Junius favoured English, which "having a neer relation to the old Gothike, Cimbrike, and Saxonike languages, is much more capable of goodly and gallant ornaments" than

> anie of the languages so much cried up and allmost wholly derived or traduced out of that corrupted barbarous Latin, which about the times of the decaying Romane monarchie came in, and since was chiefly maintained and partly forged by monkes.[45]

It should be borne in mind that Junius's disgust concerned not the Romance languages *per se* – of which French, after all, had been his father's mother tongue – but rather their barbarous deviation from the uncorrupted, ancient form of the language; Latin, in the case of Romance languages.

No doubt Junius's keenness with respect to barbarisms was also stimulated by the current studies of his brother-in-law Vossius. At the time of Junius's return to Holland, Vossius was not only adding to his Latin etymological dictionary, which Junius was to use extensively for his first Germanic publication *Observationes Willerami* (1655),[46] but also preparing a study on barbarisms in Latin, which involved the early medieval stages of the northern vernaculars. In *De Vitiis sermonis* (1645), he discussed a hoard of impure or incorrect words in mainly later Latin, many of which had entered the language as barbarisms or loans from Germanic languages.[47] He explained that the term barbarism was not intended to be pejorative, but just meant "foreign," and would therefore equally apply to Latin words borrowed into the vernaculars.[48] So as to be able to identify the source language from which such barbarisms in Latin had come, he had familiarised himself with texts in the older Germanic languages as best he could. His Old English material came from William Lambarde's *Archaionomia* (1568), the first edition of Anglo-Saxon laws, and Spelman's *Archaeologus*. Although his principal interest was the Latin language, Vossius had paid serious attention to the early medieval vernaculars.

In his own studies, Junius was to go further in his desire for language purity than Vossius had done. Whereas Vossius had not concerned himself with loanwords in the field of religion and the Church, because they had been established by tradition,[49] Junius openly regretted that loanwords such as "catholic" and "orthodox" had been adopted in the language, and that the loanword *evangelie* "gospel" was used in Dutch instead of a native Germanic word or loan-translation, such as there was in English in Old English *godspell* or contemporary "gospel."[50] With respect to such terminology, Junius even remarked that "it is deplorable that the best part of the ancient Dutch tongue has been lost for us, since we let the ancient and serviceable [parts] become wholly obsolete and perish because of our too great quirks for exotic and novel words."[51]

The principal stimulus for Junius to embark on the compilation of an etymological dictionary of Dutch, however, was probably the 1642 re-edition of the current dictionary of Dutch, the celebrated Kiliaan.[52] First published in 1599, Cornelis Kiliaan's *Etymologicum Teutonicae linguae* was the first Dutch-Latin dictionary which contained etymological and comparative material from a whole range of languages and dialects to explain the Dutch entries.[53] Its five reprints in the first half of the seventeenth century are indicative of its popularity. However, in 1642 – the year Junius had moved to the Low Countries again – the publishers

Johannes and Jodocus Jansonius brought out a re-edition in Amsterdam, *Kilianus auctus seu dictionarium Teutonica-Latino-Gallicum*,[54] which, according to Junius, had been "nominally enlarged [i.e. *auctus*], but actually mutilated and corrupted."[55] Junius's objection concerned the publishers' decision to replace the wealth of etymological and dialectal information with French translations of the Dutch entries. It is telling of the current situation in the Low Countries that the publishers expected such a design to have a wider appeal than the original historical and dialectal material. Junius seems to have been most disturbed that this would become the new standard edition used by young people, "who should only accustom themselves to the best authors of their mother tongue,"[56] and that now "really so many exceptionally talented illustrious Dutchmen, who have endeavoured to recover the pristine splendour, wealth and power of expression of our tongue for several years now, have been to no avail."[57] Junius may have wished to resume the thread where the Jansoniuses had failed, by improving on the original Kiliaan with the addition of evidence of a venerable history and ancestry for his mother tongue.

*Junius's study of Old English for the "Etymologicum Teutonicum"*

Junius seems to have envisaged his "Etymologicum Teutonicum" both as a replacement and emulation of the Kiliaan of 1642. Most of its entry words which Junius quoted in his other work occur in Kiliaan's 1599 edition as well. In her review of Voorwinden's re-edition of Junius's *Observationes Willerami*, Van der Wal has observed that the correspondences between Junius's aforementioned list of Dutch monosyllabic words truncated from Greek and the relevant entries in Kiliaan's 1599 edition are too obvious to be coincidental.[58] Furthermore, the (working) title of the dictionary is reminiscent of Kiliaan's *Etymologicum Teutonicae linguae*.[59] Nevertheless, even a superficial comparison of the entries of Junius's Dutch etymological dictionary and Kiliaan's of 1599 reveals that the former was by no means a mere copy of the latter. Not only did the "Etymologicum Teutonicum" include different entries,[60] Junius's etymological discussions and the suggestions for Greek origins of the words are much more substantial than what can be found in Kiliaan. The entry TEMMEN may serve as example:

> Kiliaan: TEMMEN, TAM MAKEN to tame, subdue, vanquish, restrain; to make tame, to make gentle. English "tame."[61]
> Junius: TEMMEN to tame, make tame, make gentle. The

English say "to make tame." The Anglo-Saxons formerly seem to have said *teman*; thus we may read in the venerable Bede 5.13, "*he temede ðone ealdan lichoman*," "he subdued the old body;" and in Cotton's and Rushworth's Mark 5.1 is written, "*nænig mæhte hine temma*," "nobody could tame him." Therefore we suspect not unjustly that the word is derived from Greek τέμμειν, which is translated by Hesychius as πείθειν "to persuade, to handle reluctant people with some skill and urge them to complaisance by the sweetness of a serious and embellished speech." [Junius added a quotation from Cicero and one from Horace to support this proposition.][62]

The entry is exemplary of the dictionary as Junius had described it, with its dependence on Old English to derive the word from Greek. It reveals that Junius emulated Kiliaan's achievement exactly by adducing and relying on evidence from early medieval Germanic languages. The reason that especially Old English had such a prominent place in the dictionary, as Gronovius had noted, can be explained by both Junius's etymological method and by the material he had at his disposal at the time of writing, as we shall see.

Junius's use of early medieval Germanic material was inspired by his etymological method. In recovering the etymologies of Dutch, he followed the true humanist course of examining the oldest, most authentic documents available.[63] In his dedicatory letter prefixed to his *Observationes Willerami*, Junius explained that "I noticed that the true origins of 'Teutonic' words can be derived from nowhere with more certainty than from the ancient spelling of such [i.e. ancient 'Teutonic'] documents."[64] His method of searching for these origins was first to trace contemporary Dutch words back to their earliest yet uncorrupted attestations, and then to propose Greek origins which he believed to correspond to these attestations. In other words, he felt one should postulate etymologies only on the basis of the earliest language forms. This view appears from his rejection of Clauberg's etymological method because it was based on contemporary words:

the gentleman most diligent in examining the elegancies of his mother tongue [i.e. Clauberg] has this peculiarity, as it were, that he mostly searches the origins [of words] from the contemporary use of the German language; whereas it remains always fixed and steadfast for me to swerve not even a finger's breadth from the ancient orthography of more authentic documents.[65]

Such a tenet seems sound enough, but it was much harder to live up to it in practice.

When setting out to write the etymological dictionary, Junius faced two main difficulties. In the first place, Dutch lacks a written heritage in Old Dutch, which hampers the finding of early forms of Dutch words. Secondly, the ancient manuscripts which should offer the primary material were known to be full of errors due to careless copying and thus to be unreliable sources for authentic vocabulary.[66] Junius's handling of both problems brought him to Old English.

The lack of substantial attestations of Old Dutch compelled Junius to turn to manuscript evidence of other early medieval Germanic languages. Though there is a wealth of Dutch manuscripts from the high Middle Ages, Old Dutch literature is barely extant.[67] As he recollected in his dedication to De la Gardie, Junius accordingly had "bestowed all of my pains and attention to the 'Theotiscan' and Anglo-Saxon documents to examine whether I would perceive any opening in them for finding what I sought [i.e. the origin of Dutch]."[68] First, he had been discouraged from searching for ancient "Theotiscan," or Old High German, sources by an (incorrect) remark from the ninth-century Otfrid von Weissenburg that that language had simply not been committed to writing.[69] He had then proceeded with Old English, for "the Anglo-Saxon documents, the extraordinary treasure-house of Great Britain, appeared to arouse higher hopes [at finding the origin of Dutch]."[70] He had noticed that "evident traces of an exceptional eloquence are manifest here and there in the texts which the monk Cædmon, the Bishops Warnfrid [i.e. possibly Wærferth], Ælfric and Wulfstan, and also Alfred, the famous king of the Anglo-Saxons, and many others left to posterity,"[71] although he had had to conclude that there was "also here deep silence on the origin of the northern languages."[72] What concerns us here for the reconstruction of the course of Junius's researches for the "Etymologicum Teutonicum," is that he explained in these recollections that his involvement in Old English was instigated by his searches for the origins of Dutch.

The idea that Old English might reveal the origins of Dutch was based on Junius's assumption that it was the ancestor of Dutch. In his "Letter to the Reader" in *Observationes Willerami*, Junius explained the affinity of these languages as follows:

> From Anglo-Saxon there has proceeded a major part of English and Scots, as well as all Dutch, yet especially that ancient Frisian, which is hardly understood by the other inhabitants of all Netherlands, since it has retained very clear traces of

Anglo-Saxon in many words, and also in the very spelling and pronunciation of many words, up to this day.[73]

The view that Dutch, Frisian and Old English were closely related was current in the sixteenth and seventeenth centuries. In an instructive article, Bremmer has described how Frisian was considered an ancient dialect of Dutch which was particularly closely related to Old English.[74] For this reason, Junius took the unusual step of going to Friesland, probably during one or more periods in the years between 1646 and 48, to be instructed in this tongue and collect Frisian data for the Dutch dictionary.[75] Yet, he did not have the occasion to study Old Frisian then, nor to study ancient Frisian manuscripts, as Breuker has observed.[76] Since Junius's study of Frisian has been appreciated elsewhere,[77] let it suffice to observe the connection Junius made between Frisian, Dutch and Old English and the relevance he found in this language for his Dutch etymologies. The proximity between Dutch and Old English was also repeatedly referred to at the time. Among Junius's acquaintances, for instance, William Boswell (d. 1649), the English resident in Holland, intimated to the antiquary Sir Simonds D'Ewes (1602–1650) in 1636 that "I have often thought how much the knowledge of this present Low-Dutch language would advantage your intelligence of our old Saxon";[78] and in 1640, Sir Henry Spelman (1564?–1641) suggested that the Dutchman Johannes de Laet (1581–1649) was best equipped for the compilation of an Old English dictionary "both for his knowledge and great travell in the Saxon tongue and also for the proximitiue which his owne language [i.e. Dutch] and the Frisian have to the ancient Saxon."[79] Possibly De Laet, whose life and studies run so curiously parallel to Junius's without any sign of their having been in touch, may also have taken up the study of Old English out of an interest in the origins of his mother tongue Dutch, yet some decades earlier than Junius. Whereas the results of his studies seem to have solely concerned Old English, De Laet observed in 1616 that "I am used to while away my leisure time by investigating the antiquities of our native tongue."[80]

Junius coped with the second difficulty, the unreliability of late medieval manuscripts, by classifying certain manuscript documents as bearing witness to a primeval period of pristine language forms. Initially, he had doubted the possibility of being able to find the origins of Dutch words at all by relying on manuscripts. In the aforementioned dedication of the Gothic Gospels to De la Gardie, he continued his praise of Dutch and desire to find its history and origin with the exclamation:

But to what extent, I ask, must one attempt something one doubts to be able to attain? Where must one search? . . . . Finally, how can one elicit from the obscurity and ignorance of the Middle Ages, after so many and such great attacks, overthrows and transmigrations of most warlike tribes, something trustworthy which is not confused or doubtful, but pure and manifest?[81]

Once he had used and valued early medieval Germanic texts, however, Junius came to distinguish between untrustworthy, because faulty, manuscripts of the later Middle Ages, and pristine manuscripts of the early Middle Ages. He explained the distinction as follows in a letter to Johann Clauberg from 1660:

books of the Middle Ages are indeed mostly rather full of faults, but the more ancient ones still preserve numerous traces of undefiled antiquity; and I think I cannot offer any more preferable service to the lovers of "Teutonic" than to show pristine writing to the reader everywhere, and present this reverend splendour of pure antiquity to the eyes of the studious at every possible opportunity.[82]

This quotation suggests that Junius reserved the term "antiquity" for the early Middle Ages, no doubt in imitation of classical antiquity and its textual treasures, with which he had been raised and which had previously formed the subject of his studies. Just as he conceived the paradigm of the Latin language as a period of pure antiquity succeeded by the spoiled forms of Romance languages, he appears to have visualised the paradigm of Dutch, and of the other Germanic languages, as consisting of three stages, a Germanic antiquity, in which the language had been pure and venerable, followed by a stage of corruption in the Middle Ages, succeeded in turn by the contemporary vernacular. Thus, Junius construed a Germanic antiquity for his mother tongue, to which it would be no more than natural to turn for the elevation of the contemporary form of the vernacular.

When undertaking the writing of the "Etymologicum Teutonicum," Junius's access to this pure Germanic antiquity consisted predominantly of Anglo-Saxon material. Only upon his finding of Franconian hymns and study of the Gothic Gospels some years later, did his testimonies of this stage in the ethnic history become more varied. The prominent place of Old English evidence in the dictionary, which Gronovius had noticed, is accordingly explained by the relative abundance of material in this language, both published and in manuscript, which Junius had at his disposal at the time.

The entries of the "Etymologicum Teutonicum" which Junius quoted in his other work reveal what Old English evidence Junius had consulted for and included in the dictionary. As indicated earlier, the entries retrieved to date comprise one and a half dozen quotations in his publications and MS Junius 116c, and a list of brief entries of Dutch monosyllabic words, which need not have had exactly their current form in the "Etymologicum." While the Old English included in the one and a half dozen quoted entries must have been present in the "Etymologicum," some of the Old English in the brief entries of monosyllabic Dutch words may have been added by Junius at a later date, when he compiled the list for inclusion in *Observationes Willerami*. In the following presentation of the Old English evidence in the "Etymologicum," I have therefore distinguished between (1) Old English attestations undisputedly from entries of the "Etymologicum," and (2) those taken from the list of Dutch monosyllabic words, which were presumably, but not undisputedly, present in the dictionary.

1) *ceahhetan* at KICHEN, KICHELEN; *ceorian* at KARIEN, KORIEN, KOERIEN; *freond* and *freoh* at VRIEND; *teman* at TEMMEN.

2) *ar* at EER; *æl / el* at EL; *æs* at AES; *æx* at AX / AXE; *beom* at BOOM; *blod* at BLOED; *breost* at BORST; *ceaf* at KAF; *ceaster* at BURG; *ceol* at KIEL; *chor* at KOOR; *cin* at KIN; *corn* at KORN; *craw* at KRAY; *cu* at KOE / KOEY; *cup* at KOP; *deaw* at DAUW; *dwæs* at DWAES; *eag* at OOG; *earc / erk* at ARCK; *earn* at ARN; *faest / fest* at VAST; *feoh* at VEE; *feol* at VIJL; *flint* at VLINT; *fot* at VOET; *full* at VUL / VOL; *gæst / gest / gyst* at GAST; *geal* at GAL; *ger / gear* at JAER; *geoc / ioc* at JOK; *glid* at GLAD; *hana* at HAEN;[83] *hat* at HEET; *hæm / ham* at HEYM; *heard* at HARD; *heg / hig* at HOY; *hill* at HIL; *hleow / hliw* at LAW / LOW; *hlud* at LUYD; *hof* at HOEF; *hraðe* at RAD; *hricc* at RUGH / RUGGE; *hweol* at WIEL; *ic* at IK; *læp* at LAP; *lam / lim* at LIJM; *leac / leah* at LOOK; *mæl* at MAEL / MAEL-TIJD;[84] *meolc / melc* at MOLK; *mit* at MET; *mos* at MOS / MOSCH; *myltestra / myltestreona, myltenhus, myltan* at MOT; *nett* at NET; *niw / neow* at NIEW; *ora / ore* at OOR; *ord* at OORT; *ost* at OEST; *oxa* at OS; *pað* at PAD; *pyt* at PUT; *rap* at REEP / ROOP; *reaf / reof* and *reofera* at ROOF; *rocc* at ROCK; *rum* at RUYM; *scæb* at SCHAB; *scalc* at

SCHALCK; *sceap* at SCHAEP; *scern / sciern* at SCHERN; *scrin* at SCHRIJN; *scyleage / sculeaged / sceoleag* at SCHEEL; *sealm* at PSALM / SALM; *seað* at SAAD / SAD; *smec / smyc* at SMOOK; *snaw* at SNEE / SNEEW; *spere* at SPER / SPERE; *stæf* at STAF; *stif* at STIJF; *storc* at STORK; *stræt* at STRAET; *streng* at STRENG / STRING; *streon / gestreon* at MOT; *swet* at SOET; *swin* at SWIJN; *tas* at TAS; *tid / tyd* and *tydder* at TEER / TEEDER / TEDER;[85] *toll* at TOL; *treow / trew / triw* at TREE / TERE / TIER; *tylian / tyligean* at TUYL;[86] *ðic* at DICK; *ðinn / ðynn* at DUN; *up* at OP; *wærm / werm* at WERM; *wahl* at WAEL / WALE; *wald / weald* at WALD / WOUD; *wall / weall* at WAET / VERWAET; *weg / wæg* at WEG; *weorc / werc* at WERK; *wic* at WIJK; *wif, wifmann / wimman, wifhades man* at WIJF; *win* at WIJN; *wis* at WIJS; *worm / wyrm* at WORM; *wul* at WOL / WUL; *ymb* at OM.

Of these, the words *cup, craw, eag, hill, hliw, myltestra, myltestreona, scæb, scalc, sculeaged, sceoleag, tyligean, wahl* and *werm* do not occur in this form in the corpus of Old English.[87] Junius must either have construed them himself, or have copied them from unfaithful transcripts. I have not had the opportunity to determine Junius's exact source for each of the words, but I do wish to consider the information available on the Old English material he may have seen during the period he was working on the "Etymologicum" in order to appraise the sources on which the Old English component of the dictionary was based. My discussion of them here does not claim to be exhaustive or detailed, but is rather an invitation for further research.

In several instances, Junius explicitly referred to the sources in which he had found the Old English attestations. For *teman* Junius mentioned Bede, the Rushworth Gospels and the Lindisfarne, or Cotton's, Gospels, as quoted earlier. About *reof* and *reofera* he observed that these forms occur in the Rushworth Gospels. For *mæl* he gave the source as the Laws of Cnut. Finally, for *hana, trew, triw, wifman* and *wimman* he alluded to the particular Gospels in which they can be found. These references indicate that Junius used both printed editions, such as Abraham Wheelock's edition of Bede and the Anglo-Saxon Chronicle (1643) and John Foxe's edition of the Old English Gospels (1571), and Anglo-Saxon manuscripts, such as the Rushworth and Lindisfarne Gospels (now MS Auct. D.2.19, Bodleian Library, Oxford, and MS Cotton Nero D.iv, British Library, London, respectively), for the writing of the "Etymologicum."

Junius may have acquired the printed books while he was still in the Low Countries, while he probably did not have access to any Anglo-

Saxon manuscripts. He had his own copies of Wheelock and no doubt also of the Gospels, though the latter has not been retrieved.[88] Vossius's copies of Lambarde and Spelman were also available for consultation. Furthermore, several of the above Old English attestations occur in the psalms, among other sources. Junius may have taken them from his copy of John Spelman's edition of the Old English psalter (1640).[89] These three printed books, as Dekker has demonstrated, also formed the sources of the earliest quotations in Junius's Old English-Latin manuscript lexicon (now MSS Junius 2 and 3, Bodleian Library, Oxford), which he seems to have begun to compile soon after beginning to study Old English.[90] This suggests that Junius had them at his disposal at an early moment in his studies.

The Old English evidence in the ancient manuscript form Junius desired was to be found in England. He was not in a position, however, to go there immediately when he had begun to write his "Etymologicum." His tutorship to Aubrey de Vere compelled him to stay in the Low Countries for some years. I have not been able to find whether Junius remained in England when he accompanied de Vere back there at some point in 1647, or first returned to the Low Countries – for instance by order of Lady Aletheia Howard (d.1654) – to go to England once more one year later. Yet, for some three years, from 1647/8 until 1651, Junius delighted in the treasure-house which England must have been to someone with his lexicographical interests, and in a circle of old and new antiquarian friends who helped him to the Anglo-Saxon manuscripts.[91] He cheerfully wrote to his nephew in Amsterdam that "the English especially favour me for my examining their antiquities and drawing much from them to elucidate the northern languages."[92] It is hard to assess exactly which of all the Old English sources Junius examined, collated or transcribed he consulted during this visit rather than later, when he was no longer working on the "Etymologicum Teutonicum." Besides, Junius's activities in the field of Germanic studies in England in these years need not have been exclusively directed to the compilation of the Dutch etymological dictionary. For instance, the Old English–Latin lexicon presumably also took part of his time. Nevertheless, there is some information on the sources he studied for the "Etymologicum."

For several months in 1648 and 1649, Junius stayed with the D'Ewes, to whom he may have been introduced by their joint friends Patrick Young (1584–1652), the former royal librarian, or John Selden (1584–1654), the antiquary and parliamentarian.[93] At the time, D'Ewes was trying to compile an Old English dictionary and to make ready for the press Ælfric's glossary and grammar of Old English and the laws of

King Edgar, and he was accordingly an obvious choice for Junius to co-operate with.[94] Presumably, Junius went to D'Ewes not yet as an expert of Old English, but rather as the interested etymologist of Dutch who wished to increase his understanding of Old English with the help of the material D'Ewes was using. By the end of January 1649, some time after a first stay with D'Ewes, Junius professed to be familiar with Anglo-Saxon characters, which he was comparing with runes, yet the extent of his proficiency in Old English then is not known.[95] In her discussion of D'Ewes's dictionary, Hetherington has listed the sources D'Ewes had at his disposal.[96] Besides the Old English manuscript lexicon of John Joscelyn (1529–1603), which served as a model and the main source of information, and those of Sir William Dugdale (1605–1686), Richard James (1592–1638), and Laurence Nowell (d.1571/2), they include the wills of Ælflæd and Æþelflæd, unspecified charters, the laws of King Edgar and some of Cnut, the Gospels from the manuscript now Corpus Christi College, Cambridge, 140, and Psalms from the manuscript now Trinity College R.17.1. From all of these texts, as well as from Ælfric's glossary and grammar, Junius may accordingly have derived material for his "Etymologicum."

Junius also collected Old English evidence from elsewhere. He consulted the Rushworth Gospels, which D'Ewes had on loan until March 1650,[97] and about which Junius wrote to his nephew in Amsterdam two months later:

> Even very recently indeed, the excellent gentleman John Rush-worth most kindly lent me the Vulgate version of the four Gospels [i.e. the Rushworth Gospels] interlineated with Anglo-Saxon by a glossator eight or nine hundred years ago, I believe. . . I have inserted much information from this most friendly gentleman's treasure, hitherto unknown and especially useful for my purpose, in my etymological work.[98]

It is not clear whether Rushworth had lent the Gospels to Junius in particular, or whether Junius referred to the loan of the manuscript to D'Ewes, with whom he had used it. Junius made excerpts from the Rush-worth Gospels in what is now MS Junius 76, Bodleian Library, Oxford, which also comprises excerpts from the Lindisfarne Gospels. Kees Dekker imparted to me that the information in MS Junius 76 is remarkably succinct in comparison with Junius's other transcripts and annotations. I therefore assume the notes were among the earliest excerpts Junius made from Anglo-Saxon manuscripts. He probably gained access to the

Cottonian library to consult the Lindisfarne Gospels with the assistance of Selden. In May 1654, Junius still reminded Selden of "these Anglo-Saxonick monuments I transcribed by your favour out of divers Cottonian manuscripts."[99] The many other transcripts from Cottonian manuscripts he may have made on subsequent visits.[100] Possibly also at this visit to England, Junius consulted Cambridge manuscripts, probably by the agency of Abraham Wheelock (1593–1653), to whom he may have been introduced by D'Ewes or by their joint friend James Ussher (1581–1656), the Primate of Ireland.[101] As Hetherington has observed, Junius presumably made his transcript of the pseudo-gospel of Nicodemus (now MS Ii.2.11, Cambridge University Library), when he cooperated with D'Ewes.[102] Finally, Ussher put the famous so-called Cædmon manuscript (now MS Junius 11, Bodleian Library, Oxford) at Junius's disposal.[103] Junius was interested in it because of its poetic vocabulary rather than its literature, just as before him De Laet, William Somner, for whom see below, and presumably D'Ewes had examined it for their respective lexicographical projects.[104]

In turn, Junius seems to have promoted Kiliaan among his English friends. Probably at D'Ewes's house, he met William Somner (1606–1669), who had begun to study Old English some time before on the advice of Meric Casaubon (ca.1599–1671), a joint friend of him and Junius, and was at the time engaged in drawing up the glossary *Ad verba vetera Germanica* for Casaubon's treatise *De Quatuor linguis commentationis* (London, 1650) and assisting D'Ewes in preparing the Old English dictionary and grammar for the press.[105] The nature of Somner's and Junius's cooperation during these years is not known,[106] but it seems rather likely that Junius promoted Kiliaan to Somner. As Dekker has demonstrated, Somner made substantial use of Kiliaan for the glossary.[107] Then, Somner, and possibly Junius, may have encouraged Casaubon to introduce the few references to Kiliaan in his treatise.[108] Likewise, Junius presumably acquired his copy of Casaubon's and Somner's work right upon its publication in 1650, so that the various references to Kiliaan and Dutch in his marginalia to Somner's glossary[109] fall into place if one considers they were made in the period when Junius was working on his "Etymologicum Teutonicum."

*Conclusion*

Junius was inspired to study early medieval Germanic languages by a desire to contribute to the elevation of his mother tongue Dutch. His interest in Old English was not motivated by attempts to trace the history of English or to study Anglo-Saxon culture and literature, but to uncover the ancient splendour of his own vernacular. Initially, at least, his study of Old English was embedded in his research for a Dutch etymological dictionary. His exertions reveal a connection between Anglo-Saxon studies and Dutch lexicography which has not been recognised as yet – neither by Anglo-Saxonists, who tend to consider Junius first and foremost an Anglo-Saxonist, nor by historians of Dutch, who do not consider him at all.

Junius's motivations for devoting himself to Old English were parallel to those of his English friends. Both English Anglo-Saxonists and Junius were aroused by feelings of national identity – but their "nationalisms" differed. Whereas the Englishmen sought to legitimise the contemporary English constitution and Church, Junius strove to establish the prestige of his mother tongue Dutch with the help of Old English. His incentives must therefore be sought in the contemporary discourse in the Low Countries on the status of the vernacular as part of a wider search for the definition of a national or ethnic identity. For his contribution to this discourse, a Dutch etymological dictionary, Junius turned to the study of Old English. He conceived Old English documents as witnesses of a pure antiquity, which he distinguished from the spoiled renderings of the later Middle Ages. Thus, in his paradigm of languages, he construed a Germanic antiquity which preceded the northern Middle Ages on lines comparable to the succession of classical Latin by the Romance vernaculars. The "Etymologicum Teutonicum" was never published; but Junius became an Anglo-Saxonist, and his Old English material has proven of great value in its own right, for his later studies, and for students of Old English ever since.

## NOTES

1. I read an adaptation of this contribution at the 33rd International Congress of Medieval Studies, Kalamazoo, MI, May 1998. The research was initially executed for my edition of Junius's correspondence, *For my Worthy Freind Mr Franciscus Junius: An Edition of the Complete Correspondence of Francis Junius F.F. (1591–1677)* (forthcoming). I am grateful to Rolf Bremmer and Kees Dekker for making helpful suggestions and giving encouragement during the preparation of this contribution, to Chris Heesakkers for assistance with the Latin, and to Han Nijdam for proofreading an earlier version.

2. Junius's year of birth has been a matter of uncertainty. For some time, Kees Dekker and I have contested the generally accepted year 1591, insisting it should be 1590. A reinterpretation of the evidence has now led me to see that the

odds are in favour of the year 1591, although I am still not fully convinced it is the true year; see Van Romburgh, *For my Worthy Freind*.

3. For a brief survey of Junius's Germanic achievements, see Rolf Bremmer's contribution to this volume. The course of Junius's Germanic studies is presented in more detail in Ph.H. Breuker, "On the Course of Franciscus Junius's Germanic Studies, with Special Reference to Frisian," in Rolf H. Bremmer Jr, ed., *Franciscus Junius F.F. and his Circle* (Amsterdam and Atlanta, GA: Rodopi, 1998): 129–57. A slightly earlier version of the article appeared with the same title in Rolf H. Bremmer Jr, Geart van der Meer and Oebele Vries, eds., *Aspects of Old Frisian Philology* [= *Amsterdamer Beiträge zur älteren Germanistik* 31/32, = *Estrikken* 69] (Amsterdam, Atlanta, GA, and Groningen: Rodopi, 1990): 42–68.

4. Breuker, "On the Course," 145.

5. Recent surveys of Junius's life can be found in Keith Aldrich, Philipp Fehl and Raina Fehl, eds., *Franciscus Junius: The Literature of Classical Art 1, The Painting of the Ancients* (Berkeley, Los Angeles and Oxford: University of California Press, 1991), xxvi–xlix; Colette Nativel, ed., *Franciscus Junius, De Pictura veterum libri tres (Roterodami 1694): Edition, traduction et commentaire du livre I*, Travaux du Grand Siècle 3 (Geneva: Droz, 1996): 25–80, though she has not always interpreted Junius's Germanic studies correctly; Breuker, "On the Course," and Bremmer, *Franciscus Junius*. More details will be found in my *For my Worthy Freind*. The article in the *Dictionary of National Biography* 30 (1892): 227–28, will be superseded by my contribution for the *NewDNB* (Oxford, 2004).

6. For a brief appreciation of the Leiden philological tradition, with references to further literature, see Kees Dekker, *The Origins of Old Germanic Studies in the Low Countries*, Brill's Studies in Intellectual History 92 (Leiden, Boston and Cologne: Brill, 1999): 41–43.

7. *Painting* has been reprinted, with introduction and commentary, in Aldrich, Fehl and Fehl, *Literature*.

8. Breuker, "On the Course," 139–40.

9. Dekker, *Origins*, 93–94.

10. See Dekker, *Origins*, 94 n225.

11. In his discussion of *irminsul*, described in *Painting* 2.8 as "an image in compleat Armor, honoured by the ancient Saxons with divine worship," Junius added references to both Gerardus Vossius, *De Origine et progressu idololatriae* (1641) and Henry Spelman, *Archaeologus in modum glossarii* (1626) in the second, posthumously published edition of *De Pictura* (Rotterdam, 1694); see Aldrich, Fehl and Fehl, *Literature*, 147 n264, from which I took this quotation.

12. The ideological and political motivations of Englishmen for the study of Anglo-Saxon culture and Old English have been clearly analysed in a detailed article by Angelika Lutz, "The Study of the Anglo-Saxon Chronicle in the Seventeenth Century and the Establishment of Old English Studies in the Universities," in Timothy Graham, ed., *The Recovery of Old English: Anglo-Saxon Studies in the Sixteenth and Seventeenth Centuries* (Kalamazoo: Medieval Institute, 2000).

13. See Eric Stanley, "The Sources of Junius's Learning as Revealed in the Junius Manuscripts in the Bodleian Library," in Bremmer, *Franciscus Junius*, 159–76, esp. 160–61; and also Lutz, "Study of the Anglo-Saxon Chronicle," 41.

14. Breuker, "On the Course," 142.

15. They were incorporated as "six year old" ["ante sexennium"] annotations in Junius's *Observationes in Willerami Abbatis Francicam paraphrasin Cantici Canticorum* (1655), 294–97, which was printed during the winter of 1654 and has a dedicatory letter dated January 1655. A facsimile reprint has been prepared by N. Voorwinden, Early Studies in Germanic Philology 1 (Amsterdam and Atlanta, GA: Rodopi, 1992).

16. *Observationes Willerami*, 7, 176–233. Breuker takes a remark by Junius in *Observationes Willerami*, 273, as another reference to his Dutch etymological dictionary. It presumably does allude to the dictionary indeed, but it does not literally mention it: "we will perhaps discuss the reasoning of this etymology more fully some time in the etymology of Dutch *man* 'man' " ["cuius etymologiae rationem aliquando forte fusius trademus in etymologia Teutonici *man* 'homo' "]. Likewise, it cannot be fully ascertained that the entries of Dutch monosyllabic words, "*monosyllaba Teutonica e Graecarum vocum initiis detruncata*," were actually taken from the Dutch etymological dictionary, for Junius did not introduce them as such. They most likely were, but they need not have had their current form in the "Etymologicum Teutonicum," on the one hand because in the entries *boom* "tree," *haen* "cock," and *oog* "eye" Junius quoted the Gothic Gospels, which he did not yet have when he was working on the dictionary, and on the other because the list merely serves to illustrate Dutch words supposedly truncated from Greek, so that the entries of these words may have been more elaborate in the dictionary itself. See below.

17. Kees Dekker, " '*Vide Kilian. . ..*:' The Role of Kiliaan's *Etymologicum* in Old English Studies between 1650 and 1665," *Anglia* 114/4 (1996): 514–43.

18. Junius's Dutch etymological dictionary is the topic of a paper in progress, in which I will present an edition of the dictionary entries as I have retrieved them to date and discuss their aspects and context in more detail.

19. "Totus nunc in eo sum ut prima quaque occasione. . . praelo subiiciam etymologicum, in quo chiliades aliquot vocum Teutonicarum ad Graecas origines refero; originum ratione plerumque petita ex veteribus Franco-Celticae, Anglo-Saxonicae, Gothicaeque linguae monumentis," draft, University Library Amsterdam, M 92c verso.

20. See Breuker, "On the Course," 142. "Franc. Iunium. . . habet paratum lexicon originum linguae patriae, in quo multa praeclara ex Anglosaxonum veteribus monumentis," Gronovius to Nicolaas Heinsius (1620–1681), printed in Petrus Burmannus, ed., *Sylloges epistolarum a viris illustribus scriptarum*, 5 vols. (Leiden, 1723–27), 3: 286.

21. "luculentam illam tuam in Saxonicis, immo omnium propemodum Europae vulgarium hodie linguarum, originibus operam," original, University Library Amsterdam, M 89b.

22. See Breuker, "On the Course," 142–43, and Dekker, "*Vide Kilian*," 528–29.

23. For this episode of Junius's service to the Arundel family, see Rolf H. Bremmer Jr and Reina Rácz, "Junius's Case against William Howard, Viscount Stafford," in Bremmer, *Franciscus Junius*, 121–27.

24. See Bremmer and Rácz, "Junius's Case," 124, and Breuker, "On the Course," 139–40 n38.

25. "On the Course," 145–7.

26. In particular, Junius had still confused Cimbric, or Old Norse, and Gothic – one of his major sources of evidence for the etymologies in the "Etymologicum," as quoted earlier – until he had thoroughly studied the Gothic Gospels. In the entry OWNDIE in the *Etymologicum Anglicanum*, he admitted that "also I myself formerly confused Gothic with Cimbric, until I learnt from repeated reading of the Codex argenteus [i.e. the Gothic Gospels] that the Cimbric dialect differs greatly from ancient Gothic" ["et ipse olim confudebam Gothica cum Cimbricis, usque dum ex Arg. codicis frequentiore lectione didici plurimum a vetere Gothico discrepare dialectum Cimbricam"].

27. See, for instance, Junius's remark following his excerpt of Dutch *vyand* in *Observationes Willerami*, 297.

28. A comprehensive survey of Junius's manuscript legacy in the Bodleian Library, Oxford, will no doubt yield more material.

29. "Non gravabor interim ex disiectis etymologiarum Belgicarum schedis hunc in locum transferre, quae pluribus abhinc annis de hac voce in mentem venerant," *Etymologicum Anglicanum*, s.v. COCK.

30. Cornelis Kiliaan, *Etymologicum Teutonicae linguae* (1599), for which see below, adds an explanation from Johannes Goropius Becanus (1518–1572).

31. "iam in Belgicum etymologicum retuleram hanc meam qualemcunque de tota re coniecturam, quam non pigebit hic adscribere, ut iis gratificer, quibus non ingrata solet esse coniecturarum diversitas: *karien, korien, koerien* 'gemere instar turturis vel columbae.' Vide quae de hoc verbo habet Kilian. A.S. pro eo dicunt *ceorian*; Cim. **kur** est 'murmur, mussitatio;' D. denique *kæremæl* est 'quaerimonia.' Videnturque omnia haec valde affinia isti γαϱύειν, quod apud Pindarum Dorice positum invenitur pro γηϱύειν 'canere, loqui, sonare'. . ."

32. It is quite conceivable that more information on Junius's early motivations for his studies can be recovered from his extensive manuscript legacy in the Bodleian Library, Oxford. De la Gardie had become the owner of the manuscript of the Gothic Gospels in 1662, when he had bought it back for Sweden from Junius's nephew Isaac Vossius (1618–1689), who had brought it from the royal library of the Swedish Queen Christina, whose librarian he had been, to the Low Countries in 1654. For the vicissitudes of the manuscript, see Cor van Bree, *Lotgevallen van de Codex argenteus: De wisselende waarde van een handschrift*, Vierde Bert van Selm-lezing (Amsterdam: De Buitenkant, 1995).

33. "Tanta veterem linguam Teutonicam claritas undiquaque superfluit, ut ei hoc nostro saeculo. . . primas lubentes concesserint magni nominis exteri; unde

et mihi, ad hanc praestantissimae linguae celebritatem erecto, turpe praeter caeteros videbatur nescire ultimam nobilis linguae stirpem, natales, cunabula, quibusque processibus in excelsitatem aliis quoque genetibus agnitam evecta fuerit," *Quatuor D.N. Iesu Christi Evangeliorum versiones perantiquae duae, Gothicae scilicet et Anglo-Saxonica*. . . (Dordrecht, 1665), *2–*2v.

34. "In Anglia cum incidisset in multos veteres Anglosaxonicos libros, illam coepit linguam excolere, quam cum ad Belgicam, quae ei erat vernacula, Germanicam et Anglicam illustrandam, verasque pervestigandas origines plurimum facere cognosset, multum studii et operae in illa perdiscenda collocavit. Huic addidit postea cognitionem omnium veterum linguarum Septentrionalium, Gothicae, Francicae, Islandicae, Cimbricae, quae et Runica dicitur, Frisicae, necnon Cambobritannicae," J.G. Graevius, "Vita Francisci Iunii F.F.," in F. Junius, *De pictura veterum. . . accedit Catalogus. . . artificum* (Rotterdam, 1694), [xv]–[xix], at [xvi]. In imitation of Breuker, "On the Course," 156 n100, I have translated *Belgicam* as "Netherlandic."

35. To illustrate, until well into the 1650s, Junius almost exclusively corresponded in Latin, also with his relatives. The only Dutch letters he wrote during these years were addressed to his sisters or to a few other people who did not know Latin. His only English retrieved letter of that period was the dedicatory letter to his patroness Lady Aletheia for the English translation of his art theory; see Van Romburgh, *For my Worthy Freind*.

36. See H. Burrowes Lathrop, *Translations from the Classics into English from Caxton to Chapman 1477–1620* (Madison, Wisc., 1933) and M. Kitagaki, *Principles and Problems of Translation in Seventeenth-Century England* (Kyoto, 1981).

37. See Marijke J. Van der Wal, *De moedertaal centraal: Standaardisatie-aspecten in de Nederlanden omstreeks 1650*, Nederlandse cultuur in Europese context, monografieën en studies 3 (The Hague, 1995), and van der Wal, *Geschiedenis van het Nederlands*, 2nd edn (Utrecht: Het Spectrum, 1994), 183–99, 218–25.

38. For a non-comprehensive list of seventeenth-century translations into Dutch, see Van der Wal, *De moedertaal*, 123–31.

39. See Van Romburgh, *For my Worthy Freind*.

40. See Van der Wal, *Geschiedenis*, 183–99, 218–25.

41. See Marijke J. van der Wal, "Taalidealen, taalnormen en taalverandering: Johan de Brune in linguistisch perspectief," in P.J. Verkruijsse, ed., *Johan de Brune de Oude (1588–1658). Een Zeeuws literator en staatsman uit de zeventiende eeuw*, Werken uitgegeven door het Koninklijk Zeeuwsch Genootschap der Wetenschappen, pt 6 (Middelburg, 1990): 54–68.

42. See Van der Wal, *Moedertaal*, 43–49.

43. See Van der Wal, *Geschiedenis*, 230–31.

44. "praepostere ambitiosi adolescentes, ab exteris oris in patriam reduces, facundiae minime vulgaris famam apud agrestes hispidasque plebeiorum aures

captant ex insolenti strepitu ac tumore vocabulorum e linguis notholatinis conquisitorum," original, University Library Leiden, BPL 293b.

45. Printed in William Hamper, ed., *The Life, Diary, and Correspondence of Sir William Dugdale, Knight, Sometime Garter Principal King of Arms* (London, 1827), no. 131, 354–57 (356).

46. See Dekker, *Origins*, 224.

47. See Dekker, *Origins*, 219–22, and C.S.M. Rademaker, *Life and Work of Gerardus Joannes Vossius (1577–1649)* (Assen: Van Gorcum, 1981), 296–8.

48. Vossius, *De Vitiis*, [vii].

49. See Rademaker, *Vossius*, 297–98.

50. See *Etymologicum Anglicanum*, s.vv. CATHOLICK and GOSPEL.

51. "Dolendum . . . optimam veteris linguae Teutonicae partem nobis deperiisse, dum nimia exoticarum novarumque vocum affectatione veteres probasque prorsus obsolescere atque intercidere patimur. . .," *Etymologicum Anglicanum*, s.v. GOSPEL. Junius voiced the same regret at such loanwords in *Observationes Willerami*, 7.

52. Junius's copy of Kiliaan has not been retrieved, but Kees Dekker has demonstrated that Junius made frequent use of the dictionary in his various Germanic projects; see Dekker, "*Vide Kilian,*" 522–30.

53. Cornelis Kiliaan, *Etymologicum Teutonicae Linguae sive Dictionarium Teutonico-Latinum* (Antwerp, 1599); see Lode van den Branden, Elly Cockx-Indestege and Frans Sillis, *Bio-bibliografie van Cornelis Kiliaan* (Nieuwkoop, 1978), 88–92.

54. See Van den Branden et al., *Bio-bibliografie*, 122–24.

55. "Nomine quidem auctum, at re ipsa mutilatum corruptumque," *Observationes Willerami*, [vii].

56. "quam [i.e. iuventus] nonnisi optimis patriae linguae authoribus assuescere oportebat," *Observationes*, [vii].

57. "Frustra certe hactenus fuerint tot praeclara illustrium Belgarum ingenia, quae aliquot ab hinc annis linguae nostrae pristinum splendorem, copiam, emphasin conata sunt reddere," *Observationes*, [vii].

58. Marijke J. van der Wal, review of Voorwinden, *Observationes Willerami*, in *Tijdschrift voor de Nederlandse Taal- en Letterkunde* 110 (1994): 325–28, at 327–28.

59. Dekker, "*Vide Kilian,*" 528–29.

60. Dekker has already noted that the aforementioned entry *evangelie* does not occur in Kiliaan; see Dekker, "*Vide Kilian,*" 528.

61. "domare, edomare, perdomare, coercere; cicurare, mansuefacere. Ang. *tame.*"

62. " 'domare, cicurare, mansuefacere'. *to make tame* dicunt Angli. A.Saxones videntur olim *teman* dixisse; ita legimus apud ven. Bedam V,13, *he temede ðone ealdan lichoman* 'domabat senile corpus'; et in C.R. Marc. V, 1 scriptum est *nænig mæhte hine temma* 'nemo poterat eum domare'. Non iniuria igitur suspicamur vocem derivatam e Gr τέμμειν, quod Hesychio exp. πείθειν

'persuadere hominum reluctantes animos arte quadam tractare ac gravis ornataeque orationis amoenitate ad obsequium impellere," *Etymologicum Anglicanum*, s.v. TAME.

63. For a concise survey of humanist research methods and the preference for the most authentic, ancient manuscripts, whether in classical languages or the vernaculars, see Dekker, *Origins*, 9–24. See also Anthony Grafton, *Defenders of the Text: The Traditions of Scholarship in an Age of Science, 1450–1800* (Cambridge, MA, etc.: Harvard University Press, 1991).

64. "Didici. . . neque aliunde veras Teutonicarum vocum origines certius peti posse, quam ex prisca istiusmodi monumentorum orthographia," *Observationes Willerami*, [iv].

65. ". . . hoc veluti peculiare habuit vir in perscrutandis patriae linguae elegantiis diligentissimus, quod originationes plerumque peteret ex hodierno linguae Germanicae usu; mihi contra fixum semper immotumque remansit ne latum quidem unguem a vetere antiquiorum monumentorum orthographia recedere," *Etymologicum Anglicanum* s.v. TOES.

66. See also Rolf Bremmer's contribution to this volume.

67. At the time, only the glossary of Justus Lipsius (1547–1606) from the Old Middle and Low Franconian *Wachtendonk Psalter Glosses*, and a single psalm in Abraham Mylius (Van der Mijle), *De Lingua Belgica* (1612), were available in Old Dutch; see Dekker, *The Origins*, 179–80. Junius made his own transcript of Lipsius's glossary (now MS Junius 116f), but even if he already did so on behalf of his "Etymologicum Teutonicum," it does not in the least provide enough material to satisfy Junius's requirements. Besides, he seems not to have identified the material as Old Dutch, as suggested by his use of "all of my pains" in the following quotation.

68. "omnem meam curam operamque ad Theotisca atque Anglo-Saxonica monumenta contuli, rimaturus an aliquod in iis deprehenderem initium inveniendi quod quaerebam," *Quatuor versiones*, *2v–*3. The quotation follows his rhetorical questions where to start searching for the origin and history of Dutch as quoted below.

69. "The following words by Otfrid foretold me that I would take pains in the Theotiscan ones [i.e. documents] in vain: 'This language is considered rustic, because it has been embellished by neither its own writing nor by any rhetorics of its own at any time'," ["ut in Theotiscis frustra operam sumpturum praemonebant sequentia Otfridi verba, 'Lingua haec veluti agrestis habetur, dum a propriis nec scriptura nec arte aliqua ullis est temporibus expolita' "], *Quatuor Versiones*, *3.

70. "Maiorem spem videbantur ostendere monumenta Anglo-Saxonica, peculiaris magnae Britanniae thesaurus," *Quatuor Versiones*, *3.

71. ". . . manifesta non vulgaris eloquentiae vestigia passim eluceant in iis quae Cædmon monachus; Warnfridus, Ælfricus, et Lupus episcopi, nec non inclytus Anglo-Saxonum rex Alvredus, aliique plures posteris reliquerunt," *Quatuor Versiones*, *3.

72. "Sed hic quoque altum de linguarum Septentrionalium origine silentium," *Quatuor Versiones*, *3.

73. "Ex Anglo-Saxonico vero promanavit magna pars Anglicae et Scoticae, tota quoque Belgica, praecipue tamen Frisica illa vetus, reliquis universi Belgii incolis vix intellecta, propterea quod in plurimis vocibus, atque in ipsa quoque plurimorum vocabulorum orthographia et pronuntiatione manifestissima Anglo-Saxonicae vestigia usque in hunc diem retinuerit," *Observationes Willerami*, [xi]. See also Dekker, *Origins*, 258.

74. Rolf H. Bremmer, "Late Medieval and Early Modern Opinions on the Affinity between English and Frisian: the Growth of a Commonplace," *Folia Linguistica Historica* 9 (1989): 167–91. See also Breuker, "On the Course," 141.

75. See Breuker, "On the Course," 141.

76. Breuker, "On the Course," 150–51. Junius's first Old Frisian notes date from the next decade, and were all derived from a printed text he received in 1657.

77. See Breuker, "On the Course," also for further references.

78. Quoted from B.J. Timmer, *The Later Genesis: Edited from Ms Junius 11* (Oxford: The Scrivener Press, 1948): 5; the original is BL, Harley 374, f. 92.

79. Quoted from Timmer, *Later Genesis*, 7; the original is BL, Add. 34601, f. 6. See also Bremmer, "Growth of a Commonplace," 177–78.

80. "soleo otium in lingua[e? SvR] nostratis antiquitatibus indagandis fallere," quoted from J.A.F. Bekkers, *Correspondence of John Morris with Johannes de Laet (1643–1649)* (Assen: Van Gorcum, 1970), xviii n5; the original is BL, MS Add. 22961, f. 161. See also Bremmer, "Growth of a Commonplace," 176, and "The Correspondence of Johannes de Laet (1581–1649) as a Mirror of his Life," *Lias* 25 (1998) 139–64, esp. 154–58.

81. "Sed quorsum, quaeso, experiatur quis, quod se assequi posse diffidat? Ubi locorum quaerat? . . . Quomodo, denique, ex medii saeculi obscuritate atque ignorantia, post tot tantasque pugnacissimarum gentium incursiones, excidia, transmigrationes, eruere quis valeat quod non turbidae nec ambigae, sed purae liquentisque sit fidei?" Junius, *Quatuor Evangeliorum versiones*, *2v.

82. "Mendosiores quidem plerumque aetatis mediae libri, sed antiquiores plurima vetustatis adhuc intemeratae vestigia servant; neque potiorem ullam videor mihi operam philoteutonibus posse navare, quam ut priscam ubique scripturam lectori praestem, ac reverendum illum sincerae vetustatis colorem quavis occasione studiosorum oculis ingeram," original, Leiden University Library, BPL 293b.

83. In his substantial discussion of Dutch *haen*, Junius also mentioned *hancred*, but since this reference occurs in a discussion alluding to the Gothic Gospels, which he did not have at the time of the compilation of the "Etymologicum," as indicated earlier, it is presumably a later addition.

84. The reference to the entry Old English *reord* later in the *Observationes Willerami* is a later addition.

85. These references may be later additions to the entry. *Tydder* is found only in the manuscript now Cotton Tiberius A.iii, British Library, London.

86. The substantial quotation of the Alfredian translation of Boethius, *De Consolatione philosophiae*, at the end of this entry is presumably a later addition. Junius introduced the quotation as: "the remarkable translation of this verse [i.e. Boethius], prepared by the most exalted King of the Anglo-Saxons Alfred, just as I copied it from the aforementioned manuscript of the famous Oxford library [i.e. now MS Bodley 180]" ["insignem huius metri paraphrasin ab augustissimo Anglo-Saxonum rege Alvredo elaboratam, prout eam descripsi ex supra memorato inclytae Oxoniensis bibliothecae codice manuscripto"].

87. As made available online by *The Dictionary of Old English Project*, Toronto.

88. Junius's annotated copy of Wheelock is now MS Junius 10, Bodleian Library, Oxford.

89. Junius had two copies of Spelman, one is now MS Junius 33, Bodleian Library, Oxford, and the other MS 499 D 16, University Library, Leiden, for which latter, see Rolf H. Bremmer Jr, "Retrieving Junius's Correspondence," in Bremmer, *Franciscus Junius*, 199–235, at 233.

90. See Kees Dekker, " 'That Most Elaborate One of Francis Junius': An Investigation of Francis Junius' Manuscript Old English Dictionary," in Graham, *Recovery of Old English*.

91. I have not yet found information as to whether Junius was already friendly with the antiquary Sir William Dugdale (1605–1686), with whom he later corresponded on Germanic studies, and Gerard Langbaine (1609–1658), who was to make numerous suggestions to the etymologies for Junius's *Etymologicum Anglicanum*, during this visit to England, or only on a subsequent one.

92. "Unice mihi favent Angli antiquitates suas perscrutanti atque ex iis nonnulla ad illustrationem Septentrionalium linguarum depromenti," draft, University Library Amsterdam, M 92c verso.

93. D'Ewes also entertained contact with other Dutchmen, among whom Johannes de Laet; see Andrew G. Watson, *The Library of Sir Simonds D'Ewes*, British Museum Bicentenary Publications (London: The Trustees of the British Museum, 1966), 9.

94. See M.S. Hetherington, *The Beginnings of Old English Lexicography* (privately published, 1980), 102–24; Watson, *Library of D'Ewes*, 10–12; and Lutz, "Study of the Anglo-Saxon Chronicle," 27 n91.

95. In a letter of 29 Jan 1649, Junius wrote that "I have begun to compare the ancient Cimbric characters [i.e. runes] with the Anglo-Saxon ones here" ["Ego hic veteres Cimbricas literas cum Anglo-Saxonicis coniungere coepi"], original, University Library Amsterdam, I 89b.

96. Hetherington, *Beginnings*, 108–16.

97. See Watson, *Library of D'Ewes*, 11, and Hetherington, *Beginnings*, 111.

98. "Quinetiam nuperrime adhuc Quatuor Evangelia vulgatae versionis a

glossatore quodam ante annos, credo, octingentos nongentosve Anglo-Saxonice interlineata humanissime suppeditavit mihi vir optimus Io. Rushworth. . . ex hoc amicissimi viri thesauro multa recondita et proposito meo apprime utilia operi etymologico inserui," draft, University Library Amsterdam, M 92c verso.

99. Printed in George Hickes, *Linguarum vett. Septentrionalium thesaurus grammatico-criticus et archaeologicus*, 2 vols. (Oxford, 1703–05), xliii–iv.

100. See Stanley, "Sources," 162–76.

101. Junius and Wheelock had become or were already acquainted during this visit of Junius to England, for Junius's German friend Christoph Arnold (1627–1685), who had stayed in London in the summer of 1651, referred to Wheelock – as well as Ussher and Selden – as a joint acquaintance in a letter of 1652; see Van Romburgh, *For my Worthy Freind*.

102. Hetherington, *Beginnings*, 108–09.

103. In reply to an apparent inquiry from Junius, Ussher also explained to him the present state of knowledge on Gothic in a letter of July 1651, printed in R. Parr, *A Collection of Three Hundred Letters, Written between. . . James Ussher. . . and Others* (London, 1686), no. 263; Junius's copy of the letter is MS Junius 55, f. 4, Bodleian Library, Oxford. See Van Romburgh, *For my Worthy Freind*.

104. Now MS Junius 11, Bodleian Library Oxford. Junius took the manuscript to the Low Countries and made its *editio princeps* in 1655, *Caedmonis monachi paraphrasis poetica* (Amsterdam, 1655). It is reprinted in facsimile, with an edition of Junius's manuscript commentary, by Peter J. Lucas, *Early Studies in Germanic Philology* 3 (Amsterdam and Atlanta, GA: Rodopi, 2000). De Laet, who had the manuscript on loan from Ussher for some years in the early 1640s in Holland, enthusiastically described it to Worm as a manuscript "of which the diction differs considerably from other manuscripts. . . and there occur many nouns and verbs which I have not found in other manuscripts" ["codicem MS cuius dictio multum ab aliis MSS discedit. . . et occurrunt multa nomina et verba, quae in aliis MSStis non inveni"]; see B.J. Timmer, "De Laet's Anglo-Saxon Dictionary," *Neophilologus* 41 (1957): 199–202, at 200. Likewise, Somner, who made a transcription of it when it was with D'Ewes's, presumably in the late 1640s, used it for his lexicographical work, as has been demonstrated by Angelika Lutz, "Zur Entstehungsgeschichte von William Somners Dictionarium Saxonico-Latino-Anglicum," *Anglia* 106/ 1–2 (1988): 1–25, at 17–20. D'Ewes must also have had the manuscript on loan in the hope to benefit from it for his current projects in the late 1640s; see Watson, *Library of D'Ewes*, 9–10. With D'Ewes, Junius probably noticed its usefulness for his "Etymologicum Teutonicum." Ussher must subsequently have given it, possibly also on loan, to him to take it to Holland either for examination or publication. Junius's manuscript commentary (now MS Junius 113, Bodleian Library, Oxford) reveals that his interest too was primarily in the vocabulary of the text, although he christened the poetry Cædmonian; see further Van Romburgh, *For my Worthy Freind*, and Lutz, "Study of the Anglo-Saxon Chronicle," 31–35.

105. For a discussion of Casaubon's treatise, see John F. Eros, "A

17th-century Demonstration of Language Relationship: Meric Casaubon on English and Greek," *Historiographia Linguistica* 3:1 (1976): 1–13.

106. See Lutz, "Study of the Anglo-Saxon Chronicle," 34–32, and Hetherington, *Beginnings*, 130.

107. Dekker, "*Vide Kilian*," 520–22.

108. Dekker, "*Vide Kilian*," 520–21.

109. Dekker, "*Vide Kilian*," 523–24. Junius's annotated copy is now 766 F 8, University Library Leiden.

# Franciscus Junius reads Chaucer: But Why? and How?

*For Larry Benson and Derek Pearsall*

## Rolf H. Bremmer Jr

Franciscus Junius F(rancisci) F(ilius), that eminent seventeenth-century Dutch philologist,[1] is perhaps best known in the field of Anglo-Saxon studies, and foremost as a collector and copyist of Old English texts and manuscripts. Shortly before his death he generously bequeathed his collection to the Bodleian Library, Oxford, where they have since been kept as the Junius Manuscripts.[2] The value of these documents has changed little in the course of time, and they serve much the same function for us today as they did for Junius, who firmly upheld the humanist principle of *ad fontes*. His edition (1655) of the famous Caedmon Manuscript, now Junius 11, for example, is the first published book of Old English poetry.[3] Besides Anglo-Saxon, he was equally active in the study of related Old Germanic languages, especially Old High German; this activity resulted, among other feats, in the publication of a thorough investigation into the vocabulary of Williram of Ebersberg's paraphrase of the *Song of Songs*,[4] and in the preparation for the press of a similar work on the Old High German *Tatian*, a synopsis of the Gospels of Matthew, Mark and Luke; this project also included an edition of the text.[5] His *opus magnum* was his edition of the Codex Argenteus, which contained Bishop Wulfila's fifth-century translation of the Gospels in Gothic, in conjunction with a revised edition of the West-Saxon Gospels, and accompanied by a voluminous Gothic dictionary.[6] Lexicography, indeed, was the main aim of his philological endeavours; besides the Gothic dictionary, several others – including a copious Old English–Latin one in two volumes – though well-nigh completed for the press, remained unpublished.[7]

Junius's *Etymologicum Anglicanum* was only brought to the press almost seventy years after his death by Bishop Edward Lye.[8] Not only did Lye prefix a Life of Junius to the dictionary proper, he also included testimonies to the excellence of the *Etymologicum* from George Hickes ("certainly a better work than Skinner's *Etymological Dictionary* [of 1668]"), Humphrey Wanley ("a very elaborate and most useful work"), Bishop William Nicolson ("a work. . . which will be also of singular use to our English Antiquary") and Bishop White Kennett ("The want of a new edition [of Somner's Old English dictionary of 1659] would indeed be superseded, could the world at last enjoy the *Etymologicum Anglicanum* completed by Fr. Junius").

Less familiar among neophilologists is Junius's first publication, *De pictura veterum*, which dealt with a completely different subject, viz. a learned and detailed analysis of the visual arts of the Romans and Greeks. *De pictura* not only reveals the author's intimate knowledge of the depth and breadth of Classical literature, but also his sensitivity for the visual and literary arts. The book had a profound influence on the spread of Neoclassical aesthetical ideals, and has earned Junius the distinction of being one of the first modern art-theoreticians.[9]

Hardly anyone in the field of English studies, however, is aware of Junius's having spent considerable energy on Middle English language and literature[10] – this ignorance, no doubt, being due mainly to his never having published any monograph on the subject. Yet Junius, it would seem, was as fully at home with Chaucer as he was, for example, with the Old English poems contained in the Caedmon Manuscript. It is the purpose of this paper to bring Junius's Chaucer researches into the spotlight. In doing this, I shall discuss the motivation of this aspect of Junius's philological pursuits, together with the methods which he employed.

### *Chaucer's reputation amongst Dutch seventeenth-century philologists*

Perhaps we should not be surprised to hear about Junius's interest in Middle English literature. After all, he lived in England consecutively from his thirtieth to his fiftieth years, in the household of Thomas Howard, Earl of Arundel, as tutor to the latter's son and, afterwards, grandsons. This position caused him to move among the cultural and political elite of England. Open-minded as he was, he became completely acculturated to the English way of life, developing a taste, among other things, for such sixteenth-century authors as Sir Philip Sidney and Edmund Spenser.[11] Later on in his life, after his return to Holland in 1642, he frequently visited England, and, when he was eighty-three, he again took up residence in that country. He died in the house of his nephew Isaac Vossius in Windsor, in 1677, at the age of eighty-six, and was buried in St George's Chapel there.

Junius, however, was neither the first nor the only Dutchman in the seventeenth century to have taken a keen interest in the medieval literary heritage of England. The honour of being the first to show familiarity with Chaucer must go to Richard Verstegen. Verstegen's life, much like that of Junius was intricately tied up with England, although his career differed much from that of the later author. Verstegen was born in London in c.1550, of Dutch descent. He studied at Oxford, but because of his ardent Roman-Catholic convictions, was forced to leave the country in the 1580s. He spent the rest of his life mainly in Antwerp, and it was there, in 1605, at the publishing house of Robert Bruney, that he published his *A Restitution of Decayed Intelligence in Antiquities. Concerning the Most Noble and Renowned English Nation.* This book may deservedly be seen as the first textbook on Anglo-Saxon and post-Conquest England in English. Verstegen's main concern was to show the English nation that their roots were Germanic rather than Celtic or Romance, as was the current opinion. By comparison with his contemporaries, his knowledge of Old English was formidable, and he was the first to print a lengthy Old English–Modern English glossary.[12]

When, in chapter five "Of the Great Antiqvitie of Ovr Ancient English Tovng," he comes to dwell on the origin of the term "Romance," Verstegen explained that Frenchmen and Spaniards used to call verses written in their vernacular (as opposed to Latin) *Romances*, or "Roman tongue," and he illustrated this, for example, by referring to Jean de Meung's *Romant de la Rose*, "afterward translated by Geffrey Chaucer with the tytle of *The Romant of the Rose.*" Likewise, he has been informed that Walloons who live in the district of Liège say to strangers: "*parlé Romain*," by which they mean: "speak French."[13] From the Conquest onwards, many Romance words had entered the English language, which left an ineradicable effect upon the language, Verstegen claimed:

> Some few ages after [i.e. the Conquest] came the poet *Geffrey Chaucer*, who writing his poesies in English, is of some called the first illuminator of the English tongue: of their opinion I am not (though I reuerence *Chaucer* as an excellent poet for his tyme). He was in deed a great mingler of English with French, vnto which language by lyke that hee was descended of French or rather Wallon race, hee caryed a great affection.[14]

Whilst admitting Chaucer's greatness as a poet, Verstegen had greater difficulties in following those who acclaimed Chaucer as the first author to have given splendour and lustre to the English language.[15] Such a claim, in his opinion, would be too much honour for a poet who "mingled," not to say corrupted, pure English with French words, and in so doing helped to obliterate the Germanic texture of the language. Verstegen continued by claiming that the situation had grown ever worse since Chaucer's time, so much so that in his own days foreigners did not even consider English to be a language in its own right, but "the scum of many languages." According to Verstegen, the English had borrowed so many words from other languages, that "yf wee were put to repay our borrowed speech back again, to the languages that may lay claim to it; we should bee left litle better then dumb, or scarcely able to speak any thing that should be sencible." Verstegen's argument ended with a plea for a proper use of English, avoiding French words as much as possible. To do so, a thorough awareness of the Germanic roots of the language was needed, and that is why he concluded this chapter with the afore-mentioned Old English– English glossary, amounting to twenty-seven pages, illustrating simultaneously what words had disappeared from the language to be replaced by French loans, and what words, though changed by time, had survived.

Verstegen's *Restitution* was a great success, and went through several reprints in the seventeenth century, though not every reader agreed with his critical assessment of the mixed character of the English language. George Tooke, in 1647, boasting of the advantages of the foreign element in English, scorns Verstegen who "will indeed upbraid *Chauc[er]* with it [viz. the foreign element] as prejudicial; and anothore Netherlander has objected our English to me, for made up of several shreds like a Beggars Cloake."[16] The growing animosity between England and Holland, which would lead to three naval wars that century, is barely hidden in these lines. Tooke casually alludes to Verstegen's Dutch origin in the words with which the second spokesman are indicated: "anothore Netherlander." The latter's opinion of the mixed quality of the English language expressed in tailor's terminology stands in a long tradition of such comments.[17] Thomas Fuller, in his *Church History* of 1655,[18] also signals Verstegen's censure upon Chaucer's language:

> Indeed, Verstegan, a learned Antiquarian, condemns [Chaucer], for spoiling the purity of the English tongue, by the mixture of so many French and Latin words. But he who mingles wine with water, though he destrois the nature of the water, improves the quality thereof.

Where Verstegen saw the abundance of Romance loanwords in English as a detriment to that language, Fuller appreciated their presence as an improvement.[19]

Verstegen's *Restitution* was also read in Holland by historians with a particular interest in England's past, and the author's opinionated remarks did not fail either to generate or fortify their prejudice against the debased quality of English. Perhaps not surprisingly, we find that both Verstegen and Chaucer were staple diet for the small, if active, number of Dutch Anglo-Saxonists. One of those was Johannes de Laet (1581–1649), another major Dutch Anglo-Saxonist, as we know from the auction catalogue of his library.[20] De Laet is a typical representative of the Dutch seventeenth-century merchant-scholar. Having completed his studies at the University of Leiden in 1603, he settled in London, of which town he became a denizened citizen in 1604 upon his marrying a London girl of Dutch descent. After the death of his young wife in 1606, he moved again to Leiden in 1607, where he lived until his death. From there, he visited England at least twice, in 1638 and 1641.[21] Not only was he deeply interested in a wide range of scholarly disciplines, he also appears to have developed some interest in contemporary English literature, especially in that characterised by religious or moral overtones. De Laet's library was well-stocked and included, beside numerous English theological books mostly of Puritan character, Owen Feltham's *Resolves* (London, 1636), Francis Bacon's *Essayes* (London, 1634) and *The Temple* (Cambridge, 1634), by the metaphysical poet George Herbert. He also owned a copy of Thomas Speght's edition of Chaucer of 1602, but we have no idea how de Laet appreciated Chaucer as a poet. Nor do we know whether he annotated his Chaucer copy, because, after the auction of de Laet's library in 1650, all traces of this book have been lost. It would seem, though, that de Laet was especially interested in the linguistic side of Chaucer. In the 1630s and 1640s, de Laet was deeply involved in a competition to bring out the first Anglo-Saxon dictionary. Other competitors were Sir Henry Spelman, Abraham Wheelock and Sir Simonds D'Ewes. At least once in his correspondence with D'Ewes, de Laet illustrates with the help of Chaucer that the meaning of words is not static but changes through time.[22] It also appears, from his correspondence with the Danish antiquary Ole Worm, that de Laet shared Verstegen's low opinion of the mixed character of English – the *Restitution* was also included in his library. De Laet knew that at least some of the Anglo-Saxons when they invaded Britain, originated from Denmark and had brought their language along with them; therefore it occurred to him that the people who were living in, or close to, Denmark, might use that language in a less corrupted way than did the English in his day.[23]

Further evidence of an acquaintance with Chaucer in the Low Countries at this time appears from the writings of Marcus Zuerius Boxhorn (1602–1653), professor of History and Rhetoric at Leiden. Boxhorn was a man of broad scholarly interests, one of which was comparative linguistics. He was also acquainted with Old English, and indeed intended to publish on the Anglo-Saxon laws, of which he possessed an edition.[24] In an appendix to his edition of a chronicle of the province of Zeeland, whose capital is Middelburg, he illustrates the town's flourishing international trade in the fourteenth century by quoting from Chaucer's portrait of the Merchant in the *General Prologue*, though – curiously – he attributed the lines to John Gower:

> In these times Middelburg flourished greatly in trade, which was carried on from England to Zeeland, and from Zeeland to England. I have learnt this from an English author and knight, called John Gower, who lived under Richard II, by that name, King of England, and who wrote many remarkable poems, dying in 1402. . . . *His reasons spake hee full solemnely // Shewing alway the encrease of his winning // He would the Sea were kept for any thing // Betwixt Middleborough and Orewely.*[25]

How Boxhorn came to confuse Chaucer with Gower is not clear to me, but the appreciative tone of the quality of Gower's / Chaucer's work is striking for someone whose mother-tongue was not English. It may well be that de Laet, a good friend of his, alerted him to Chaucer's mentioning Middelburg in these lines.

Finally, I should like to call attention to Jan van Vliet (alias Janus Vlitius; 1622–1666), another Dutch Anglo-Saxonist, who also made a study of Chaucer. Van Vliet was especially interested in Chaucer's language, and he compiled a glossary of some 225, usually unreferenced words, most of which, upon closer scrutiny, appear to be hapax in Chaucer. Apparently, van Vliet had a keen eye for such exceptional words. His work, therefore, can best be seen as belonging to the study of so-called "hard words" in Chaucer which was beginning to emerge in the seventeenth century, although etymology also played a part, as appears from his frequently adding cognate forms from Dutch, Danish and contemporary English.[26] Van Vliet, by the way, also was familiar with Verstegen's *Restitution*, to which he occasionally refers in his unpublished studies.[27]

*Junius's appreciation of Chaucer*

It is against this ambivalent background of the current opinion concerning the allegedly dubious quality of Chaucer's language, on the one hand, and, on the other, of Chaucer's well-established reputation as a great poet, that we must view Junius's work on Chaucer. Exactly when Junius took up his study of Chaucer is difficult to determine. From his heavily annotated copy of Sir Philip Sidney's collected works, preserved in the Leiden University Library, and which he extensively used for *The Painting of the Ancients* (1638) – his own, English translation of *De pictura*[28] – it appears that Junius was already familiar with Chaucer's reputation as a great poet in the late 1630s. While reading Sidney's famous essay, *The Defence of Poesie*, Junius underlined those passages that seemed of particular interest to him. Sidney comes to treat of Chaucer at the point where he discusses the difficulty of expressing thoughts in words. Quoting a line from Ovid, *Quidquid conabor dicere, Versus erit* ("Whatever I shall try to say, will be a verse"), Sidney carries on: "Neuer marshalling it [i.e. thought] into any assured ranke, that almost the Reader cannot tell where to find themselues." From this point on, Junius underscored the following:[29]

> *Chawcer* vndoubtedly did excellently in his *Troilus* and *Creseid*; of whom truly I know not whether to marruell more, either that he in that mystie time could see so clearly, or that wee in this clear age, goe so stumblingly after him. Yet he had a great want, fit to be forgiuen in so reuerent an Antiquitie.

According to Sidney, and apparently with Junius's subscription, Chaucer is looked upon as an excellent poet, albeit one suffering from a "great want." To Sidney, according to Derek Brewer, this would seem to imply "the absence of the dominant criteria of Neoclassical taste, i.e. regularity, unity of plot and tone, realism, moral improvement, [and] high seriousness of the poetic *vates*."[30]

In any case, Junius resumed and intensified his Chaucer studies after he had finally seen his edition of the Gothic and West Saxon Gospels through the press in 1665. On 3 June, 1667, he wrote to his friend and pupil, Thomas Marshall, to thank him[31]

> for the comment upon Chaucer, which I finde not otherwise then I expected, seeing I knew not how to looke for a commentator[32] that should give anie light to Chaucers old language, and

so putt us in a way for to understand better the meaning of that inventive poët.

What exactly Junius had asked Marshall for is not clear, for the letter in which he had addressed Marshall about Chaucer has not been retrieved. It is possible that there was no letter at all, but he had raised the question during one of their meetings. However it may be, three points raised by Junius in this letter require some clarification. Junius needed a commentator to "give anie light to Chaucers old language."[33] From these words it becomes clear that Junius looked upon Chaucer as a writer of a bygone age, whose language could no longer be readily understood, and hence was no longer capable of being read meaningfully. Such a supposition would be in line with the opinion prevailing in the seventeenth century. The phrase "anie light" also seems to suggest that Junius had only just embarked on Chaucer, and that therefore any help in coming to grips with Chaucer's text was welcome to him. Most interestingly, it is not so much the Middle English language as such that is the object of Junius's curiosity. Had that been the case, Junius could just as easily have resorted to other manuscripts in his library, such as Wycliffe's translation of the New Testament (MS Junius 29), *The Prick of Conscience* (MS Junius 56),[34] or a Lydgate anthology (Leiden University Library, MS Vossius Codex Gallicus Q 9); as for the *Ormulum* (MS Junius 1), Junius, like his contemporaries, probably considered its language to be Old English.[35] What mattered to him was the unlocking of the full significance of Chaucer's language, the restoring of corrupted passages, as well as the providing of a commentary – where necessary – to elucidate certain passages. This was because Chaucer was a poet who, more than any other, *deserved* to be studied. To Junius – and here we have an appreciative evaluation of Chaucer the author – he was an "inventive poët." This qualification, for Junius, referred to "invention," a concept in Rhetoric which he had frequently used in his *Painting of the Ancients*, and on which he expounded in great detail in its Book III, ch. 1, 1–6. According to Fehl and Fehl, the term has three meanings in Junius's writings: (1) The act of finding – inventing or conceiving – an appropriate and just means to present a subject in a way that will ring true; (2) the faculty of invention; (3) the result, that is the conceit, especially the developed conceit in the mind of the artist as he means to represent it or as he has represented it.[36]

Essential for "invention," according to Junius, was the artist's proper use of his memory and his imagination. To his creative work the artist should bring, in as skilful and orderly a manner as he can, whatever he has observed with his senses or has read in authoritative writers. "Invention," then, implied qualities which for us would be subsumed under "imagina-tion," "creativity" or "originality," but also certainly "craftsmanship." It was the opposite of "convention," the ideal of imitating one's predeces-sors as much as possible. Junius, it is clear, was fully aware of Chaucer's prominent position amongst other medieval English authors as an inno-vator.

Some six months after he had written to Marshall, Junius again referred to Chaucer, this time in a letter of 3 February 1668 to his friend and fellow Anglo-Saxonist, Sir William Dugdale.[37] The second Anglo-Dutch Sea War (1665–1667) had been concluded a few months earlier, and Junius was musing about the negative effects which the war was having on the book and publishing-trade. The passage gives us some further insight into his motivation and method:[38]

> Thus sitting still, as dwelmed by the universal confusion of manie nations, two or three years are slipped away over my head stealingly; which in these high yeeres [Junius was seventy-seven by then!] I find to be more then six in my younger years, though I was not alltogether idle since I returned to the Hague from Dordrecht [this was early in 1666]. But first of all gott my great worke of Teutonic Glossaries in a perfect order for the presse; but seeing them as it were lie dead by me, I had neither heart nor lust to hoorde up more workes of that nature in my studie; but for a chaunge I took your archpoet Chaucer in hand; and though I thinke that in many places he is not to bee understood without the help of old manuscript copies, which England can afforde manie, yet doe I perswade my selfe to have met with innumerable places, hithertoo misunderstood, or not understood at all, which I can illustrate. To which work I hold the Bishop of Dunkel his Virgilian translation to be very much conducing, and in my perusing of this prelate his book (to say so much by the way) I stumbled upon manie passages wherein this wittie Gawin doth grosly mistake Virgil, and is much ledd out of the way by the infection of a monkish ignorance then prevailing in Church and common wealth; yet is there verie good use to be made of him. All this mentioned change of worke gave me a sweet entertainment, and was to me some kind of solace to my griefe in the most sad times.

This is admittedly a long quotation, but I will show how well it serves to reveal Junius's frame of mind.

It would seem that Junius, after the publication in Dordrecht in 1665 of the Gothic Gospels and Gothic Glossary – his greatest undertaking – had fallen into a state of dejection. True, he had finally come round to preparing yet another lexicographic project for the press, a comparative Germanic dictionary on which he had been working off and on for almost ten years, but due to the economic situation in Holland he was not in a position to furnish the money necessary to have it published. This in its turn discouraged him from carrying on with his other lexicographical projects, of which the *Etymologicum Anglicanum* was the most ambitious one. In this temporary stalemate position he had taken up reading the "archpoet" – in the sense of "principal poet"[39] – which promised to be an enjoyable diversion. But blood is thicker than water, and before long the philologist in Junius had taken over from the leisurely reader. As he read, Junius gradually became aware that Chaucer's text as he found it in Speght's edition frequently could, and indeed should, be emended – in other words, was greatly in need of a critical text edition. This, however, could only be achieved by collating that edition with the oldest available manuscripts. This realisation betrays Junius the humanist, and a true member of the Leiden school of text editors.

As a student at Leiden,[40] Junius had been trained in the method of textual criticism promoted especially by Joseph Scaliger – whom he had personally known – of how to establish a classical text's most authentic redaction by collating all extant manuscript versions and selecting from these the best textual variants. Sometimes, in the absence of reliable textual witnesses, resort had to be taken to conjecture in order to make sense of a passage. Since Junius was living in The Hague at the time when he took up the serious study of Chaucer, the option of collating Chaucer manuscripts, of which he realised there must be many in England, was not open to him. Hence, the only alternative for emending what he thought were nonsensical passages was conjecturing improvements, conjectures sometimes based on his familiarity with English, whether Old, Middle or contemporary, or simply based on intuition and common sense.

Even without the indispensable Chaucer manuscripts, Junius felt sufficiently confident to explain many passages that had hitherto remained obscure. When he mentioned the Chaucer he took "in hand," he was no doubt alluding to the then standard edition by Thomas Speght, *The Workes of Our Ancient and Learned English Poet, Geoffrey Chaucer,* which had appeared in 1598, and again, revised, in 1602. Speght's edition was based on that of William Thynne, first published in 1532, and reprinted in 1541, 1550 and, expanded with some new items by John

Stowe, in 1561.[41] Speght had been the first Chaucer editor to accommo-
date the reader by providing a lengthy introduction to Chaucer the man
and his work, an extensive glossary, as well as some annotations to clarify
certain obscure passages. Since Speght's 1602 edition, however, no
dramatic progress had been made in Chaucer studies, and the passing of
time had only contributed to rendering Chaucer less and less accessible.

What Junius appears to have had in mind, when he wrote to
Dugdale, would seem to have been some kind of commentary on
Chaucer. I cannot help thinking that such a commentary would have
looked much like his *Observationes* on Williram's Old High German Paraphrase of the Song of Songs. The latter book came out in 1655, and was
the first fruit of his Germanic studies. These "Observations" are mainly
concerned with discovering the precise meaning of Williram's use of
words. According to Junius, the precise meaning of a word could only be
established by comparing it with as many cognates as possible – the older,
the better. To him, the etymology of a word was the key to its original
meaning. Junius compiled other such "Observations," notably on the Old
High German Tatian (MS Junius 13 and 42) and on the Old English
Caedmon poems (MS Junius 73*), both of which remain in the Bodleian
Library unpublished.[42]

## Junius's annotations in Speght

Junius's annotated copy of Speght's Chaucer edition (now Bodleian
Library, Junius MS 9) does not show signs of having been read by
someone who merely sought a pleasant diversion. Everything rather
points to Junius taking his approach to Chaucer seriously and profession-
ally. The way Speght's edition was printed, without proper numbers to
refer to the individual texts, and provided with foliation numbering –
excluding the prefatory matter and the *General Prologue*, beginning only
with "Fol. 1" with the *Knight's Tale* – instead of continuous pagination,
made it a tool that was too crude for Junius to work with. Instead, he set
about clarifying matters. First of all, the structure of Speght's edition had
to be laid bare. To this end, Junius provided the individual items in its
two tables of contents with an appropriate numbering. Furthermore,
rather than numbering the pages consecutively, Junius opted for a more
convenient solution and numbered continuously at the bottom of each
page the individual columns (two per page) containing the actual text of
Chaucer's works, beginning with the *General Prologue*. As the columns
themselves in Speght's folio edition were too long for his purposes – the
greatest length is fifty-five (unnumbered) lines – he subdivided them

mentally into "*i., m., s.,*" indicating "*infra, medio, supra,*" respectively. Having applied this system of column numbering and column subdivision, Junius was ready to embark on a detailed reading of the text. His heavy cross-referencing gives ample evidence of this purpose. For his convenience he added an octavo quire of ten sheets at the end of his copy on which he wrote down a detailed "Syllabus operum hoc libro Chauceri contentorum," with references to the appropriate column numbers.

It appears that Junius's approach to Chaucer's language was above all heuristically based. Some examples may illustrate this observation. In line 36 of the *General Prologue*,[43] "Or that I ferther in this tale pace," Junius underscored "Or" and wrote in the margin: "27, s. 46, m." Following these references, we find in column 27 (*KnT* 1155): "For paramour I loued her first or thou," with a cross-reference to "1, i." and in col. 46 (*KnT* 2209): "The sonday at night, or day began to spring," with further cross-references to "1, i. 35, i. 49, i. 51, i.". Following this lead to col. 35, we find line 16 (*KnT* 1595): "Chese which thou|wilt, or thou shalt not astert." Apart from a slightly pedantic vertical line indicating a space between "thou" and "wilt," Junius wrote "for" in small letters over "or." His reading meanwhile had taught him, we must assume, that *or* in Chaucer could be a variant of "ere, before," but that in this particular line that meaning did not apply. He therefore felt sufficiently confident to read "for," a reading now found in all editions.

As we have seen in his letter to Dugdale, Junius boasted that he had "met with innumerable places, hithertoo misunderstood, or not understood at all, which I can illuminate." His emendation of "or" to "for" illustrates such an illumination. Time and again, we see Junius venturing a better reading, ranging from simple to ingenious. Simple but sensible are the following: col. 28 (*KnT* 1206) Duke ~~Thebes~~ let him out of prison" (*KnT* 1206) into Theseus; in col. 89 (*MLT* 92) he suggested improving "Piriades" to "Piërides"; in col. 112 (*SqT* 10) "Surrie" to "Russie." Slightly less obvious was his emendation of Speght's "The vertu expulsed" (col. 56, *KnT* 2749) to "expulsive", or "Denmark" in col. 219 (*FranT* 801: "In Denmark, ther his dwelling was") into "Penmarke." Modern editions confirm that Junius was justified in making such alterations. Notably clever was the emendation / explanation he gave for the following line in col. 31 (*KnT* 1374–75):

> Of Hereos, but rather lyke many
> Engendered of humours melancolike

For Hereos, Junius suggested to read "Eros, i.e. Cupido," while for many, his suggestion was "Manie, i.e. Phrenesis." The same information, basically, is still found in the *Riverside Chaucer* edition. It is difficult to resist the temptation to tabulate all the felicitous emendations made solely by intuition, without any help from a manuscript, which all lead me to the conclusion that Junius was a reader with a sensitive eye, discerning awkward places in the text he was reading. Of course, he also sometimes blundered, even though he might be right in spotting a corrupted text. Where the *Riverside Chaucer* text of *KnT* 2075 has "This goddess on an hert ful hye seet," the line in Speght's text in col. 44 reads "This goddess full well vpon an hert <u>shete</u>." Junius underlined the last word and wondered in the margin: "videtur contractum ex <u>she sete</u> sedebat" ["It seems [this word] is contracted from <u>she sete</u> 'sat'."] Occasionally, Junius ventured an explanatory note. After Constance had been rescued from the shipwreck, she was able to communicate with the constable who had saved her, but "A maner <u>latin corrupt</u> was her speche." At this line in col. 98 (*MLT* 519), Junius wrote, whether in earnest or jokingly I cannot say: "Italian." However, modern editors also add an explanatory note at this line.

One of the aspects of Chaucer's language as it was known to Junius through Speght's edition was its bewildering amount of spelling variants. Such a state of affairs ran counter to his idea that a language should have some kind of uniform appearance. From Junius's work on Old English and Old Frisian, as Kees Dekker has demonstrated, we know that when he was copying texts he often silently eliminated spelling variants so as to achieve a greater uniformity of forms.[44] That is why he noted in the margin of col. 883 (*Bo* ii, p3, 43) at a line containing the word <u>warned</u>: "malum <u>werned</u>." Apparently, <u>warned</u> was the form to be preferred because it concurred with the English of his own day, and therefore <u>werned</u> was "ugly." In Speght's version, *MLT* 1095 reads: "That all was redy he loked besily." Junius was rightly puzzled with this reading, and wrote in the margin of col. 110: "l[ege 'read'] <u>And already he cam</u>, <u>and looked busily.</u>" At three points in this (infelicitous) emendation he modernised the spelling. Similarly, for Speght's "As is depainted in the <u>certres</u> aboue" (*KnT* 2037), Junius, in col. 43, proposed to emend <u>certres</u> into "starres." His guess was right, but in Chaucer's English the spelling was *sterres*, according to the *Riverside Chaucer*.

Another word that Junius found fault with appears in the following quotation (col. 48; *KnT* 2290): "A crowne of a grene oke <u>vnseriall</u>." Here Junius was not satisfied with a mere conjecture, but also added his arguments: "l. <u>cerriall</u>. for <u>cerrus</u> is a kinde of tree like an oke, and bereth maste. Vide Plinium." This reference to Pliny provides a good indication of how Junius was reading and interpreting Chaucer, viz. through the filter of the Classical authors. And these he seemed to know by heart, dozens of them. Pliny the Elder's *Natural History* was of course a well-known text in the seventeenth century, but what is striking is that the word *cerrus* occurs only three times in it.[45] This classical baggage, then, emerges regularly from the margins of Junius's Chaucer copy, through one or several quotations from or references to such famous works as: Ovid's *Metamorphoses, Fasti* and *De arte amoris*; Vergil's *Æneid* and *Georgics*; Boethius's *De consolatione philosophiae*; Seneca's *Epistolae morales ad Lucilium, De clementia*, and *De beneficiis*; Juvenal's *Satires*; Horace's *Ars poetica* and *Epistolae*; Plautus's dramatical works *Truculentus* and *Pseudolus*; Terence's *Eunuchus*; Tibullus's *Eligiae*; Petronius Arbiter's *Satyricon*; Ausonius's *Ludus septem sapientium*; Cato's *Distichs*; or to works now lesser known but well read in the Renaissance, such as: Aulus Gellius's *Noctes Atticae*; Valerius Maximus's *Facta et dicta memorabilia*; and Publilius Syrus's *Sententiae*. There is one lengthy Greek citation, from Hippocrates's *Aphorisms*, with which Junius identified the source of the opening lines of the *Parlement of Foules*. Junius also occasionally quoted from or referred to early Christian works, such as: Origen's *Hymn on Mary Magdalene*; Prudentius's *Hymn to the Holy Virgin*; and St. Augustine's *De civitate Dei*. On only one occasion did he write a reference to the Gospel of St. Matthew, a remarkably low figure for someone who had studied theology and had served as a minister of the Divine Word.[46]

Junius's annotations on the whole rarely give meanings of words. An example such as the following is exceptional: "That cost of gold largely a fother" (*KnT* 1908). The underlined word is given the following definition in the bottom margin of col. 40: "a fother is a twentie hundred weight, which is a cartes or waines load." The reason why hardly any glosses are to be found among his annotations is that he included these in a separate glossary, now Junius MS 6, which was erroneously subtitled by an eighteenth-century librarian as *Dictionarium Veteris Linguae Anglicanae*, i.e. "Dictionary of the ancient English Language." As this two-column glossary of ninety-eight folios contains few etymological remarks or references to cognate languages, contrary to Junius's usual practice in his dictionaries, it appears to have been conceived of as being intended only for the disclosing of Chaucer's language.

For a proper understanding of the latter, the most obvious approach for Junius was to consult Speght's list of hard words, appended at the very end of his edition. Speght's list, however, is highly eclectic, and does not give any line or page reference whatsoever. Junius's definition of "Fother," for example, is not to be found in the 1602 edition.[47] As a matter of fact, Junius never referred to Speght's glossary, whereas he did mention other lexicographic authorities, such as Gilles Ménage, *Les origines de la langue françoise* (Paris: Augustin Courbé, 1650); a glossary of barbaric, i.e. vernacular, words in Matthew Paris's chronicles, appended to the revised edition of 1640;[48] Henry Spelman's *Archaeologus*, a voluminous dictionary of Germanic words in Latin texts;[49] the *Etymologicum linguae Latinae* (Amsterdam, 1665) of his brother-in-law Gerard Vossius; and, occasionally, his own published and unpublished lexicographical works, e.g. his *Etymologicum Anglicanum*, mentioned three times.[50] Not altogether surprisingly in the context of Chaucer, references to Junius's *Glossarium Gothicum* are conspicuously rare. I have found only one: in col. 1011 (*LGW* 1289) at "shapeth" Junius noted down "Vide Goth. gloss. in *skapian.*" What is striking, though, is that for all his unrivalled knowledge of Old English, Junius drew no parallels in his Chaucer marginalia with words from that language. Only on one occasion did he refer to Old English. In col. 677 (*Tr* 2.1495), the text has "And al this thing he told him word and end," where he marked it with a sign referring to the top margin. There he wrote: "And all this thing he told him word and end. Omnino lege ord and end. Ac vide Observationes nostras ad Willerami paginam 248, ubi agimus de Saxonico *ord*." Indeed, on that page Junius discussed the meaning of Old English *ord*, including the collocation *ord 7 ende* which he translated with "*initium ac finem*."[51] He suggested therefore that Chaucer's phrase is a corruption of the Old English one, an opinion still held today.[52] References to non-lexicographical works are rare. In col. 1144 (*HF* 689–91: "And mo berdes. . . Ymade,"), Junius remarked: "Vide Gatakeri Cinnum, p. 323 partis primæ." Modern editors still give a note at these lines to explain the expression "to make a beard" as "to cheat."[53]

A clever way of tackling Chaucer's language was by means of another, related text. For this purpose, Junius diligently used Gavin Douglas's *Eneados*, a Middle Scots versified translation of Vergil's *Aeneid*. This work had the advantage of allowing Junius to compare it with the Latin source text. Junius esteemed Douglas for his "wit," a term comparable to "inventive" as he applied it to Chaucer. No matter how much Douglas might have erred in his translations through "monkish ignorance" – what Junius means is that from a humanist point of view Douglas's Latin was defective – it proved of great help to him in understanding Chaucer, and reading these two authors even gave him "sweet entertainment" and "solace" in those dark, depressing days. Among the Juniana in the Bodleian Library, the 1553 edition of Douglas's *Eneados* has also been preserved; it is heavily annotated with references to both Vergil's Latin text and to Chaucer: Junius rarely read without a pen.[54] Instrumental, too, for his reading of

Chaucer was his consultation of the French text of the *Roman de la Rose*. At the top of this text in Speght's edition, Junius wrote the title "*Le Rommant de la Rose*, imprimé à Paris l'an 1528. fol. 1.*" Throughout the text of Chaucer's translation of the *Roman de la Rose*, Junius wrote numbers in the left-hand margin corresponding to the numbers of the pages ("feuillets") of the French edition of 1529. As no edition of *Le Rommant de la Rose* is known for the year 1528, the latter date is probably a mistake, and Junius must actually have used the 1529 edition. This supposition is borne out not only by Junius's referring to the latter edition in the *Etymologicum Anglicanum*, for example, s.v. *saylours*,[55] it is also confirmed by his sparingly annotated copy of this edition, which I recently discovered in the Leiden University Library.[56] Junius, whose father was French, was as proficient in French as he was in English, and must have found the French text a welcome help in his reading of Chaucer's version of the *Roman of the Rose*. Interestingly, it is only for his marginal annotations to the *Roman* that he seems to have consulted Gilles Ménage's *Les origines de la langue françoise*, and that four times in all.

For his reading of Chaucer's *Boece*, Junius could, of course, rely on his great familiarity with Boethius's Latin text, as he has indeed been shown to have done.[57] Throughout the text in Speght, Junius inserted the appropriate section numbers of the prose and metrical subdivisions. On occasion, he observed that Chaucer's Latin exemplar had suffered from textual corruption. For example, where in col. 919 (*Bo* iii. m9, 39–40), Speght has "into thy straite seat", Junius remarked: "Interpres noster legit <u>angustam</u> pro <u>augustam</u>," or in col. 931 (*Bo* iii. p12, 73–74) at "he is as a key and a styere": "Interpres noster legisse videtur <u>clavis</u> pro <u>clavus</u>." As for the post-Classical sources, Junius seems to have been unaware of, or indifferent to, Chaucer's great indebtedness to, for example, Boccaccio, Dante and Deschamps.

Before reaching this point, I have mentioned several books carrying Junius's annotations in the Leiden University Library, something that requires an explanation. Until recently, it was generally assumed that Junius had bequeathed his entire library to the Bodleian Library, an assumption probably deriving authority from the remark in the Bodleian's *Summary Catalogue* that Junius donated "his philological collections" to Oxford University.[58] In view of the forty-five printed books included among the Bodleian Junius collection of 122 items – original manuscripts, transcripts, commentaries and lexicographical works, quite a few of which were ready for the press – this would be a poor library for a scholar who in his published and unpublished work displayed such an intimate knowledge of both Classical authors and secondary, contemporary literature.

Over the past decade it has become clear that Junius in fact bequeathed only a small portion of his library to the Bodleian, mainly books concerning Germanic philology and dictionaries of various Germanic languages. The major part of his collection, including the theological and Classical books, but also books of which he possessed two copies, was inherited by his nephew, Isaac Vossius, who incorporated them within his own vast library.[59] Upon Isaac's death in 1689, Leiden University purchased the collection from Vossius's heirs, and since 1690 these books and manuscripts have formed an invaluable part of the university library. Over the past ten years, some forty books in the Vossius collection have been identified as items formerly belonging to Junius. A problem complicating the identification is that Junius did not mark his books with his signature or with any other sign of ownership. It is only his annotations in them that betray his ownership, and sometimes, scholars have failed to recognise his hand. Since one of the stipulations of Vossius's heirs was that each book of the collection should be marked as such – and indeed they usually carry a printed strip on the title page "*Ex bibliotheca Cl. V. Isaaci Vossii*" – Junius's hand-writing has been misidentified. So it happens that the annotations in the only Middle English manuscript in the university library of Leiden, a fifteenth-century anthology of poems by John Lydgate – but also including Chaucer's short poem *Truth* – were erroneously attributed to a "hand from the second half of the sixteenth century."[60] In fact, the hand is clearly and unmistakably Junius's. His annotations mainly concern short titles in Latin, based on an English table of contents written on the front fly-leaf.

For example, where the list of contents has "The Danish warres in Ethelstans time with the story of Guy of Warwicke," Junius wrote at the top of the text "Danica invasio regnante Ethelstano, una cum historia Guidonis de Warwik" (p. 17). At one point in the manuscript we can see how Junius familiarised himself with the script. As is known, Junius took a particularly close interest in the presentation of text. Especially for his philological publications he had made a variety of type fonts, enabling him to use the Gothic uncial for Gothic words, the insular script for Anglo-Saxon, runes for Old Norse and a variety of black-letter types for contemporary languages.[61] On p. 232 of the "Leiden Lydgate," which was left blank by the scribe, we can see how Junius tried to imitate the fifteenth-century hand of the scribe by copying on an empty page the title and three stanzas from the facing page. The result is fair enough.

*Epilogue*

Taking Junius's study of Chaucer into consideration, we can see a three-pronged approach:
    (a) he strove towards establishing a better text by making the spelling uniform and by improving corrupt passages by way of conjecture;
    (b) he compiled a glossary to be used as a key to words which were obscure or had become obsolete. Meanings were established either by comparing one passage in Chaucer's texts with one or more other passages, with Gavin Douglas's Middle Scots and with the *Roman de la Rose*, or with the help of existing lexicographical works;
    (c) he identified sources and analogues of certain passages through his vast knowledge of the Classics.
More than a century ago, the Harvard Chaucer critic Mark Liddell, with evident enthusiasm, announced his discovery of Junius's Chaucer material in the Bodleian in a less than one-page article in the English gentleman's monthly *The Athenaeum*, and suggested that Junius intended to prepare a new Chaucer edition.[62] Although modern scholars have regularly repeated this suggestion on Liddell's authority,[63] I seriously doubt whether Junius ever fostered such an ambition. Junius was certainly aware of the need for a new edition, and he was undoubtedly qualified to carry it out, but he simply could not comply with the most important condition: he lacked authoritative manuscripts with which to establish a reliable scholarly text based on collation and emendation.[64] The best that he could have achieved would have been a commentary, a kind of "Observations on Chaucer." Death, however, prevented him from bringing the material together into a coherent monograph.

When Junius donated his most valuable philological treasures to the Bodleian, part of his stipulation was that his works that were ready for the press should be published. Indeed, shortly after his death, a group of Oxford scholars, including Bishop John Fell and Thomas Marshall, both devoted friends of Junius, set about carrying this out.[65] On 26 July 1684, Marshall sent the following report (naturally in Latin) from Lincoln College, Oxford, to Isaac Vossius in Windsor, where the latter was canon:[66]

> Most illustrious Sir,
> On the occasion of having sent this, I have not been able to ensure you how much progress we have made in preparing the collected works of Mr. Junius of blessed memory, with which purpose a Lexicon Septentrionale [Dictionary of Northern

Languages] will be compiled. The work has been almost finished by a certain good editor; nothing, as far as I know, will stop its completion, except the Observations on Chaucer by the excellent author [i.e. Junius]. This Chaucer is with me amongst other works left by the illustrious Junius. Its running marginalia refer the Reader to an enriched Index, which I have long and much searched for here in vain. Lest this great work [i.e. the Lexicon Septentrionale], moreover to be printed at our not mediocre expenses, be published incomplete and mutilated in this part, I may hope that you will leave not unseen to us the copy of the Index of this Chaucer, which is now part of your most instructive library.

This was written in haste, Yours obligingly, Thomas Marshall.

What exactly Marshall is referring to here is not entirely clear: he appears to have Junius's annotated Speght edition, and he must have had the Chaucer glossary. But what does he mean by "the enriched Index"? Curiously, Junius's Oxford copy of the 1598 Speght edition is lacking the "old and obscure words of Chaucer explained," together with the other end items, viz. "The French in Chaucer translated," "Most of the Authours cited by G. Chaucer in his workes, by name declared," "Corrections of some faults and Annotations vpon some places," "Faults escaped," and the final note. These pages were cut out, but the stubs still testify to their formerly having been there. As we have seen, Junius also owned a copy of the 1602 Speght edition, which still has the expanded glossary intact, but this copy contains far fewer annotations in his hand,[67] of which two are worthy of mention. The first is an explanatory note on fol. 113, 4 (*RR* 1093): "Worth all the gold in Rome and Frise," where Junius wrote in the margin "intellige Phrygia*m*." Whether by experience – he had spent some time in Friesland[68] – or, more likely, through his knowledge of the Classics, Junius realised that "Frise" did not refer here to the northernmost area of the Netherlands, but was rather an allusion to Phrygia, the opulent kingdom of Midas.[69] The other remark shows Junius's impatience with the way Chaucer mutilated Classical names. On fol. 181, 3 (*Tr* 5.1792): "Of Uergil, Ouid, Homer, Lucan, and Stace," he wrote right below this line: "In lingua Anglicana ejus orthographiæ ingens est diversitas, multisque erroribus obnoxia est" ["In his (i.e. Chaucer's) English language the variety of spelling is enormous, and liable to many errors"]. In seventeenth-century Dutch, most likely with Junius's approval, these names had been restored from their vernacular to their Latin forms. At the same time, Junius made his remark to apply to Chaucer's spelling in general.

The printing quality of his 1602 copy was rather poor, and throughout the book Junius has dotted the "i"s where the dot did not appear, and touched up letters that had come out printed only half, occasionally correcting a printing error along the way. We can also see Junius employing a method of cross-referencing similar to that in his Oxford copy, but he did not apply the consecutive column numbering. Instead, he used Speght's folio numbering with the refinement of dividing each folio into four columns, so that, for example, "3, 2" refers to "fol. 3, col. 2." Since Junius's Chaucer glossary (MS Junius 6) throughout displays the reference system as set up in his Oxford copy, it is clear that he obtained his 1602 copy only when he had advanced very far in his Chaucer project – too far in any case to find it convenient to make adjustments. In what measure Junius used the 1602 edition to improve the text of that of 1598 is a moot point. Some of Junius's improvements in the latter copy can also be found in print in the edition of 1602, and he may have carried them over into his working copy without proper acknowledgement; but many other of his corrections are not to be found in the second edition. Concerning Speght's revised text, Derek Pearsall remarked that "[m]any of them are obvious and straightforward. . . and could have been introduced independently by an intelligent editor with an ear for Chaucer's verse."[70] Junius qualifies as such an intelligent reader, if anyone does.

Junius's 1602 copy does not include the "Enriched Index" that Marshall referred to in his letter to Isaac Vossius. Could Marshall have been referring to a separate copy-book containing a list of annotations? On over fifty occasions, the margins in the Oxford Speght copy bear a note saying vide Annotationes, as if Junius had compiled a list of notes which were too large to write down in the margin. Most of these brief notes, forty-five to be precise, are to be found in the part containing the *Canterbury Tales*, the remainder being scattered over the other texts. For example, such references appear at *palmers* (col. 1; *GP* 13), *Magike naturell* (col. 10; *GP* 416), or *ascendent tortuous* (col. 94; *MLT* 302).[71] None, however, are found in the margins of the *Roman of the Rose* or Chaucer's translation of Boethius's *De consolatione*, as if Junius had other explanatory resources for these texts that made annotations redundant. What Marshall had not noticed is that all these references relate to Speght's "Corrections and some faults and Annotations vpon some places," appended at the very end of his 1598 edition. These pages, as we have seen, were removed from Junius's Oxford copy. In the 1602 edition, Speght had incorporated the "Annotations," which served much the same purpose as the modern explanatory notes, into his revised glossary.[72] Much to our disappointment, the glossary and annotations cut out from

Junius's 1598 Speght are exactly what is missing among his legacy to the Bodleian, with the result that we can only guess to what extent Junius might have "enriched" these pages. It is, however, still possible that we may yet be able to gain an idea of the kind of annotations it would have contained, presumably on sheets added to the pages he had removed from his 1598 copy. At the top of col. 253, Junius – or the early eighteenth-century binder[73] – pasted a rather large slip of paper, with a comment on *CYT* 1047–51 which runs as follows:

> Chaucerus 254, i.
> Beleveth this as siker as your crede.
> God thanke I, and in good time it be saied,
> That there nas never man yet evill paied
> For gold ne silver that he to me lent:
> Ne never falsehede in mine harte I ment.
> Observa hoc in loco illam bene precandi formulam, qua utebantur se suaq*ue* impensius laudaturi, ad invidiam deprecandam vel ad advertendum fascinum, in good time be it saied, Absit verbo invidia.
> Prorsus ut vetustiores Romani præfiscine vel præfiscini dicebant; est enim præfiscine ex præ et fascino, atque ad verbum sonat ἁ βασκάντως ac citra invidiam. Vide his doctissimi Vossii etymologicum Latinum, in Fascinum.[74]

Such an explanatory note is precisely appropriate, and, though somewhat verbose, contains essentially the same information as that of the *Riverside Chaucer*.[75] The only difference is that Junius reveals his etymological mind by adding a remark on the derivation of *præfiscine*, with reference to his brother-in-law's huge Latin etymological dictionary, published post-humously in Amsterdam and London in 1662.

Isaac Vossius, unfortunately, was not able to help Marshall. The *Lexicon Septentrionale* was never brought to the press – the fruits of Junius's learning were simply too large to handle – but it is preserved unfinished in the Bodleian Library among the Fell manuscripts.[76] There can be little doubt, though, that Chaucer studies would have been furthered considerably in the eighteenth century, if Junius's annotations to Chaucer had been published, preferably in conjunction with his glossary. As this was not the case, Chaucer criticism virtually had to start all over again in the nineteenth century – in particular concerning allusions to or hidden quotations from Classical authors. In this respect it is curious that the anonymous editor of Urry's Chaucer edition – this was in fact Timothy Thomas[77] – played down the quality of Junius's Chaucer studies:[78]

> There is a copy of the Edition 1597 [sic] with MS. notes of *Junius* in the *Bodleian* Library amongst his MSS (N°. 5121.9) but neither did those notes nor his other Papers there of that nature (which I likewise consulted) afford that assistance which might be expected from so great a Name; most of them being very imperfect, or drawn up rather for his own use than for the information of others.

One of Urry's intentions with his edition had been to demonstrate the sources of Chaucer's learning. Timothy Thomas, however, had not been able to find anything concerning this part of the project amongst Urry's papers, apart from a note which identified the source of *Eight Goodly Questions with Their Answeres*, the poem (now no longer considered part of the Chaucer canon) printed in Speght's edition immediately before the *General Prologue*, as being Ausonius.[79] The same had been done by Junius, who wrote over the first line of each stanzaic question the name of Ausonius together with the original question in Latin. Is it possible that Urry, a student of Christ Church College, had seen Junius's annotated copy? One of the preparatory steps he had taken towards his edition was to write a letter, on 5 December 1711, to consult the doyen of historical linguists, George Hickes, upon whose advice he studied the Junius Manuscripts in the Bodleian, as Hickes had informed him that "an Edition of Chaucer was there in great measure in [Junius's] hands."[80] But apart from his possible indebtedness to Junius's identification of Ausonius, Urry's edition shows no trace of having seized the opportunity to make use of the rich material he had had in his hands.

Junius's detailed occupation with Chaucer, nevertheless, was not wholly without impact. Many of his lexicographical observations found their way into his *Etymologicum Anglicanum*. In all, this dictionary includes some 468 illustrations from Chaucer, seventy-nine of which were added from his handwritten Chaucer glossary (MS Junius 6) by his editor Edward Lye, as is indicated by square brackets.[81] These entries show Junius to have read Chaucer with empathy and care, and, on occasion, with a little mischievous delight for the bachelor he was (see Appendix II). Impressive though the amount of Chaucer quotations in his *Etymologicum* may seem, it must be viewed against Junius's Chaucer glossary which contained about 4,000 entries, almost twice as many as did Speght's glossary in the 1602 edition.[82] As it is, Junius did not manage to finish his glossary, since his pious wish, expressed in the second entry (on *A per se*), was never fulfilled. Having compared the use of this expression in both Chaucer and Douglas, Junius went on with a quotation, in Greek, from Revelations 1: 8: "I am the Alpha and Omega, the beginning and the ending, etc.," and continued, in Latin:[83]

> What the Highest Judge of things wanted to indicate with this statement, you can clearly gather from the following words, viz. that God is the same, and always has been and will be from now on; accordingly, his promises are certain and unchangeable. These [promises] also tell me to hope that this project of mine will one time be carried to a conclusion, (which project) the inexhaustible giver of all good things, God, has granted that the day has dawned for me to undertake it.

Oh happy morning! The evening, however, was not given to Junius to see, but would we not all wish for the same productive longevity that the Highest Judge bestowed upon this great philologist?

**Appendix I**

In this list, I have recorded only the source identifications which Junius made to those works by Chaucer in Speght's edition which are now recognised as canonical, with the exception of the first item. Identifications are marked † when they are accepted by Robinson's 1957 edition, and marked * when accepted by the *Riverside Chaucer.*

*Eight Goodly Questions with their Answers*
Above stanzas 2 to 9, Junius wrote down in Latin the question, and the
    beginning of the answer from Ausonius. At the third stanza he
    wrote: "Auson. explicat hic dictum Seneca epistola CIII: <u>Ab homine
    quotidiarum periculum</u>. etc."
†At col. 27 (*KnT* 1162: "Loue is a gretter law. . ."): Boëth. III de Consol.
    metro 12; <u>Quis legem det amantibus? Major lex amor est sibi</u>.
†*At col. 31 (*KnT* 1387: "His slepy yerd. . ."): <u>Somniferam virgum</u> vocat
    Ovidius Metam. I, 672. vide quoque Metam. II, 736.
†*At col. 35 (*KnT* 1625–26: "Full soth is saied, that loue ne lordship /
    Woll nat his thankes haue any feliship;"): <u>Non bene eum sociis regna
    Venusque manent</u>. Ovid. III de Arte, versu 564.
At col. 38 (*KnT* 1773–75: "fie / Upon a lorde that woll haue no mercie, /
    But be a Lion both in worde and dreede"): <u>Non decet Regem sæva
    nec inexorabilis ira</u>. Vide Senecam de Clementia.
†At col. 38 (*KnT* 1798–99: "Now loketh, is not this a great folie? / Who
    may be a foole, but if he loue?"): Mimijambus P. Syri; <u>Amans quid
    cupiat, scit; quid sapiat, non videt</u>. Plautus Pseudolo, Act. I, Sce. 3; –
    <u>non jucundum est, nisi amans facit stulte</u>.
†*At col. 43 (*KnT* 2056: "Calistope"): Ovidius II Fast. versus 158. sicuti
    et II Metam. versu 409.
†*At col. 43 (*KnT* 2065: "Atheon"): <u>Aetæon</u>. Ovidius Trist. II, vers. 105.
    et Metam. III, 190.
†*At col. 43 (*KnT* 2070: "Athalant"): Atalanta & Meleager. Ovid.
    Metam. VIII, 299.
†*At col. 49 (*KnT* 2389: "Whan Uulcanus had caught the in his laas"):
    Ovid. Met. IV, 184. & II de Arte, versu 180.
At col. 50 (*KnT* 2448: "In elde is both wisdome and usage."): <u>Seris venit
    usus ab annis</u>; Ovid. Metam. VI, 29.
At col. 61 (*KnT* 3029–30: "in youth or else in age. / He mote be dedde, a
    king as well as a page"): <u>Mors per omnes it</u>; Seneca ep. XCIII.
At col. 65 (*MilT* 3227–28: "He knew nat Cato (for his wit was rude)
    [parentheses added by J.] / That bad men wed her similitude."):

Solon apud Ausonium: Par pari jugator conjux: quicquid impar, dissidet.

At col. 103 (*MLT* 776–77: "There dronkenesse reigneth in any rout, / There nis no counsaile hid, [comma added by J.] withouten dout."): Horat. Quid enim ebrietas designat? sic.

†*At col. 122 (*SqT* 518: "a tombe is all the faire aboue,"): Matth. XXIII, 27.

At col. 158 (*WBTProl* 572–74: "I hold a Mouses wit not worth a Leke? That hath but one hole to sterten to, / And if that faile, than is all idoe."): Plautus Trucul. Actu IV, scena 4; Cogitato, mus pusillus quam sit sapiens bestia, / Ætatem qui uni cubili nunquam committi suam, / Quia si unum ostium obsideatur, aliud perfugium gerit.

At col. 169 (*WBT* 1117: "Christ wuld we claimed of him our gentilnesse,"): Aurelii Prudentii Hymnus in laude Romani martyris; Generosa Christi secta nobilitat viros. &c.

*At col. 170 (*WBT* 1183–84: "Glad pouerte is an honest thing certaine, / This wol Seneck and other clerkes saine."): Honesta res est, læta paupertas. Seneca epist. II.

†*At col. 170 (*WBT* 1192–94: "Iuuenal saith. . .: The poore man, whan he goeth by the way / Before theues, he may sing and play."): Cantabit vacuus coram latrone viator.

At col. 170 (*WBT* 1195–97: "Pouert is. . ./ A great amender eke of sapience,"): Bonæ mentis soror est paupertatis; Arbiter.

At col. 186 (*SumT* 2067: "And up the string he pulled to his ere"): Virgil IX Æneïd. Ecce aliud summa telum librauit ab aure.

At col. 212 (*ClT* 993–94: "That him to seen þe people had cauȝt plesance, / Commendyng now the Marques gouernance"): Claudianus, Mobile mutatur semper cum Principe vulgus.

At col. 219 (*FranT* 829–31: "By processe, . . ./ Men mowen so long grauen in a stone, / Till some figure therin printed be:"): Quid magis est durum saxo? quid mollius unda? Dura tamen molli saxa cavantur aqua. &c. Ovidius I de Arte. v. 477.

At col. 230 (*FranT* 1409: "The eight maidens of Melesy also"): Vide Aulum Gellium.

At col. 487 (*Rom* 343–45: "For who so sorrowful is in harte, / Him lust not to plaie, . . . ne to sing."): Difficile est tristi fingere mente jocum. Tibullus Eligia 6 libri. Tertii. vide locum.

†*At col. 578 (*Rom* 5234–35: "For good dede done through praiere / Is sold and bought to dere iwis"): Seneca de benef. II,1.

†*At col. 668 (*Tr* 2.1030–36: "For though the best Harpour upon liue / . . . and of his strokes full."): Citharoedus ridetur chorda qui semper oberrat eadem. Horatius de Arte.

†*At col. 716 (*Tr* 3.1634: "As great a craft is to kepe well as winne."):
Ovidius circa initium libri II de Arte am. Non minor est virtus quam
quærere parta. / Casus inest illic, hic erit artis opus.

†*At col. 724 (*Tr* 4.197: "O Juuenal lord, trew is thy sentence,"):
Juvenalis Satyra X, circa finem Satyræ(:) Permittes ipsis expendere
Numinibus, quid / Conveniat nobis rebus*que*, sit utile nostris: /
Nam pro quæundis aptissima quaq*ue*, dabunt Di/ Carior est illis
homo, quam sibi — &c. Socrates humanæ sapientia*m* quasi
quoddam terrestre oraculum, nihil utora a Diis immortalibus
petendu*m* arbitrabatur, quam ut bona tribuerent. Quia ii clemu*m*
scirent quid uniique esse utile. &c. Val. Maximu*m* VII, 1.

At col. 725 (*Tr* 4. 258–59: "That wonder is the body may suffise / To
halfe this wo, which that I you deuise."): Mirandum est unde ille
oculis suffecerit humor; Juvenalis Satyra X, versu 32.

At col. 730 (*Tr* 4.501: "O death, that ender art of sorowes all,"): mors
ultima linea reru*m* est. Horat libro Primo, epist. 16.

†*At col. 730 (*Tr* 4.503–04: For sely is that death, . . . / That oft ycleped,
cometh and endeth pain."): Mors hominum felix, quæ nec se
dulcibus annis / Inserit, et miseris sæpe vocata venit. Boëthius libro
I, metro 1.

†*At col. 749 (*Tr* 4.1408: "Eke drede fond first goddes, I suppose."):
Primus in orbe Deos fecit timor; Arbiter.

†*At col. 754 (*Tr* 4.1645: "That loue is thing ai full of busie drede."): Res
est solliciti plena timoris Amor. Ovidius, Penelope Vlyssi. vers. 12.

†*At col. 838 (*LGW* 1690: "The great Austyn," etc.): Vide Augustinum
libro 1 de civitate Dei, cap. 19.

†*At col. 848, before the opening line of the Legend of Philomena (*LGW*
2282): Vide Boëthium de Consolatione philosophiæ et confer cum
initio hujus legendæ.

†*At col. 1011, written over the first line (*PF* 1): ὁ βίος βραχὺς, ἡ δὲ τέχνη
μακρὴ, ὁ καιρὸς ὀξυς, ἡ δὲ πεῖρα σφαλερὴ, ἡ δὲ κρίσις χαλεπὴ – Tale
est initium aphorismorum Hippocratis.

At col. 1016 (*PF* 225: "In such arraie as when the Asse him shent"):
Ovid. Fast. 1, 437.

†*At col. 1017 over stanza (*PF* 275–77: "And Bacchus. . . lay Cupide"):
Terentius Eun. Act IV, sce 5. Verbum herile verum hoc est: Sine
Cerere et Libero frigat Venus.

†At col. 1018 (*PF* 343: "The Oule eke, that of deth the bode bringeth;"):
Ignavus bubo, diru*m* mortalibus omen; Ovid. Met V, 555. Tristia
mille locis Stygius dedit omina bubo; Met XV, 791.

At col. 1018 (*PF* 353: "The Swalowe, murdrer of the Bees smale"): Virg. Georg. IV, 15.

At col. 1018 (*PF* 358: "The waker Gose;"): Ovidius Met XI, 600.

**Appendix II**

THINGS videntur Chaucero dici illæ pulchrarum feminarum partes, quibus sunt id quod sunt, quibusque viros ad sui amorem præcipue pelliciunt. **Let Ladies worken with her things**. RR. 6037. Huic affine quoque est Chaucerianum **bellechose**, pro quo tamen idem Chaucerus aliquanto post **bely chose** scribit.

— If I wolde sell my belle-chose,
I couth walken as fresh as any rose.
        W.B. 447.

—— he couth so wel me glose,
Whan that he wold, he had my bely-chose,
That though he had me bete on every bone,
He couth winne agen my love anon.
        ibid. 509.

Ac priore quidem in loco **bellechose** videtur satis manifeste Bellam rem, posteriore vero Rem ventris denotare: eadem compositionis ratione, qua huic nostro Poetæ Ma.T. 114 **bely naked** est Totus nudus. i.e. "Ita ut quisque nostrum e bulga est matris in lucem editus," ut loquitur Lucillius apud Nonium. Latinis etiam Res denotabat Veneream rem. . . .

(From this point Junius proceeds to dwell extensively on Latin, French, Dutch and, especially, Old English words for "things" and "copulation.")

[" 'THINGS' seems to be what Chaucer calls those parts of beautiful women by which they are what they are, and with which they especially entice men to love them. . . . Related to this (word) is also the Chaucerian **bellechose** for which the same Chaucer writes **bely chose** a little later. . . . But in the former passage **bellechose** seems quite manifestly to denote 'beautiful thing', whereas in the latter it means 'belly thing': using the same way of writing as when in our Poet (*MeT* 1326) **bely naked** is 'completely naked'; i.e. 'Just as each of us is given to light from the mother's belly,' as Lucillus says in Nonius. In Latin 'Thing' signified 'what pertains to sexual love'. . . ."]

(N.B. The phrase *bely chose* rests upon an error in Speght's edition.)

## NOTES

1. See Rolf H. Bremmer Jr, ed., *Franciscus Junius F.F. and his Circle* (Amsterdam and Atlanta, GA: Rodopi, 1998), as well as Sophie van Romburgh's contribution to the present volume. A shorter version of this paper was read at the 34th International Congress of Medieval Studies, Kalamazoo, MI, May, 1999. Part of my researches on Junius were conducted at Harvard University when in 1994 I held the post of Erasmus Professor of Dutch History and Culture as a guest of the Department of English and American Literature. Hence my dedication. I would like to thank Bart Veldhoen, Sophie van Romburgh, Alasdair MacDonald and Kees Dekker for their help and suggestions.

2. F. Madan, H.H.E. Craster and N. Denholm-Young, *A Summary Catalogue of Western Manuscripts in the Bodleian Library at Oxford*, 2: 11 (Oxford: Oxford University Press, 1937), 962–90, nos. 5113 to 5232*. For a further discussion of a number of these items, see E.G. Stanley, "The Sources of Junius's Learning as Revealed in the Junius Manuscripts in the Bodleian Library," in Bremmer, *Junius and his Circle*, 159–76. The description in *SC* of the Junius MSS is much in need of revision.

3. Franciscus Junius F. F., *Caedmonis Monachi paraphrasis poetica Genesis ac praecipuarum Sacrae paginae Historiarum* (Amsterdam: Christophel Cunrad, 1655). Also available in a facsimile edition with an introduction by Peter J. Lucas, *Early Studies in Germanic Philology* vol. 3 (Amsterdam and Atlanta, GA: Rodopi, 2000).

4. Franciscus Junius F. F., *Observationes in Willerami Abbatis Francicam Paraphrasin Cantici canticorum* (Amsterdam: Christophel Cunrad, 1656), also available as a facsimile edition with an introduction by Norbert Voorwinden, *Early Studies in Germanic Philology* vol. 1 (Amsterdam and Atlanta, GA: Rodopi, 1992).

5. The text proper and part of Junius's commentary were published posthumously by Johann Phil. Palthen, *Tatiani Alexandrini harmoniae Evangelicae antiquissima versio Theotisca* (Greifswald: Johann Wolfgang Fickweiler, 1707). Also available as a facsimile edition with an introduction by Peter Ganz, *Early Studies in Germanic Philology* vol. 2 (Amsterdam and Atlanta, GA: Rodopi, 1993).

6. Franciscus Junius F. F., *Quatuor D. N. Jesu Christi Evangeliorum versiones perantiquae duae, Gothica scilicet et Anglosaxonica* (Dordrecht: Hendrik and Johan van Esch, 1665); and *Gothicum Glossarium* (Dordrecht: Hendrik and Johan van Esch, 1665).

7. MSS Junius 2 and 3. On this dictionary, see Kees Dekker, " 'That Most Elaborate One of Francis Junius': An Investigation into Francis Junius's Handwritten Old English Dictionary," in Timothy Graham, ed., *The Recovery of Old English: Anglo-Saxon Studies in the Sixteenth and Seventeenth Centuries* (Kalamazoo, MI: Western Michigan University Press, 2000), 310–54.

8. Franciscus Junius F. F., *Etymologicum Anglicanum ex autographo descripsit & accessionibus permultis auctum edidit* Edwardus Lye (Oxford: Sheldonian Theatre, 1743; facsimile repr. Los Angeles: Sherwin and Freutel, 1970). The original, in two volumes, is MSS Junius 4 and 5. The testimonies are to be found on p. *E3v.

9. Franciscus Junius F. F., *De pictura veterum* (Amsterdam: Johannes Blaeu, 1637). Junius himself translated this book into both English and Dutch as *The Painting of the Ancients* (London: Richard Hodgkinson, 1638) and *De Schilder-konst der Oude* (Middelburg: Zacharias Roman, 1641), respectively. Junius completed an enlarged revision of *De pictura* which was published posthumously by Johannes Georgius Graevius, augmented with Junius's *Catalogus artificum*, unpublished until then, a kind of encyclopaedia of Classical art and artists (Rotterdam: Van Leer, 1694). For a modern edition with an excellent introduction, see Franciscus Junius, *The Literature of Classical Art*. Vol. 1: *The Painting of the Ancients*, Vol. 2: *A Lexicon of Artists and Their Works*, ed. and transl. Keith Aldrich, Philipp Fehl and Raina Fehl (Berkeley, Los Angeles and Oxford: University of California Press, 1991), and Franciscus Junius, *De pictura veterum libri tres (Roterodami 1694). Edition, traduction et commentaire du livre I*, ed. Colette Nativel (Genève: Librairie Droz, 1996).

10. With the exception of a brief, exploratory study by Johan Kerling, "Franciscus Junius, 17th-Century Lexicography and Middle English," in R.R.K. Hartmann, ed., *LEXeter '83 Proceedings. Papers from the International Conference on Lexicography at Exeter, 9–12 September 1983* (Tübingen: Max Niemeyer Verlag, 1984), 92–100.

11. See Judith Dundas, " 'A Mutuall Emulation': Sidney and *The Painting of the Ancients*," in Bremmer, *Junius and His Circle*, 71–92.

12. On Richard Verstegen, or Verstegan, see extensively Rolf H. Bremmer Jr, "The Anglo-Saxon Pantheon According to Richard Verstegen (1606)," in *The Recovery of Old English*, ed. Timothy Graham, 147–75. Add to the secondary literature mentioned there: Christine Fell, "Norse Studies: Then, Now, and Hereafter," in Anthony Faulkes and Richard Perkins, eds., *Viking Revaluations: Viking Society Centenary Symposium 1992* (London: Viking Society for Northern Research, 1992), 85–99.

13. Verstegan, *Restitution*, 200.

14. Verstegan, *Restitution*, 203–04.

15. *OED* s.v. *illuminator* (4): "one who makes resplendent or illustrious," with reference precisely to this passage in Verstegen.

16. George Tooke, *The Belides, or Eulogie of that Noble Martialist Major William Fairefax. . .* (London: [n.p.], 1647), 22.

17. This notion already had some tradition in the Netherlands. As early as the first quarter of the sixteenth century, a Frisian chronicler remarked that "gente Anglice moderne mixtum est idioma, nam ex Teutonico, Phrisionico, Gallico et ex alijs quibusdam linguis consarcinatum" (the present-day English people have a mixed vocabulary, for it is patched together from German, Frisian,

French and various other languages). See my "Late Medieval and Early Modern Opinions on the Affinity between English and Frisian: The Growth of a Commonplace," *Folia Linguistica Historica* 9 (1989): 167–91, at 172–73.

18. *The Church-History of Britain from the Birth of Jesus Christ until the Year MDCXLVIII* (London: John Williams, 1655), Bk IV, p. 152.

19. On Tooke and Fuller, see Caroline F.E. Spurgeon, *Five Hundred Years of Chaucer Criticism and Allusion 1375–1900* (Cambridge: CUP, 1925; repr. New York: Russell & Russell, 1960), 1: 225 and 230, respectively.

20. See Paul G. Hoftijzer, "The Library of Johannes de Laet (1581–1649)," in Rolf H. Bremmer Jr and Paul Hoftijzer, eds., *Johannes de Laet (1581–1649): A Leiden Polymath*, special issue of *Lias: Sources and Documents Relating to the Early Modern History of Ideas* 25/2 (1998): 201–16.

21. On de Laet, see extensively Bremmer and Hoftijzer, above.

22. On de Laet's part in the making of an Anglo-Saxon dictionary, see, with further references, Rolf H. Bremmer Jr, "The Correspondence of Johannes de Laet (1581–1649) as a Mirror of his Life," in Bremmer and Hoftijzer, 139–64, at 154–62. His letter to D'Ewes, dated 24 August 1640, is British Library, MS Harley 374, fol. 154; and cf. J.A.F. Bekkers, *The Correspondence of John Morris with Johannes de Laet (1634–1649)* (Assen: Van Gorcum, 1970), xxiii.

23. *Olai Wormii et ad eum doctorum virorum epistolae, medici, anatomici, botanici, physici & historici argumenti: Rem vero literariam, linguasque & antiquitates Boreales potissimi illustrantes*, 2 vols. (Copenhagen, 1751), II, no. 781 (De Laet to Worm, 4 April 1642): "Quia autem scio Anglo-Saxones illos e parte Dania in Angliam venisse, eoque linguam portasse, venit in mentem, non posse me auxilium melius expectare, quam ab iis qui illas partes aut saltem illis incolunt, e quibus illi primum venerunt, quique ad huc eandem linguam incorruptius, quam hodie Angli utuntur." See Bremmer, "The Correspondence of Johannes de Laet," 158–59.

24. See Kees Dekker, *The Origins of Old Germanic Studies in the Low Countries* (Leiden, Boston and Cologne: Brill, 1999), 213–14. Boxhorn owned an edition of the Anglo-Saxon laws as appears from the auction catalogue of his library, *Catalogus variorum et insignium librorum, celeberrimi ac eruditissimi viri Marci Zueri Boxhornii. . .* (Leiden: Petrus Leffen, 1654), where it is listed as no. 6 in the section "Libri Rariores & Manuscripti" as "Veteres Anglorum Leges. Saxonicum cum interlineari versione Latine & Notis marginal. viri Erudit. in Script.," an annotated copy, therefore, indicating Boxhorn's engagement with the topic. This entry does not allow us to identify the book as the original edition of William Lambard's *Archaionomia* (London: John Day, 1568), or Abraham Wheelock's revised edition of this book (Cambridge: Roger Daniel, 1644), though its listing in the section "Rare books" invites one to think of the former possibility. Boxhorn also possessed John Spelman's *Psalterium Davidis Latino-Saxonicum* (London: R. Badger, 1640) and two (!) copies of Verstegen's

*Restitution*, but the catalogue lists neither Gower nor Chaucer, at least not in any recognisable form.

25. Marcus Z. Boxhorn, *Chronijck van Zeelandt, eertijds beschreven door d'heer Johan Rygersbergen, nu verbetert, ende vermeerdert* (Middelburg: Zacharias Roman, 1644), II, 170: "Te deser tijdt heeft Middelburch seer gefloreert in koopmanschappe, die van Engelandt op Zeelandt, en van Zeelandt op Engeland sterck gedreven wierdt. Dit leert my een Engels schrijver ende Ridder, ghenaemt Ian Gouwer, die onder Ritsaert den tweeden van dien naeme, Conink van Engelant gheleeft, ende vele aardige Dichten gheschreven heeft, ghestorven in het jaer 1402. . . ."

26. Van Vliet's glossary, headed "E Chaucero," is preserved in London, Lambeth Palace MS 738, fol. 276 r+v. See further Dekker, *Origins*, 138, 251, 314–15. For further information on van Vliet, see extensively Dekker's book.

27. For example, Dekker, *Origins*, 167, 321–23.

28. Dundas, " 'Mutuall Emulation'," *passim*.

29. Sir Philip Sidney, *In Defence of Poesie*, in his *The Covntess of Pembrokes Arcadia*, 4th edn. (London: 1613), 513 [Leiden, Universiteitsbibliotheek 766 A 15].

30. Derek Brewer, *Chaucer: The Critical Heritage, Vol. I: 1385–1837* (London, Henley and Boston: Routledge and Kegan Paul, 1978), 118.

31. Oxford, Bodleian Library, MS Marshall 134, fol. 8. Thomas Marshall (1621–1685) studied theology at Lincoln College, Oxford, and came to Holland in 1650 to serve as a minister to the English Company of Merchant Adventurers first in Rotterdam, and later, from 1656 to 1669, in Dordrecht. During his time in Dordrecht, he became befriended with Junius. In 1669, Marshall was appointed Master of Lincoln College, Oxford, and it was most probably because of Marshall that Junius settled in Oxford towards the end of his life. Marshall cooperated with Junius on the publication of the Gothic Gospels, taking care of the edition of and commentary on the West-Saxon Gospels that faced the Gothic text. On Marshall, see *Dictionary of National Biography* 36: 247–48; Vivian Green, *The Commonwealth of Lincoln College* (Oxford: Oxford University Press, 1979), 275–80; and Kees Dekker, "The Old Frisian Studies of Jan van Vliet (1622–1666) and Thomas Marshall (1621–1685)," in Rolf H. Bremmer Jr, Thomas S.B. Johnston and Oebele Vries, eds., *Approaches to Old Frisian Philology*. Amsterdamer Beiträge zur älteren Germanistik 49 (Amsterdam and Atlanta, GA: Rodopi, 1998), 113–33, at 121.

32. *OED*, 2a: "A writer of expository comments or critical notes on a literary work; the writer of a commentary." First attestation 1641.

33. Possibly, Junius used "anie" here as the equivalent of Dutch *eenig* in the sense of "some".

34. On these two manuscripts, see Stanley, "Sources," 163, 167.

35. Dekker, *Origins*, 169, 250.

36. Junius, *The Literature of Classical Art*, ed. and transl. Aldrich, Fehl and

Fehl, I, 395. See also p. [liv]: ". . . *invention*, that is, the choice of subject and the appropriateness of the manner in which it is to be treated."

37. On William Dugdale (1605–1686), see *DNB* 16: 136–42. Like Junius, Dugdale was also employed by Thomas Howard, Earl of Arundel.

38. The letter is printed in William Hamper, ed., *The Life, Diary, and Correspondence of Sir William Dugdale*. . . (London: Harding, Lepard, 1827), 146.

39. "archpoet," first recorded according to the *OED* in 1612 with the meaning of "principal poet." Junius's usage of the word would be the third in the seventeenth century, and, as far as I can see, he is the first to apply it to Chaucer. Elsewhere he calls Chaucer "poëtarum Anglorum olim princ[eps] (in former times the foremost of the English poets)," *Etymologicum Anglicanum*, s.v. *a per se*.

40. On Junius's education, see C.S.M. Rademaker, "Young Franciscus Junius: 1591–1620," in Bremmer, *Junius and his Circle*, 1–17, at 4–10.

41. See Geoffrey Chaucer, *The Works 1532, with Supplementary Material from the Editions of 1542, 1561, 1598 and 1602*, facsimile edition, ed. D.S. Brewer (London: Scolar Press, 1978), Introduction; Johan Kerling, *Chaucer in Early English Dictionaries. The Old-Word Tradition in English Lexicography down to 1721 and Speght's Chaucer Glossaries* (Leiden: Leiden University Press, 1979), chap. 3; and especially, Derek Pearsall, "Thomas Speght," in Paul G. Ruggiers, ed., *Editing Chaucer: The Great Tradition* (Norman, OK: Pilgrim Books, 1984), 71–92.

42. On the former, see Peter Ganz, "Ms. Junius 13 und die althochdeutsche Tatianübersetzung," *Beiträge zur Geschichte der deutschen Sprache und Literatur* 91 (1969): 28–76; the latter is published in facsimile as an appendix to Lucas's facsimile edition of Junius's *Caedmon* (see above, note 3).

43. All my references to the Speght 1598 edition are by Junius's column numbering. For the standard edition, I have consulted Larry D. Benson, ed., *The Riverside Chaucer*, 3rd edn. (Boston: Houghton Mifflin, 1987), including the conventional abbreviations for Chaucer's individual texts. For the appendix to this article I have also consulted the edition upon which the *Riverside Chaucer* is based, F.N. Robinson, ed., *The Works of Geoffrey Chaucer*, 2nd edn. (Oxford: Oxford University Press, 1957). Especially in their explanatory notes, these two editions differ at times.

44. Kees Dekker, "Francis Junius (1591–1677): Copyist or Editor," *Anglo-Saxon England* 29 (2000), forthcoming.

45. The word *cerrus* occurs only four times in the entire electronic corpus of Classical and late-Classical Latin texts (*Pandora*), of which thrice in Pliny's *Natural History* (§ 17 l. 4, § 19 l. 2, § 218 l. 10). The other instance is to be found in Vitruvius's *De architectura* (Bk II, ch. 9, § 9 l. 4). In both works, which Junius had extensively used for his *De pictura* and *Catalogus artificum*, *cerrus* is each time identified as a kind of oak. Interestingly, *cer(r)ial* is hapax in Chaucer.

46. For a complete survey of Junius's source identifications, see the appendix below. On the recovery of Chaucer's indebtedness to the Classics, see

Richard L. Hoffman, "The Influence of the Classics on Chaucer," in Beryl
Rowland, ed., *Companion to Chaucer Studies*, rev. edn. (New York and Oxford:
Oxford University Press, 1979), 185–201.

47. That it was a word in need of elucidation by that time appears from its
lengthy treatment in the glossary with Urry's edition (see note 64).

48. *Historia maior, iuxta ex. Londinense 1571 verbatim recusa. . .* (London:
Richard Hodgkinson, Cornelius Bee and Lawrence Sadler, 1640). The glossary,
on pp. 267–310, was compiled by William Watts, and contains nineteen refer-
ences to Chaucer – hitherto unnoticed as far as I know – in the following entries:
*Anelacius, Aurifrisia, Brennium, Brudatus, Burdare, Burdones, Burnettus, Capa,
Cointises, Cordewon, Costrelli, Escheccum, Gisarma, Goliardensis, Grisei,
Haubercum, Heuses, Parvisium,* and *Ribaldus.* The copy in Leiden University
Library [406 A 6], shows no visible signs of Junius having consulted it.

49. *Archaeologus in modum glossarii ad rem antiquem posteriorem, continentis
Latino-Barbara peregrina, obsoleta et novatae significationis vocabula* (London:
Alice Warren, 1625). The Leiden University Library copy [362 A 2] is Junius's
own heavily annotated copy. At the end of his Oxford Speght copy, a small
octavo quire has been pasted, on which Junius identified all the five occurrences
in which Spelman referred to Chaucer.

50. They are, in order of occurrence: *rote* (col. 5; *GP* 236), *Epicure* (col. 8;
*GP* 336), and *tapinage* (col. 618; *Rom* 7361). Inspection of *rote* in the
*Etymologicum Anglicanum* is illuminating. Here Junius calls it "Musicum
instrumentum". After a quote of the relevant passage in Chaucer, he mentions
Laurence Nowell who, in his (unpublished) "A.Saxonic[um] exegetic[um]," s.v.
*rote*, appears to refer to precisely this locus in Chaucer, calling it "a kind of harp."
Junius then proceeds to adduce further supporting evidence from Old English
and Old High German to consolidate Nowell's explanation.

51. *Observationes in Willerami* (1655).

52. Cf. *Riverside Chaucer*, 1036, note on *Tr* 2.1495.

53. Cf. *Riverside Chaucer*, 983. Junius's reference is to Thomas Gataker,
*Cinnus. Sive adversaria miscellanea. . .* (London: J. Flescher and L. Sadler, 1651),
a voluminous kind of exegetical encyclopaedia on the Bible. On this Cambridge
theologian, see *DNB*. I had access only to the edition included in Gataker's post-
humous *Opera critica* (Utrecht: F. Halma, 1697–98), where Chaucer's beardless
Pardoner is mentioned in the commentary on *Hym.* 49: 13. Junius made a
similar note on the additional quire, [fol. 396r]: "qualis apud Chaucerum
Indulgentiarum proxeneta: Gatakeri Cinnus, pagina 196 – parte prima."
Gataker's reference to Chaucer has not been noticed before, as far as I know.

54. *The .xiii. Bukes of Eneados of the famose Poete Virgill Translatet. . . into
Scottish metir bi. . . Gawin Douglas* (London: [William Copland], 1553). Junius's
copy is Bodleian Library, MS Junius 54; cf. Stanley, "Sources," 167. Junius, in his
censure of Douglas's command of Latin, did not take into account that Douglas
had to work with a Vergil edition much inferior in quality to the one he himself
was familiar with. In all likelihood, Douglas translated from the edition by

Jodocus Dadius Ascencius (Paris, 1501). "Many 'howlers' in Douglas's transla-
tion are attributable to imperfections in Ascensius's edition," according to
Priscilla Bawcutt, *Gavin Douglas. A Critical Study* (Edinburgh: Edinburgh
University Press, 1976), 97–102. Junius also compiled a glossary of Douglas's
Middle Scots, now MS Junius 114.

55. In the margin of his Oxford Speght copy (col. 495), Junius wrote "In
poëmate Gallico dicuntur batelleurs, vide Menagium, in Bastelleurs." With
Menagium, Junius referred to Gilles Ménage, *Les origines de la langue françoise*
(1650), which served as one of the models for his *Etymologicum Anglicanum*.

56. *Le Rommant de la Rose nouuellement Reueu et corrige oultre les presedentes
Impressions* (Paris: Galliot du pre, 1529) [Leiden University Library 1369 G 6].

57. Much earlier, Junius had copied the Old English translation of
Boethius's *Consolation* from MS Cotton, Otho A. VI, one of the manuscripts to
be damaged in the Ashbourne House fire. He published the passage from the OE
Boethius in his *Observationes in Willerami*, 46–47 and 229–30. The entire text
was published posthumously from Junius's transcript (now MS Junius 12) by
Christopher Rawlinson, *An. Manl. Sever. Boethi Consolationis Philosophiae libri V.
Anglo-Saxonice redditi ab Alfredo, inclyto Anglo-Saxonum Rege. Ad apographum
Junianum expressos. . .* (Oxford: Sheldonian Theatre, 1698). His transcripts of
the *Metres* are published in facsimile by Fred C. Robinson and Eric G. Stanley,
*Old English Verse Texts from Many Sources: A Comprehensive Collection*. EEMF 23
(Copenhagen: Rosenkilde and Bagger, 1990), item nr. 5.

58. Madan et al., *Short Catalogue*, 962.

59. In 1656, Junius boasted to Dugdale of Isaac's library: "my kinsman
Vossius is held to have a more exquisite librarie of rare bookes, and especially of
manuscripts, then anie other private man in all High and Low Germanie." Cf.
Bremmer, "Retrieving Junius's Correspondence," 213. Junius lived together with
Isaac in The Hague from 1652 until Isaac's move to England in 1673, when he
was appointed Canon of Windsor. Junius followed his nephew to England in
1674. It was in Isaac's house in Windsor that Junius died on 17 November 1677.

60. J.A. van Dorsten, "The Leyden 'Lydgate Manuscript'," *Scriptorium* 14
(1960): 315–25. The manuscript is MS Vossius Codex Gallicus Q 9.

61. Cf. Peter J. Lucas, "Junius, His Printers and His Types: An Interim
Report," in Bremmer, *Junius and His Circle*, 177–97.

62. "Junius's Edition of Chaucer," *The Athenaeum* (12 June, 1897): 779.

63. For example, Eleanor Prescott Hammond, *Chaucer: A Bibliographical
Manual* (New York: MacMillan, 1908; repr. 1933), 508; Spurgeon, *Five Hundred
Years*, 253; Madan, *SC*, 962; William L. Alderson and A.C. Henderson, *Chaucer
and Augustan Scholarship* (Berkeley, Los Angeles and London: University of California Press, 1970), 41; Kerling, *Chaucer in Early English Dictionaries*, 16–17, 20
(but denied in Kerling, "Junius," 97); Dekker, *Origins*, 96 n.235.

64. This was done by John Urry, *The Works: Compared with the Former
Editions, and many valuable MSS., / Geof. Chaucer; out of which, three tales are
added which were before printed by John Urry, together with a glossary; to the whole*

*is prefixed the author's life, newly written, and pref.* (London: B. Lintot, 1721). On this edition, see Alderson and Henderson, *Chaucer and Augustan Scholarship*, chapter 5.

65. See Richard L. Harris, ed., *A Chorus of Grammars: The Correspondence of George Hickes and his Collaborators on the* Thesaurus linguarum septentrionalum (Toronto: PIMS, 1992), 6–8.

66. Amsterdam, Universiteitsbibliotheek, MS III E 10, 37: "Cl. Vir, Hac data occasione, non potui non Te certiorum facere quantos progressus fecerimus in digerendis D. JUNII τοῦ μαϰαρίτου Collectaneis, ad conficiendum Lexicon Septentrionale paratis. Opus jam pene ad umbilicum est productum a dispositore quodam Germano: nec aliquid, quod sciam, desineratur ad ejusdem perfectionem, praeter summi Authoris Observata ad Chaucerum. Ipse Chaucerus, inter alia Cl. JUNII legata, penes me est: cujus perpetua Marginalia Lectorem relegant ad Indicem locupletatum, diu multumque a me hic frustra quaesitum. Ne itaque opus hoc grande, et sumptibus nostris non mediocribus imprimendum, hac ex parte imperfectum prodeat ac mutilum; sperare licet Te nobis non invisurum copias Indicis illius Chauceriani, qui jam pars est instructissimae tuae Bibliothecae. Hoc raptim scribebat, Tui observatissimus Tho. Mareschallus. Oxoniae e Coll. Lincoln. Julii 26 1684."

67. Leiden, Universiteitsbibliotheek, 364 A 13; the annotations in this copy were erroneously attributed to Isaac Vossius by Johan Kerling, cf. Rolf H. Bremmer Jr, "Retrieving Junius's Correspondence," in Bremmer, *Junius and His Circle*, 199–235, at 233.

68. See Philippus H. Breuker, "On the Course of Franciscus Junius's Germanic Studies, with Special Reference to Frisian," in Bremmer, *Junius and His Circle*, 129–57, at 139–41.

69. A similar suggestion was made independently by Albert S. Cook, "Two Notes on Chaucer," *Modern Language Notes* 31 (1916): 441–42, at 442. Both Robinson and the *Riverside Chaucer* are reluctant to adopt this interpretation, but unjustifiably so, cf. Rolf H. Bremmer Jr, "Friesland and Its Inhabitants in Middle English Literature," in Nils R. Århammar et al., eds., *Miscellanea Frisica. A New Collection of Frisian Studies* (Assen: Van Gorcum, 1984), 357–70, at 363–64.

70. Pearsall, "Thomas Speght," 87.

71. Most of the words at which Junius placed this reference are not included in his *Etymologicum Anglicanum*.

72. Pearsall, "Thomas Speght," 89–90.

73. The book was evidently rebound after Junius's death: towards the end annotations disappear in the gutter and marginal notes have been partly lost through trimming.

74. "Observe in this place that formula for wishing well, which people used to use when they were about to praise themselves or their achievements immoderately, to ward off envy or to avert witchcraft, *in good time be it saied*; may envy not attend upon the word. Precisely as the more ancient Romans said *præfiscine* or *præfiscini*; for *præfiscine* is from *præ* and *fascin[um]*, and corresponds

to the word *abaskantōs* and without envy. See about this the most learned (Gerard) Vossius's *Etymologicum Latinum*, s.v. *fascinum.*"

75. See p. 950: "*in good time*: A formula to avert evil consequences, similar to 'touch wood'."

76. Bodleian Library, MSS Fell 8–18; Madan et al., *Short Catalogue*, nos. 8696–8706. In the early eighteenth century another attempt was made to publish the dictionary, and finally a much abbreviated version, compiled by Edward Lye, was published in 1772, see Dekker, *Origins*, 305 n. 30.

77. Alderson and Henderson, *Chaucer and Augustan Scholarship*, 97–103.

78. Urry, *The Workes*, "Preface," sig.L4, M1.

79. Urry, *The Workes*, "Preface," sig.I4.

80. Alderson and Henderson, *Chaucer and Augustan Scholarship*, 93 and n. 43.

81. Hammond, *Chaucer*, 508; Spurgeon, *Five Hundred Years*, 390, remarks: "Continuous reference to Chaucer," but cites only four entries. On Junius's use of Chaucer in his *Etymologicum Anglicanum*, see also Alderson and Henderson, *Chaucer and Augustan Scholarship*, 35.

82. The glossary in the 1598 edition contained 2034 entries, increased in that of 1602 to 2607). On Speght's glossaries, see Kerling, *Chaucer in Early English Dictionaries*, ch. 3; on the scope of Junius's glossary, see Kerling, "Junius," 95–97.

83. *Etymologicum Anglicanum*: "Quid vero hac locutione significare voluerit Summus rerum arbiter, ex sequentibus manifeste colligas: Deum nempne eundem & esse & semper fuisse ac porro futurum esse; proinde quoque certa atque immutabilia esse ejus promissa; quae me quoque sperare jubent ad finem aliquando perductam iri hanc nostram operam, ad quam inchoandam hunc mihi diem illucescere passus est inexhaustus bonorum omnium largitor Deus."

# Transportation to Canterbury: The Rival Envisionings by Stothard and Blake

## Betsy Bowden

In 1807 and 1809, respectively, two London artists alike in age and upbringing each portrayed Geoffrey Chaucer's pilgrims all riding toward Canterbury. Comparative scholarship so far has addressed circumstances of the two paintings' production, via William Blake's angry accusation that his lifelong friend and colleague Thomas Stothard had stolen his idea.[1] The present article will analyze the two pictures themselves, as artistic artifacts rather than biographical bones for contention. (See figures 1 and 2, after endnotes.)

Concerning these two contemporaneous interpretations of one medieval literary work, the stark discrepancies pose for reception aesthetics the question of sociohistoric context vs. personal creativity.[2] To what degree does one aspect or the other cause someone's specific response to a given item of literature? For the two artists under consideration here, the examination of public expectation vs. individual intention runs parallel to current Chaucerians' debate about secular vs. religious elements within the *Canterbury Tales* itself. Each early-nineteenth-century artist found in Chaucer exactly what each was seeking: Stothard a secular light-heartedness that would encourage everyone to buy prints, Blake a heartfelt religious fervour misunderstood (so he believed) by everyone except himself. The contrast implies that we who study medievalism must beware temptations to underestimate the personal while investigating, for example, the Victorian or the Augustan attitude toward something in the Middle Ages – for it was just such a tendency that induced overgeneralisations about "the" Middle Ages in the first place.

Studies in Medievalism XI, 2001

From the two artists' conceptions, among countless visual details ripe for comparison I glean those related to a major, yet neglected, component of pre-twentieth-century culture. Only lately has the primary mode of land transportation been displaced, such that a person now can choose whether or not to interact with horses. During previous millennia, anyone who wanted to travel very far on land or move a large object or even safely cross a city street had to recognise the basic equine emotions of fear, pride, and anger. In the nineteenth century and earlier, therefore, viewers of visual art would readily notice connotations of horseflesh and horsemanship (i.e., equitation) that may elude present-day observers. By beginning with equestrian elements in the two pictures, I hope to establish cross-disciplinary scaffolding for future work on other minute particulars of the two disparate fellowships going on pilgrimage to medieval Canterbury, while remaining in the context of visual art in London during the transition circa 1800 from patronage to sales as artists' principal funding source.[3]

For writers, such a transition had been under way since the Copyright Act of 1709. By Blake and Stothard's time, commercial printers were producing modernisations of Chaucer's work as aids or substitutes for Middle English folio editions. Also available and affordable were unauthorised reprints of the 1775 edition by Thomas Tyrwhitt, whose philology and commentary set the precedent for twentieth-century attempts to read Chaucer's work within the fullest possible re-creation of its own historical milieu.[4]

Tyrwhitt's methodology, which coordinates with the goals of history painting at the time, appears in the series of Canterbury pilgrims depicted by yet a third exactly contemporary artist, James Jefferys. He did a separate brown-wash portrait of every pilgrim, some with their horses, all featuring carefully researched late fourteenth-century clothing, weapons, furniture, architecture, and other details. The fate of Jefferys' work, completed in 1781 for a private patron, may imply lack of public interest in historical accuracy: never reproduced, the drawings were presumed lost until 1987, when I happened upon them at the Houghton Library.[5]

Jefferys died young, however. Perhaps he, like Stothard, would have gone on to establish a market for his artistic output. Stothard studied humbly at the Royal Academy for the requisite seven years, starting in 1777, and kept up connections thereafter with London's artistic elite. Occasional wealthy patrons commissioned works of art. Far more often Stothard did book illustrations, silverwork, separate prints, engravings of others' drawings, and his own paintings and engravings funded by subscription. His art agent, on commission, arranged such subscription drives and also exhibitions of Stothard's work, preferably at venues visible en route to and from the Royal Academy.

Blake, in contrast, defied authority and did not work well with others. Although his middle-class parents apprenticed him to a well-placed engraver, Blake in 1779 both entered and left forever the Royal Academy. He earned a living as a printer while creating and attempting to sell his "illuminated" books, which express verbal and visual art as one. Friends sometimes acted as intermediaries, explaining Blake's temperament to potential patrons or employers. Primarily, though, he went his own way in pursuit of his own vision. As a sort of one-man Bakhtinian carnival, upsetting social norms, William Blake provides an extreme but essential *caveat* for any study in medievalism that might generalise about sociohistoric context.

Within this particular context, in what forms did each artist encounter Chaucer? We know that Blake quoted from the 1687 Speght edition, and copied three portraits from the 1721 Urry edition; of Stothard's sources we know less.[6] Must we deduce that Blake formulated his ideas only after deciphering Middle English from Thomas Speght's black-letter type and John Urry's garbled guesses? My previous studies establish otherwise, by beginning to document the entangled visual and oral traditions about Chaucer that had developed alongside written ones.[7] Even limiting the late eighteenth-century interpretive context to printed Chauceriana, it is noteworthy that public perception came far less from scholarship than from modernisations of separate Canterbury tales, reprinted in mass-marketed miscellanies. In 1700 John Dryden became first to publish modernisations. Alexander Pope soon followed, doing the "Merchant's Tale" and "Wife of Bath's Prologue," then other modernisers for three versions of the "Miller's Tale," three of the "Reeve's Tale," and four of the "Shipman's Tale." The less bawdy tales prompted but one ill-distributed modernisation apiece, or none in the case of the "Parson's Tale."

Besides the predominance of easy-to-read fabliaux in accessible publications, at the turn of the nineteenth century, additional factors documented by Caroline Spurgeon contributed toward the common perception of Chaucer as "a comic poet chiefly remarkable for the scurrility of his verses."[8] Thus Stothard, his principal motivation being the need to earn a living, gladly fulfilled the contemporary public's expectations for secularised, merry, somewhat risqué Canterbury pilgrims. (See figure 1.) In contrast, Blake spent his life striving in vain for any public comprehension of his verbal/visual art – in his view, a divinely inspired art meant to challenge observers' complacent acceptance of contemporary expectations as to poetry, painting, religion, commerce, history, personal lifestyle, and everything else assuredly including Chaucer. (See figure 2, which shows Blake's fourth-state engraving for reasons to be explained.[9]) The "Father of English Literature," meanwhile, would have smiled benignly both at Stothard's pragmatism and at Blake's fiery enthusiasm and idiosyncratic interpretation of his work, which has retained popularity for over six hundred years for a remarkable range of reasons.

Prior to the renderings by Blake and Stothard, verbal descriptions had never accompanied visual depictions of Canterbury pilgrims. It is invaluable, therefore, that just such evidence does survive for both artists. In the *Descriptive Catalogue* for his only exhibition, staged at his brother's hosiery shop, Blake devotes far more detail to "Sir Jeffery Chaucer and the nine and twenty Pilgrims on their journey to Canterbury" than to any other of the sixteen pictures.[10] He specifies that in it "the Horses he has also varied to accord to their Riders" (E 533). Blake purposely uses no more words to describe the horses. As I will show, his visual art acts alone to usurp the long-familiar metaphor whereby Reason, as a rider or charioteer, uses human language to keep mute equine Emotion under control. Instead, in Blake's picture, the emotionally expressive horses proceed toward Canterbury in spite of each human rider's distortion or dearth of control.

Throughout the *Descriptive Catalogue* and elsewhere, Blake manipulates words in order to challenge the pre-eminence of words over visual art within society's complacent expectations. He superficially praises each pilgrim using the abstract, generalised verbiage associated with Urizen, a recurring figure in Blake's poetry, who embodies the rational mindset that would limit or restrain creative genius. Here and elsewhere, especially in his later work, Blake is trying to convert wary readers of empty verbal abstractions into careful viewers of his visual art, which displays the abhorrent spiritual nature of the "grand, terrific, rich and honoured" Summoner and his ilk.[11] By having the undescribed but precisely portrayed horses speak for themselves, wordlessly, Blake anticipates a revival of true artistic creativity once we humans succeed in freeing our non-Urizenic emotional powers from bridles, saddles, spurs, and other sorts of restraints.

Throughout the *Descriptive Catalogue* essay, also, intertwined with Blake's long-abiding devotion to artistic creativity based on Emotion rather than Reason, there writhes fury at the apparent commercial success of his erstwhile friend and colleague. Recent research proves Blake unjust in the bitter accusation that Stothard himself stole his idea, and wrong also to suppose that Stothard would ever earn much money from the painting, although it did gain far more recognition than Blake's.[12] Rather than accuse him in turn of stealing from Stothard a decontextualised idea, Blake specialists could step back from the fray itself in order to survey the extent to which mutual subject matter emerges from shared milieu. Besides the modernisations and folio editions noted above, both artists could have noticed new publications including William Godwin's biography of Chaucer (1803) and all of the inexpensive, because plagiarised, printings of Tyrwhitt's edition. Both also could have marked events to be mentioned below: in 1802 the arrival in London of what is now the Ellesmere manuscript, picturing all of the pilgrims on horseback (e.g., figure 3), and in 1807 the much-heralded arrival of the Elgin marbles, featuring the equestrian procession from the Parthenon frieze (e.g., figure 4).[13]

Unlike Blake, Stothard himself wrote nothing about his own painting. Several close associates did, however: his biographer and daughter-in-law Anna E. Bray; his agent Robert H. Cromek, appending to another project an advertisement for its engraving; and especially William P. Carey, a self-effacing art critic whose 75-page booklet on "The Pilgrimage to Canterbury" attracted paying viewers to exhibitions of the painting in a series of English and Scottish cities.[14] Carey's figure-by-figure description well represents contemporary response to a work of art with horses and humans equal in number. To articulate appreciation for Stothard's technique, Carey comments on every horse visible, describing several more thoroughly than he does their riders. Overall, as will be shown, he and Stothard's other associates emphasise naturalistic art and a secular atmosphere for what Cromek touts as "*a pleasurable Tour, sanctified by the name of Pilgrimage.*"[15] Thus, for example, Stothard's Wife of Bath flirts with laymen and clergy alike from her perch atop a delicate-featured, wavy-maned, long-lashed beauty (figure 1). The scene exudes genial merriment, not sinfulness or even impropriety.

In contrast Blake portrays the Wife of Bath as Whore of Babylon, who has swung her legs across from the sidesaddle's foot support in order to spread them dangling in the viewer's direction (figure 2). Like the other humans on Blake's pilgrimage fraught with sacred significance, the Wife is committing a kind of sin not recognised by Chaucer's religion nor by the Church of England circa 1800 nor by any sacrosanct system beyond Blake's own. She shares with all of the pilgrims the mortal sin of destroying or repressing artistic creativity.

"ALL RELIGIONS are ONE," declares the "Voice of one crying in the Wilderness" in Blake's earliest work in illuminated printing. "The true Man is the source [of all religions] he being the Poetic Genius" (E 1–2). In various media throughout his lifetime, Blake continued to envision a

Christianity based on poetic inspiration and freed from the clutch of established churches. His *Descriptive Catalogue* accordingly explains that the Canterbury pilgrims, like the gods of Greeks and Hebrews and others, represent

> eternal principles or characters of human life [that] appear to poets, in all ages. . . . visions of the eternal attributes, or divine names, which, when erected into gods, become destructive to humanity. They ought to be the servants, and not the masters of man, or of society. . . . for when separated from man or humanity, who is Jesus the Saviour, the vine of eternity, they are thieves and rebels, they are destroyers. (E 536)

Within Blake's private religion, Poetic Genius misused may become a force that operates against what is truly sacred. He fervently believes that Stothard and Cromek have transmuted the Canterbury pilgrims into destroyers of that true religion. Chaucer's genuinely poetic creations have been corrupted and co-opted by the art establishment, which decries Blake's own revelatory work as "eccentricity and madness" (E 538).

As an apprentice Blake had copied medieval tomb sculptures at Westminster Abbey. This and other experience, much enhanced by imagination and self-esteem, made Blake certain that he and only he could now see the spiritual meaning expressed by those who had created visual and verbal art in the Middle Ages. However, the only published review of his only exhibition dismisses "the wild effusions of a distempered brain." A few general remarks, mostly negative, occur elsewhere.[16]

During the subsequent decade, void of public recognition for the painting and his engravings of it, Blake's resentment burgeoned. To the fourth-state engraving, circa 1820–23, he added interpretive phrases in drypoint: "The Use of Money & its Wars" and "An Allegory of Idolatry or Politics" (E 687). Besides adding the inscriptions, Blake made substantive changes to visual details including one described below, the Knight's reins. The fifth-state engraving might be late impressions of the fourth, for nothing changes except disappearance of the lightly sketched inscriptions.[17] I conclude that the fourth-state engraving (figure 2) preserves Blake's fullest interpretation of the pilgrimage to Canterbury.

Two centuries ago, Blake did not foresee a future in which his oft-reproduced visualisation would stand as logo to the New Chaucer Society. Meanwhile, just outside the Tate Gallery room now dedicated to Blake's work, Stothard's painting hangs clustered with landscapes when not in storage. The two artists' contemporaries, though, profusely appreciated Stothard's version. In so doing, they took note of the horses. A painfully insipid "Sonnet on Stothard's Painting of the Canterbury Pilgrims," for example, opens thus,

> Methinks I hear their horses capering head,
> And now the merry group full blythe I see;

and continues,

> Oh! would I were a horseman by the side,
> Of you fair Nymph [the Wife of Bath!], prancing so
> courteously,
> Or I should like with you blythe Friar to ride. . .[18]

The ability to portray equine anatomy and motion was a standard measure of artistic accomplishment. Stothard's daughter-in-law is echoing others, not innovating, when she claims that "Stothard excelled in painting the horse; and in this he resembled Rubens. In the Pilgrimage, the animals are as various and as characteristic as their riders."[19] In England the high mark in equine portraiture had been set by George Stubbs, who came calling at Stothard's home very shortly before Stubbs's death on 10 July 1806. Bray may be enhancing the dialogue but would have no cause to invent the visit itself, for Stubbs remained vigorous and walked eight or nine miles a day until the end of his life:

> One circumstance connected with this work is too remarkable to be omitted. Whilst it was in progress, Stubbs, the animal painter, called on Stothard, and requested to view his Canterbury Pilgrims, saying, he felt a great curiosity to see a picture in which nearly twenty horses were introduced. On looking at it, Stubbs exclaimed: "Mr. Stothard, it has been said, that I understand horses pretty well; but I am astonished at yours. You have well studied those creatures, and transferred them to canvas with a life and animation, which, until this moment, I thought impossible. And you have also such a variety of them; pray, do tell me, where did you get your horses?"
> "From everyday observation," replied Stothard; and Stubbs departed, acknowledging that he could do nothing in comparison with such a work.[20]

The anecdote may represent only a sort of English philistinism, more concerned with animals than with art; yet to understand certain art, some understanding of animals is essential. Leaving much to be done by future analysts of the human participants in the two processions to Canterbury circa 1800, in this article I will follow Stubbs's lead and remark upon the horses.


II

Among animals admired by Stubbs, the Squire's rearing steed is the liveliest. Its whiteness serves as focal point for the front half of Stothard's procession, balanced in the back half by a rosy Wife of Bath (figure 1). Carey makes extensive comments on the Squire's equitation; Bray and Cromek make brief but relevant ones. In Blake's conception the Squire, his horse likewise rearing, rides foremost in the procession (figure 2). The Squire's steed rears also in two visual predecessors to the paintings: the fifteenth-century Ellesmere manuscript, and the 1721 Chaucer folio edited by John Urry (figures 3, 5). Thus the pilgrim whose horsemanship is directly praised in the "General Prologue" will serve to introduce equestrian issues for these two items of visual art that re-interpret Chaucer.[21] I will then follow Blake's order of riders, comparing not every figure but only those whose horses are described in especial detail by Carey and/or made strikingly significant by Blake: Knight, Prioress, Pardoner, Monk, Host, Parson, Miller, and Chaucer, with transitional remarks on Yeoman and Wife of Bath.

My previous studies have traced visual representations of Chaucer's pilgrimage up until the early nineteenth century. Nearly all relevant items were in London, viewable by artists, during the half-decade that Blake and Stothard set to work on their rival paintings. Among all of those items, though, definite evidence so far can prove only that Blake knew the lavishly illustrated Urry edition, from which he copied the head of Chaucer and two mounted pilgrims for William Hayley's library at Felpham. Stothard's life and work have been less investigated than Blake's. An unattributed pamphlet, however, does claim that Stothard based the painting on "ancient illuminated manuscripts" and other artifacts from Chaucer's time.[22]

Did either Stothard or Blake examine the only fully illustrated Chaucer manuscript extant? After 1802 it was in a collection sometimes open to the public, especially to artists, located easy walking distance from both their homes. I have encountered enough dead ends to declare definitively that this question does warrant further research.[23] Here I regard the Ellesmere manuscript only as a parallel item of interpretive interest, therefore, not as source for either painting.

In the early fifteenth century, the Ellesmere Squire is portrayed in calm control of a high-spirited courser (figure 3). As it rears, the rider keeps his eyes fixed firmly on those infallible indicators of equine moods and imminent actions: the ears. Twenty centuries earlier, riders on the Parthenon watch the ears (figure 4). Over six centuries later than the Ellesmere, beginning riders still learn to watch the ears for signs of trouble, along with other very basic principles: always mount from the left, steer with one rein on each side of the horse's neck, squeeze legs and lean forward to start, pull reins and lean backward to stop, and so on.

Probably Blake and Stothard, city boys both, never learned horsemanship beyond such minimal safety rules. Blake by no means shared his patron Hayley's passion for riding, although he did appreciate "my belov[e]d Bruno," the presumably sweet-tempered mount supplied by Miss Poole for his stay at Felpham (E 748, 709). The two artists learned from oral instruction, not from some book, how to sit and steer a horse. Nonetheless, a standard description of proper seat is useful as articulation of this three-millennium continuity in practical equitation: novice or expert, any rider must watch the ears. The following quotation, from William Cavendish's widely distributed equitation manual, describes other features also of the correct seat displayed by the Squire in the Urry edition (figure 5):

> When [the rider] is thus placed upon his twist in the middle of the saddle, he ought to advance as much as he can toward the pommel. . . holding his legs perpendicular as when he stands upon the ground, and his knees and thighs turned inwards. . . . The rider's breast ought to be in some measure advanced, his countenance pleasant and gay, but without a laugh, pointing directly between the horse's ears as he moves forward.[24]

This Urry-edition Squire, which Blake certainly and Stothard probably saw, is not just maintaining control of a high-strung, potentially unruly horse (figure 5; cf. latter situation in figure 3). He is executing a *terre à terre à main gauche* (figure 6), or perhaps a *courbette*, *pesade*, or *pirouette à gauche*. He is performing a standard movement in the *manège*, that is, the set of equestrian exercises first developed in sixteenth-century Italy and France.

During the same century that riding masters were refining this aristocratic sport, also known as dressage, some Continental writers were positing symbolic significance for rearing horses in visual art. Before we proceed with practical matters, such as watching the ears of an excitable mode of transportation, let us pause to consider any possible relevance of abstract symbolism to portrayals of Chaucer's Squire two centuries later in England.

Even during the sixteenth century on the Continent, no standard interpretation attached to depictions of the rearing pose. For some artworks the execution of a *courbette* was said to signify that the high-born rider was an ideal ruler, able to control political situations with subtle reciprocity; in reference to other items, commentators claimed that rearing denoted victory in a given battle. These two meanings had merged already by the 1630s, without affecting British art.[25] Perhaps too a folk belief alive today, and traceable as far back as the American Civil War, was orally transmitted earlier and elsewhere: in Washington, D.C. and other cities, tourists are gravely informed that a rearing equestrian statue "means" that the rider died in battle.[26]

Whether acquainted or not with symbolism ever assigned to the rearing posture *per se*, a nineteenth-century viewer of British art probably was aware that Plato, Alexander Pope, and others had compared Reason's control of Emotion to human control of a horse. A contemporary of Blake or Stothard, gazing at a painting, might wish to ruminate upon such philosophical abstractions. To do so, he would first have to determine whether the visual evidence displays an expert coaxing obedience from a high-spirited steed (i.e., Reason overcoming Emotion) or an inexperienced rider in danger of being thrown (Emotion overcoming Reason). Observation and experience, that is, must precede abstract interpretation of representational art.

Across the centuries, sculptors and graphic artists themselves have considered the successful execution of a graceful rearing posture to be an aesthetic challenge for its own sake, not a philosophical symbol. Blake is an exception. But Blake acknowledges established symbolic systems in order to overturn them – in this case, to give back to those Emotions held in check by human Reason the potential to seize control after all.

Nobody acquainted with Stothard ever assigns abstract symbolism to the rearing Squire or to anything else: not his daughter-in-law, nor his agent, nor the art critic explicating the picture's every nuance for an educated public. (See figure 1.) Among the commentators Bray notes visual effects: the Squire's "beautiful white horse," foregrounded, "relieves the whole group."[27] Cromek posits the painted Squire's motivation: "*The Fop of Chaucer's Age* is exhibited as making a display of his riding" by signalling a dressage movement.[28] Carey makes the same point, describing horse in as much detail as rider:

His spurs and stirrups are of silver. The long full tail of his steed is carefully dressed and bound across the middle, so as to give a picturesque show and form to that natural ornament. In that "age of chivalry," the pride of horsemanship was a prevailing passion. . . .

Wel coude he sitte *on hors, and fayre ride.*

This point of personal accomplishment admitted of an advantageous display upon canvas. The Painter has therefore mounted him upon a spirited white horse, of a noble figure from the *manège.* He leans back in the saddle, touching the animal with his spur, to exhibit his address and figure, to the fair Pilgrims behind.

"While his left heel, insiduously aside,

"Provokes the caper which he seems to chide."*

This stroke of character is perfectly natural in a military equestrian, an admirer of the Ladies. . . .

The horse's head is thrown back: he rears on his hind feet, and his rider, sitting with the fiery grace of a young soldier, forms an imposing object on a most conspicuous part of the fore-ground.                              *Prologue by Sheridan.*[29]

Stothard's portrayal of the Squire projects a certain artistic ambiguity, in that at least one contemporary viewer admired the scene but understood it differently than did Carey. Sir Walter Scott, whose prized Stothard print still hangs in his study at Abbotsford:

made the characteristic criticism upon it, that, if the procession were to move, the young squire who is prancing in the foreground would in another minute be over his horse's head.[30]

To Scott it looked as if Stothard's Squire, elbows flailing, is losing control of a startled, plunging steed that has tossed up its head to slacken the reins and thereby seize the bit. Meanwhile the Yeoman's horse, doing its duty, whirls to herd its overexcited charge away from the crowd before it can kick or alert its companions to the invisible horse-eating monster that it has just spotted, probably in the Host's abrupt hand gesture. To me it seems that Scott describes the visual evidence better than Carey does. Either way, the pragmatic point remains that a rider in this situation ought to watch the ears, as does Stothard's Squire, whether his horse is rearing in panic or as performance.

In Blake's visualisation the Squire contradicts both Chaucer's

description and the Urry-edition precedent. He displays equestrian inep-
titude in ways readily observable from the ground, throughout London
streets and parks, especially by an attentive artist looking to depict
"Horses. . . to accord to their Riders" (E533). Hind legs side by side show
that the Squire's horse has halted to rear in place (figure 2; cf. cantering in
figure 4). Unchecked by the drooping reins, it displays the flattened ears
and flared nostrils of an angry horse, here one twisting to snap at the
Knight's steed. Blake's Squire ought to notice the ears and the attitude.
He ought to tighten the reins, regain control of his misbehaving mount,
and steer. Instead he stares glassily off into space, oblivious to inevitable
problems and a possible stampede. Negligence and unproficiency characterise the son who ought to be learning professional riding skills from his
father, the Knight.

   Without reference to equitation, in a previous study I document
visual details whereby Blake's Knight and Squire comprise two-thirds of a
Trinity of repressive religion.[31] The ironies visible in the Knight's face,
gesture, and scale-like armor intensify with regard to his horsemanship,
for God the Father of repressive religiosity rides like a comic buffoon. At
first glance, Blake's Knight appears in control of a high-spirited steed. Its
neck arches elegantly; its eyes gaze straight forward. At first glance also his
equipment seems to include double reins, which would convey firmer
signals to a curb bit (i.e., one with leverage via extensions, as shown).
Blake's art requires much more than a first glance, however. A closer look
reveals single reins only – both held on the same side of the horse's neck!

   In sequential engravings, Blake gave increasing prominence to this
visual detail that epitomises the high-born Knight's professional incompe-
tence. Three states of the engraving may be compared in enlarged reproductions.[32] I have also examined a third-state original and two fifth-state
restrikes at the Philadelphia Museum of Art. In the first-state engraving
(1810) the Knight's uppermost rein is blended and overlaid with mane;
its origin is unclear. For the second and third states (1810–20) Blake
made alterations such that the whole of both reins do lie on the viewer's
side of the neck, unmingled with mane; he also added cross-hatching to
darken the neck, while leaving the reins a lighter shade. Same-side reins
remain well defined in the fourth (figure 2) and fifth states, ca. 1820–23.
In some impressions the mane just above them appears darker, and the
reins even lighter in contrast.

   An actual horse would panic if ever mounted with both reins on the
same side of its neck, although a very calm one (perhaps, one time, Bruno
at Felpham?) might walk tight circles until rescued. In Blake's visualisation the chivalric Father's horse is reluctantly taking care of its ignorant,

backward-looking rider. With eyes and ears aimed straight ahead, it does its best to lead him and the rest of the humans toward their spiritual goal, Canterbury. Champing the misaligned bit, though, it lashes its tail, and paws in anger. This last action, as the outthrust foreleg, stands in visual contrast to the smartly uplifted forelegs of the "collected" gaits (figure 7, to be discussed) beneath the Prioress, Wife of Bath, Clerk, and Poet.

While the Knight's horse champs the bit to protest human misman-agement, its lashing tail and pawing hoof express aggravation also at the gratuitous attack by the Squire's horse. One animal is being conscientious and the other reckless. However, the two leaders of the pilgrimage both overtly express anger – a powerful emotion that society and religion circa 1800 urged humans to repress, but that Blake expresses time and time again throughout the *Descriptive Catalogue*.

Nowadays a non-rider might spend an entire lifetime without ever seeing a horse close up. At Blake and Stothard's time, it would be difficult so to spend a single day. In today's world, a non-rider might hesitate to identify emotions displayed in a picture of a horse. Yet Carey, presum-ably no keener a rider than Blake, for an ordinary nineteenth-century audience describes in confident detail the emotions being expressed by the Knight's proud warhorse and by other animals in Stothard's painting:

> his gray stallion is. . . . a Charger, the companion of former victories; aged, but of a commanding figure: his chest powerful, his neck lofty, with a tinge of gray up its conspicuous arch. He moves with a grave and stately pace, as if proud of past services, and conscious of his master's rank.[33]

Carey has more to say about the inner life of the Knight's horse than he does about any spiritual depths to Stothard's Prioress. His description of her external appearance – a pleasing profile, a pale complexion – seems intentionally superficial in that Carey proceeds to tell how totally her companions and clothing block her horse from view:

> The Yeoman and his nag conceal the head and fore part of her horse. The upper arch, only, of his gray neck is seen. A portion of his chest is covered by the skirt of her light-coloured gown; and his body by the spreading folds of her dark cloak.[34]

A nun is a nun insofar as she wears a habit. What is beneath her outfit? We know only that her mount somewhat resembles the Knight's, for both arch gray necks. If her horse is indeed as proud and class-conscious as his, it remains covertly so. Thus Stothard showed his contemporaries the Prioress that they expected to see: upper-class, decorous, attractive, perhaps shallow and amoral but assuredly not immoral.[35]

Relationships now faded between social rank and equitation underlie both artists' visual connection of Knight with Prioress. Nineteenth-century readers of the *Canterbury Tales* encountered the idea still familiar to them that a knight's vocation is expert riding, whereas a high-born nun ought to remain in the cloister and seldom travel, certainly not mounted. Bray intends no insult, though, by noting that in Stothard's painting the Prioress "sits her horse with a quiet and graceful ease."[36]

Blake's Prioress displays a graceful, easy seat as well. In his conception, however, her riding posture and the juxtaposition of Prioress and Knight go to emphasise a significant role reversal. Blake's incompetent Knight gestures toward the one and only expert equestrian en route to Canterbury: the principal nun. Her seat is that recommended for side-saddle, with spine erect and shoulders perpendicular to the horse's back-bone.[37] She lightly holds double reins and crop, keeping her mount aware but not fearful of the aids. As demonstrated with such precision by the Prioress, equine control is an endlessly complex skill. "The perfection of a well-managed horse consists in his following the will of his rider, so that the will of both shall seem to be the same," says Cavendish, echoing oral riding instructions then and now.[38]

To display this ideal state of voluntary submission, in Blake's conception, the Prioress' mount executes a collected walk. (See figure 7.) Some of its forward impulsion converts to vertical leg motion, that is, while its neck arches to accept steady contact with the bit via reins held taut but not tight. Blake could observe high-stepping action and smartly arched necks for the collected gaits performed by a small proportion of live horses in London, and those displayed by a large proportion of the city's heroic equestrian statues, which he would have examined thoroughly in order to portray the mounted Canterbury pilgrims such that "every one is an Antique Statue."[39]

Thus the female Canterbury pilgrim who ought to remain cloistered poses instead as a sculpted war hero, as a professional equestrian in confident control of a responsive steed. Again the artist's everyday equine encounters have enabled him to transform Chaucerian possibilities into visual evidence for the Blakean worldview, whereby established religion and society neglect the work of true genius and reward instead "a class of artists, whose whole art and science is fabricated for the purpose of destroying art" (E 538). Viewers' thoughtful investigation of Blake's visual art may, however, reveal alternatives to the distorted hierarchy represented by his Prioress and Knight.

Behind the Prioress, Blake's Pardoner commands equine obedience using methods likewise observable around the streets of London, but diametrically opposed to her delicate skills. His horse evokes "Auguries of Innocence":

> A Horse misusd upon the Road
> Calls to Heaven for Human blood. (E 490)

With the cross the Pardoner threatens to strike its face, in a motion made terrifying by the limited range of equine vision. Forelegs stiffen as the horse struggles to free its head, which the Pardoner has overbent brutally and fastened to the saddle. (Neither hand holds the reins strained tight.) His posture further reveals intentional cruelty. From observation and the most basic riding instruction, Blake knew that leaning forward signals a horse to go faster; so do spurs and clenched knees. His Pardoner is ordering the horse forward with his body while holding it viciously back with the reins, and while wielding the cross to punish it for disobedience to his conflicting commands. Four hooves flat on the ground show the horse stopped while straining to walk, as forced and as prevented.

These details, of a cruel rider punishing his victim, intensify the visual effect of Blake's Pardoner as an overtly corrupted Christian – one whose evil is easy to identify, but who nonetheless is praised in Chaucer's words as "a noble ecclesiaste," and in abstract words by Blake as bearer of "his grand leading destiny." In the early nineteenth century the Pardoner's sinfulness, based on his selling false relics, was firmly established.[40] Nonetheless, as with the Prioress, Stothard in his conception avoids raising any serious religious issue. On a horse blocked from view, his Pardoner joins the circle of clergy and laymen all enamored of the Wife of Bath.

Just in front of Blake's Pardoner rides the Monk, whose "General Prologue" portrait stresses his horse-happy defiance of church regulations. In the corrupted world of Stothard's success, according to Blake, rebellious aspects of Chaucer's own characters become repressed. Therefore, not even one leg shows of the berry-brown palfrey that the Monk has chosen from many fine horses in his stables ("General Prologue" lines 207, 168). Stothard's Monk, in contrast, rides just such an animal. Carey's comment again demonstrates how closely contemporary viewers could attend to equine emotions displayed on canvas:

> His steed is of a noble shape, full of spirit, and fit to bear a
> warrior in the field. His indignation of the curb [type of bit] is

well expressed, by the haughty bend of his neck, the bearing in of his head upon his chest, and the action of champing the bit impatiently as he moves.[41]

The Host also is "well mounted," according to Carey.[42] From his position near the head of Stothard's procession, he wheels and raises his hand to announce the start of storytelling. Blake's cruciform Host, likewise inviting commencement of the tale contest, rides a placid animal. With no human guidance, it takes care to avoid collision with the Pardoner's mistreated mount, at which it pricks its ears and gazes in bovine-eyed sympathy. Its neck and face form an arch as graceful as that on the Prioress's horse, with reins as taut – on account of a gesture unrelated to steering, however, not the rider's expertise. The Host like the Prioress carries a crop, but he is oblivious to its proper use as a signal. Indeed, he is about to brush the rump, a careless move that would frighten most horses. His mount remains calm. An innkeeper, unlike a knight, appropriately rides what today is termed a "babysitter" horse. Thus the pilgrim whose posture creates an icon of established religion, and whose wide-armed gesture claims social control, owes his exalted position to the bemused tolerance of a lowly beast of burden.

In Blake's picture the Host's left hand points to the source of the secular Knight's Tale, which opens the *Canterbury Tales*. His right hand presents the Parson, whose theological treatise concludes it. Blake's Host looks backward, expecting response from the Parson. The Parson's horse awaits word also from this official representative of the established church, for it swivels its ears backward at an angle that – except during intensive fly-switching – a horse would assume to hear sounds from behind, including its rider's voice. Blake's Parson, however, says nothing to man or beast. He glares straight ahead in Urizenic magnificence, as if daring someone to tell him that his thighs will be aching within minutes if he continues to ride as if seated on a chair. Knowing it all, so he thinks, this Parson would never take advice from *Rules for Bad Horsemen*, a handbook for the reluctant sometimes obliged to travel astride, which saw frequent reprints from 1762 through 1830:

> To have a good seat. . . . Stretch not out your legs before you: this will push you against the back of the saddle; neither gather up your knees, like a man riding on a pack, this throws your thighs upwards: each practice unseats you. Keep your legs straight down, and sit not on the most fleshy part of the thighs, but turn them inwards, so as to bring in your knees and toes.[43]

Blake's Parson holds his thighs strained upward in defiance of gravity, a feat exacerbated by his pretentious disdain for stirrups. Visual art had long portrayed riding equipment among conventional indications of social class. In the Ellesmere manuscript, in the woodcuts of early Chaucer editions, and in the 1721 Urry edition known to Blake, as examples, the lowest-ranking riders can afford but the cheapest equipment: halters and lead ropes to steer, cloth pads to cover sweaty backbones. One step more expensive are iron components: a bit on a rope bridle, stirrups strapped to a pad. In visual art, as in the real world, leather implies luxury.[44] Notice now the comfortably molded leather saddle beneath Blake's Parson. Hypocritical ostentation, not humble poverty, is signified by his scorn for travel apparatus so practical as the stirrup.

The conspicuous position of Blake's Parson draws attention to the self-righteous sanctimony of organised religion. In contrast, Stothard's Parson is tucked behind the distracting foreground activity of Squire and Yeoman. The Yeoman's horse, shown reacting to the Squire's, is described in very full detail by Carey. Among several artistic functions, he notes, this horse:

> acts as a link to connect the first group or rank with the second. It accounts for the characters of the latter [including the Parson] not riding formally close to the preceding.[45]

Until the fourth decade of the twentieth century, all non-riders knew firsthand the basic safety measure that warrants Stothard's backgrounding of the Parson: keep your distance from any horse acting up. Thus Stothard employs horse-related dynamics to the effect that Chaucer's most devout pilgrim is permitted to join the jolly crew, but only if he keeps back out of the way.

The two Parsons portrayed by Blake and Stothard share one distinction besides their long beards. Stolidly, both disregard the appeal of the Wife of Bath, who across the centuries has remained Chaucer's most popular and most malleable character.[46] Blake's Miller and Merchant gaze upon the Wife of Bath as avidly as do a dozen menfolk in Stothard's picture. Both of their horses are hidden; so is that of Stothard's Merchant. Stothard's Miller leads the pack, however with his "baggepipe. . . he broghte us out of towne" ("General Prologue" lines 565–66). Carey again describes horse and tack as fully as he does the pilgrim:

> He rides without a bridle. The halter hangs loose upon his horse's neck. The knot near the end, and the three thongs into

which it is divided from thence, show that it is occasionally applied to the double purpose of a stay and a whip. There is a piece of sheep-skin spread under him on an ordinary saddle. A bald white face, hanging lip, broken look, dull, jogging pace, and dark gray coat, all give the effect to the heavy jade upon which he is mounted. The domestic drudge is in as perfect agreement with the carlish rider, as *Rozinante* with *Don Quixotte*, or *Dapple* with *Sancho Pancha*, in Coypell's admirable series of designs from Cervantes. . . . He leans or rather topples forward in his seat.[47]

Cromek likewise remarks that the Miller's "Horse is as much in character as himself."[48] Bray sees in the pair a babysitter horse taking care of its rider:

> the miller. . . appears very careless of the good people to whom he acts as piper, to bring them "out of toune;" his own tipsy music seems to be all that he heeds; his horse carries him as he lists.[49]

In Stothard's painting, Chaucer's horse seems as sedate as that of the Miller. Carey notes its tolerance for crowding that would cause many to kick or bolt. "The leading Dame," he says, using one of his many fond terms for the Wife of Bath, "follows so closely, that her horse's head appears above the hinder part of Chaucer's horse."[50]

This mounted Poet participates in another procession as well – in the diachronic one of Chaucer portraits then regarded as historically accurate, which Stothard could have known as engravings in Chaucer editions or as sixteenth- and seventeenth-century paintings owned by "Public Depositories" and "Gentlemen of the first taste."[51] Cromek makes the specific claim that Stothard's "Portrait of Chaucer is painted from that in the British Museum, done by Thomas Occleve, who lived in his time, and was his scholar."[52] The headdress and facial angle of Stothard's Chaucer do reflect the "Occleve" one. Other features, such as the forked beard, appear there and elsewhere in Chaucer portraiture. Stothard's Poet differs from other Chaucers portrayed, however, in that his eyes do not gaze "evere upon the ground" as if trying to "fynde an hare" ("Sir Thopas," lines 697, 696). Instead he looks back over his shoulder, tugged like any ordinary male into the charmed circle of the Wife of Bath: "To her gay conversation the ear of the Poet Chaucer is inclined."[53]

The eyes of Blake's Chaucer are downcast, as the portrait tradition decrees. In several details otherwise, though, Blake's conception resembles Stothard's and, in so doing, deviates from that tradition. Only the Chaucers of Blake and Stothard wear light-colored robes rather than dark ones. The elsewhere ubiquitous pencase hangs around neither one's neck. Most obviously, both are younger and thinner than any other Chaucer in the pictorial tradition, which is reinforced by the Host's teasing remark on the ample waistline of Chaucer-the-pilgrim ("Sir Thopas," line 700).

Like Stothard's Poet, his Wife of Bath is far younger and slimmer than specified in the *Canterbury Tales* – "perhaps a dozen years younger than Chaucer has represented her."[54] In portraying a youthful Chaucer enchanted by a youthful Wife of Bath, Stothard's intention goes no deeper than a display of comely characters exuding medieval morality just casual enough to titillate a typical viewer of his painting and potential purchaser of the engraving.

Stothard's self-declared rival, in contrast, creates a slim young Chaucer redolent with Blakean ideas about artistic sacrilege. His dewy-eyed Poet much resembles Blake's depictions elsewhere of Los, the spirit of Poetic Genius that gives rise to all religions. Equitation undercuts positive implications, however, for Blake's Chaucer leans backward at an angle impossible to maintain for more than minutes. Besides the curve of his body, from hips to rounded shoulders to thrusting head, awkwardness of posture appears in foot position: lifted ahead of the horse's vertical leg, the Poet's stirrup is providing no support (cf. Host's supported leg). By leaning so far backward, Los/Chaucer not only is contorting the Human Form Divine but also is signalling his mount to slow down or stop. Like the horses of Blake's Knight and Host, however, it shoulders the responsibility of carrying its untrained rider toward the spiritual goal that humans ought to be seeking.

The Poet's horse moves toward Canterbury at a collected amble, a gait never found in the real world. As discussed in reference to the Prioress (cf. figure 7), some expert riders then and now coax collected gaits from their responsive, disciplined performance partners. For many centuries, but nowadays no longer, many calm-spirited horses used to be trained to amble, i.e., to coordinate same-side strides instead of the trot's diagonal ones. On an ambler, an unenthusiastic rider could travel from one place to another without learning how to post, i.e., to rise and sit in rhythm with the jolts of a trot. Such riders would not know how to signal a collected gait, nor would such horses ever be trained to execute one. Thus Blake shows a high-spirited, highly educated horse adapting its gait to the low skill level of its undiscerning rider. Insofar as Blake recognised the amble itself as a comically inappropriate gait for a would-be hero, this portrayal seems a visual reiteration of Chaucer-the-author's joke about Sir Thopas's dapple-gray ambler, so admired by Chaucer-the-pilgrim ("Sir Thopas," lines 884–85).

## III

Whether or not Blake knew about Sir Thopas's ambler in Chaucer's Middle English text, the observant artist and occasional rider did know firsthand that human control of equine energy involves riding equipment, or "tack": a saddle, girth, stirrups, sometimes breastplate and/or crupper, and a bridle comprising headstall, bit, and reins. With the meaningful exception of the Parson's missing stirrup, the horses in "Chaucers Canterbury Pilgrims" are fully tacked. Only after comparison to all the rest of Blake's artwork does the significance of this feature emerge. Among all horses ever portrayed by Blake, it turns out, only these en route to Canterbury wear standard functional tack.

In "The Characters in Spenser's Faerie Queene" (ca. 1815), Blake's painting closest in conception to "Chaucers Canterbury Pilgrims," each equestrian lacks at least one essential item. Several Spenserian figures have no headstall, for example, without which an actual bit and reins would drop out of the horse's mouth. With incomplete gear likewise, Thomas Gray's Nordic warriors ride forth to grapple their fates. The majority of Blake's horses, such as the one in Hayley's *Ballads*, are not ridden or controlled in any way.[55] A few appear in partial harness. A catalogue of riders astride – along with those illustrating Chaucer, Spenser, and Gray – would include some bareback, several on saddled but flying horses, Saul on a kneeling horse, and one riding reinless while dwarfed by Stonehenge.[56] Also, in the same approximate year that Blake engraved one of Stothard's battle scenes with a fully tacked warhorse, Blake's sketch of another battle shows horses lacking headgear of any kind.[57]

It has not been previously noticed that full tack in and of itself marks the Canterbury pilgrims as repressive controllers of proud equine spirits, which elsewhere in Blake's artwork go free. Where did he find precedent for so many uncontrolled horses? I propose direct influence from the Parthenon frieze, on which horses are ridden bareback and, at first glance, unbridled (figure 4). Blake terms the Canterbury pilgrims "eternal principles or characters of human life [that] appear to poets, in all ages," particularly that of ancient Greece (E 536). Therefore, attention to Blake's contact with Greek equestrian art aptly concludes this account of the over-burdened, over-restrained, cruelly or heedlessly treated horses that emerge from the gates of the Tabard Inn suffering from pilgrims' Urizenic selfishness, in this "Allegory of Idolatry or Politics" that makes manifest "The Use of Money & its Wars" (E 687).

Perhaps Blake counted Lord Elgin among those who conspired to exclude him from opportunity in London art circles, for Blake's name is not recorded with artists who viewed the Elgin marbles after their arrival in 1807.[58] His definite contact with the Parthenon frieze occurred fifteen years earlier. While engraving four plates for volume 3 of *The Antiquities of Athens*, showing the Battle of Centaurs and Lapithae from the Temple of Theseus (figure 8), Blake must have examined volume 2, published five years earlier, which includes the Parthenon version of the same battle that he was engraving. Next to those plates is the ritual procession from the frieze (figure 4). In these segments and elsewhere, most Athenian horses display graceful postures as they rear or execute appropriate gaits. Exceptions, such as the centaur dying at Theseus' hands (figure 8), showed Blake the ancient artists' expertise at equine anatomy even for such an awkward position.[59]

Ancient Greek warriors indeed rode bareback. They steered, however, with headgear very like that worn by Bruno at Felpham – headgear missing from the Parthenon frieze, because it had been fashioned from metal. "The holes by which it was fixed to the marble are still distinctly visible," according to *The Antiquities of Athens*, and are reproduced in the engravings. Plate 17, for example, readily reveals that metal strips once connected a bit, a headstall (as two holes near the ears), and reins reaching the rider's hands. Is it plausible that Blake overlooked such minute particulars of visual art, then ignored statements that "the harness of the horses in this Freeze [was] of metal," so as to suppose that Athenians used neither saddle nor bridle?[60] No. Instead, Blake preferred the visual appearance and spiritual implications of unbridled horses.

This unique feature of "Chaucers Canterbury Pilgrims" – i.e., its fully tacked horses – rouses many questions suitable for Blake specialists in future. To what extent elsewhere does Blake consider the apparent control of unbridled horses to be a positive sign of Athenian skill, yet to what extent a negative sign of Greek militancy? "The Classics, it is the Classics!. . . that Desolate Europe with Wars." Throughout Blake's verbal art, to what extent is equine nature a negative element – the golden horses of Urizen, for instance – and to what extent a positive image of free-spirited Innocence?

> He who shall train the Horse to War
> Shall never pass the Polar Bar.

To Generalise is to be an Idiot, whereas this article addresses one distinct set of minute particulars. A monograph remains unwritten on the Equine Form Divine through the rest of Blake's visual art, as related to the intentionally fluctuating symbolism of his verbal horses, as related also to his attitude toward various other artists' treatments during "the classical period of horse portraiture in England."[61]

Among those other artists was Stothard, of course, whose fully tacked horses express standard equine emotions in ways easily recognised by anyone who ever encounters live horses, therefore by every viewer at the time. Stothard makes human emotions and interactions just as easy to label. In his conception Chaucer's characters are:

> now transferred to the Canvas; and with so much truth and sprightliness, and in a manner so agreeable, that the Poet's humour may, with truth, be said to be revived in the Painter . . a humour unforced, agreeable, and comic.[62]

Blake instead gives intense, serious significance to every visual detail in order to reveal how society's commercialisation of art can transform positive manifestations of the sacred Poetic Genius, as represented by Chaucer's great poem, into negative abominations of it. "Chaucers Canterbury Pilgrims," however, offers hope based outside the sphere of mankind. The Urizenic pilgrims bridle, mistreat, disregard, and in other ways repress equine spirits. Thanks to horses' pride and horse sense, the riders nonetheless proceed toward the spiritual goal that humans ought to be trying to reach.

## IV

Authoritative horses in another sort of world are not exclusive to Blake. To what extent might the artist's conception be influenced by *Gulliver's Travels*?[63] He and Jonathan Swift alter a commonplace metaphor in comparable ways. Swift inverts the concept, by re-assigning Reason to Houyhnhnms, whereas Blake leaves the two abstractions in place but portrays non-verbal equine Emotion as the superior cosmic force. At any rate, both Swift and Blake would concur with Cavendish's preference for horses' wisdom over the kind of human sense that leads to "The Use of Money & its Wars":

> What makes scholasticks degrade horses so much, proceeds (I believe) from nothing else, but the small knowledge they have

of them, and from a persuasion that they themselves know
every thing. They fancy they talk pertinently about them,
whereas they know no more than they learn by riding a
hackney-horse from the University to LONDON, and back
again. If they studied them as horsemen do, they would talk
otherwise: for example, if a man has lost his way in a dark
winter's night, let him leave the horse to himself, and the horse
will find the way to the place whither he should go. . . . As for
men of letters, tho' they study, they don't study horsemanship,
but their studies turn to better account, by procuring themselves to rule over the rest of mankind, till such time as they are
subdued by the sword.[64]

Since the advent of the iron horse and horseless carriage, men and
women of letters study equitation even less. I hope that this article's foray
into unexplored tracts of evidence will rouse further issues for scholarly
pursuit across traditional disciplinary and chronological boundaries,
always taking care to respect both public circumstances and private
concerns. As we return with the Monk to the cloister, for the time being,
we have seen how two artists within one sociohistoric context use
horse-related dynamics to display diametrically different interpretations
of the *Canterbury Tales*, and thereby two interpretations of "the" Middle
Ages that emphasize respectively its merriness and its sacredness.
   James Jefferys was born in 1751, Stothard in 1755, Blake in 1757.
They grew up with similar awareness of art and of Chaucer. We can
observe the results, and we may continue to research the causes, of their
three visual representations of the same work of imaginative literature. In
the meantime, most present-day Chaucerians intend to be taking Jefferys'
path – i.e., intend to be establishing Chaucer's meaning within the fullest
possible re-creation of its late fourteenth-century context. However, the
present study implies not only that "the" Middle Ages had at least three
completely different meanings 200 years ago, and not only that "the"
Middle Ages had an infinitude of potential meanings 600 years ago, but
also that, while purporting to Jefferys-like historical accuracy, we
medievalists may well be giving our public what it wants, Stothard-like,
and in order to do so we might even be calling upon the sacred spirit of
Poetic Genius: "For the tygers of wrath are wiser than the horses of
instruction. And every thing possible to be believ'd is an image of truth"
(E 37).

NOTES

1. Full blame on art agent Robert Cromek, and exoneration of both Blake and Stothard from charges of stealing each other's idea for the painting, is the conclusion of G.E. Bentley, Jr., " 'They take great liberty's': Blake Reconfigured by Cromek and Modern Critics – The Arguments from Silence," *Studies in Romanticism* 30 (1991): 657–84. He argues against a trend toward blaming Blake, exemplified by Dennis Read, "The Rival *Canterbury Pilgrims* of Blake and Cromek: Herculean Figures in the Carpet," *Modern Philology* 86 (1988–89): 171–90; and Aileen Ward, "Canterbury Revisited: The Blake-Cromek Controversy," *Blake: An Illustrated Quarterly* 22 (1988–89): 80–92. These three items cite the extensive earlier scholarship.

2. On reception aesthetics *qua* theory see Robert C. Holub, *Reception Theory: A Critical Introduction* (New York: Methuen, 1984). Chaucerians have long had access to basic resources thanks to Caroline Spurgeon, *Five Hundred Years of Chaucer Criticism and Allusion, 1357–1900*, 3 vols. paginated as 6 parts (1925; rpt. New York: Russell and Russell, 1960). For an overview of issues, plus pre-twentieth-century contexts for Prioress, Pardoner, and Merchant, see Betsy Bowden, *Chaucer Aloud: The Varieties of Textual Interpretation* (Philadelphia: University of Pennsylvania Press, 1987).

3. Concerning this transition see Shelley Bennett, *Thomas Stothard: The Mechanisms of Art Patronage in England circa 1800* (Columbia: University of Missouri Press, 1988); and very cautiously Alice Miskimin, "The Illustrated Eighteenth-Century Chaucer," *Modern Philology* 77 (1979–80): 26–55. Miskimin's factual errors are described by G.E. Bentley, Jr., "Comment upon the Illustrated Eighteenth-Century Chaucer," *Modern Philology* 78 (1980–81): 398.

4. See B.A. Windeatt, "Thomas Tyrwhitt (1730–1786)," in Paul G. Ruggiers, ed., *Editing Chaucer: The Great Tradition* (Norman, OK: Pilgrim Books, 1984), 117–43. On the frequent, usually uncredited reuse of Tyrwhitt's text see Eleanor P. Hammond, *Chaucer: A Bibliographical Manual* (1908; rpt. New York: P. Smith, 1933), 206–7; and Bowden, *Chaucer Aloud*, 39–40 (with further references). On other early editions see the rest of *Editing Chaucer*. For modernizations see Betsy Bowden, ed., *Eighteenth-Century Modernizations from the Canterbury Tales* (Cambridge: D.S. Brewer, 1991).

5. Jefferys' work was neglected until a 1976 exhibition at the Victoria and Albert Museum, the organizers of which list "Designs from Chaucer's Pilgrimage to Canterbury" under "Lost Works by James Jefferys": see Timothy Clifford and Susan Legouix, "James Jefferys, Historical Draughtsman (1751–84)," *Burlington Magazine* 118 (1976): 154. The drawings were up for sale in 1908, according to Spurgeon, 1:458–59; the Houghton Library bought them in 1968. I have discussed them in two articles so far: "Canterbury Pilgrims and Their Horses in the Eighteenth Century: Two Artists' Interpretations," *Harvard Library Bulletin*,

n.s. 3 (1992–93): 18–34; and "Visual Portraits of the Canterbury Pilgrims, 1484(?)–1809," in Daniel Woodward and Martin Stevens, eds., *The Ellesmere Chaucer: Essays in Interpretation* (San Marino, CA: Huntington Library Press; Tokyo: Yushodo, 1995), 171–204 (188–92 on Jefferys). Also see Martin Butlin, "The Rediscovery of an Artist: James Jefferys (1751–1784)," *Blake: An Illustrated Quarterly* 10 (1976–77): 123–24; and Jefferys' entry (which misdates his birth as 1757) in Leslie Stephen and Sidney Lee, eds., *The Dictionary of National Biography*, 22 vols. (1885–1901; rpt. London: Oxford University Press, 1937–38), hereafter cited as *DNB*.

6. On Stothard see Bennett, 44–49, and items in the controversy cited in note 1 above. On Blake's use of John Urry, ed., *The Works of Geoffrey Chaucer* (London: B. Lintot, 1721) see [William Wells,] *William Blake's "Heads of the Poets"* (Manchester: City of Manchester Art Gallery, 1969), 18–19; and Betsy Bowden, "The Artistic and Interpretive Context of Blake's 'Canterbury Pilgrims,' " *Blake: An Illustrated Quarterly* 13 (1979–80): 164–90. Blake's quotations are traced by Alexander S. Gourlay, "What Was Blake's Chaucer?" *Studies in Bibliography* 42 (1989): 272–83. I very much appreciate Prof. Gourlay's comments on two drafts of this article.

For suggestions on earlier drafts I also would like to thank Jeanne Moskal, G.E. Bentley, Jr., Robert Ryan, and A.C. Spearing. For input I also thank Carole Breakstone, Shelley Bennett, and Robert N. Essick, and for initial impetus and longterm moral support Morton Paley and Charles Muscatine. Specifically, also, Profs. Bentley and Essick both brought to my attention an exhibition of the two paintings themselves and related items at Norwich Castle Museum, October–November 1993, documented by Robin Hamlyn and Andrew Moore, *William Blake: Chaucer's Canterbury Pilgrims* (Norwich: Norfolk Museums Service, 1993). Reproduction of photographs herein was made possible by regular grants from the Research Council of Rutgers University, and by permission generously granted by the Tate Gallery, the Henry E. Huntington Library and Art Gallery, and the University of Pennsylvania library system.

7. Studies establishing interpretive context, besides those cited above in notes 2, 4, 5, and 6, include "The Oral Life of the Written Ballad of the Wanton Wife of Bath," *North Carolina Folklore Journal* 35 (1988): 40–77; "Fluctuating Proverbs in Three Eighteenth-Century Modernizations of Chaucer's Miller's Tale," *Proverbium* 9 (1992): 11–29; "Four Eighteenth-Century Modernizations of *The Shipman's Tale* as Audiovisual Performance," *Translation and Literature* 3 (1994): 30–46; and "*Chaucer New Painted* (1623): Three Hundred Proverbs in Performance Context," *Oral Tradition* 10 (1995): 304–58.

8. Spurgeon, 1:liii.

9. Blake's painting, now at Pollok House, Glasgow, was exhibited in 1809 and engraved by 1810. For a full account of states and impressions see Robert N. Essick, *The Separate Plates of William Blake: A Catalogue* (Princeton: Princeton University Press, 1983), 60–89 (68–69 on the fourth-state impression, figure 2 here). Because Essick distinguished an undetected second state to the engraving,

the fourth state is called the third (and so on) in scholarship prior to 1983, including the standard Blake edition cited here (note 10 below) and including Geoffrey Keynes, *Engravings by William Blake: The Separate Plates* (Dublin: E. Walker, 1956). Essick, *Separate Plates* (73) observes also that Keynes' plate 33 is mislabelled within that previous system.

 10. William Blake, *A Descriptive Catalogue of Pictures, Poetical and Historical Inventions*, 1809; rpt. in David V. Erdman, ed., *The Complete Poetry and Prose of William Blake*, rev. ed. (Berkeley: University of California Press, 1982), 529–51. This edition is hereafter cited as E (for Erdman) with page number. On "Chaucers Canterbury Pilgrims" see E 532–40, 567–82, 687.

 11. E 535. Blake's purposes, never stated outright precisely because he mistrusts discursive language, are described more fully in Bowden, "Artistic and Interpretive Context." Another pilgrim-by-pilgrim account of the entire procession is Karl Kiralis, "William Blake as an Intellectual and Spritual Guide to Chaucer's *Canterbury Pilgrims*," *Blake Studies* 1 (1968–69): 164–90. Less detailed studies include Orphia Jane Allen, "Blake's Archetypal Criticism: *The Canterbury Pilgrims*," *Genre* 2 (1978): 173–89; Claire Pace, "Blake and Chaucer: 'Infinite Variety of Character,' " *Art History* 3 (1980): 388–409; and Warren Stevenson, "Interpreting Blake's *Canterbury Pilgrims*," *Colby Library Quarterly* 13 (1977): 115–26.

 12. See note 1 above.

 13. Godwin's two-volume *Life of Geoffrey Chaucer* (1803) was the first biography done as a separate publication. For contents and responses see Hammond, *Bibliographical Manual*, 38–39, 207; and Spurgeon, 1:cx–cxii, 2:2.6–9, 2:2.10–23, and passim. Concerning whereabouts of the Ellesmere manuscript see note 23 below. For description of its pilgrim portraits see Martin Stevens, "The Ellesmere Miniatures as Illustrations of Chaucer's *Canterbury Tales*," *Studies in Iconography* 7–8 (1981–82): 113–30; and Richard K. Emmerson, "Text and Image in the Ellesmere Portraits of the Tale-Tellers," in *Ellesmere Chaucer* (cited in note 5 above), 143–70. Concerning whereabouts of the Elgin marbles see note 58 below. For influence on Blake see Duncan Macmillan, "Blake's Exhibition and *Catalogue* Reconsidered: On the Occasion of the Fitzwilliam Museum Exhibition and *Catalogue*, 1971," *Blake Newsletter* 5 (1971–72): 202–6. An anonymous writer ca. 1840 calls Stothard's "horses all barbs, from the Elgin Marbles," reports Bruce E. Graver, "New Voice on Blake," *Blake: An Illustrated Quarterly* 24 (1990–91): 91.

 14. Anna E. Bray, *The Life of Thomas Stothard, R.A., with Personal Reminiscences* (London: J. Murray, 1851); Robert H. Cromek, "The Procession of Chaucer's Pilgrims to Canterbury. Proposals for Publishing, by Subscription, a Print," Appendix to Robert Blair, *The Grave: A Poem* (1808; rpt. London: Methuen, 1903), 38–44; and William P. Carey, *A Critical Description of the Procession of Chaucer's Pilgrims to Canterbury, Painted by Thomas Stothard, Esq., R.A.*, 2nd ed. (London: W. Glindon, 1818). In all quotations, all italics occur in the original texts.

15. Cromek, "Procession," 39.

16. For Robert Hunt's negative review and others' remarks see G.E. Bentley, Jr., *Blake Records* (Oxford: Clarendon, 1974), 215 ff. For accounts of contemporary response to both paintings see Bennett, 45–49; and Read, 185, 189. Opinion began to shift within the half-century, however. An unpublished review of *Chaucer Modernized* (1841) briefly compares the two pictures and declares Blake's "true and vivid. . . expression" superior to Stothard's "refined and softened" style (Graver, 91).

17. Essick, *Separate Plates*, 70.

18. Enort [*sic*], "Sonnet on Stothard's Painting of the Canterbury Pilgrims," *European Magazine*, October 1821, quoted by Bennett (46) from an extra-illustrated copy of Bray's work in the Boston Public Library.

19. Bray, *Life of Stothard*, 136.

20. Bray, *Life of Stothard*, 138. On Stubbs's physical fitness see his entry in the *DNB*. Stubbs lived at Portman Square, Stothard about a mile away on Newman Street. Read (172) notes that Cromek commissioned the painting no later than November 1806, but possibly earlier, before he left London in June. This incident makes the early date likelier, unless Bray is lying outright or confusing Stubbs with his son.

21. Praise occurs at line 94 of the General Prologue to Chaucer's *Canterbury Tales*, in *The Riverside Chaucer*, 3rd ed., ed. Larry D. Benson (Boston: Houghton Mifflin, 1987), 25. This edition is hereafter cited with line numbers and the abbreviations *GP* for General Prologue and *TST* for Tale of Sir Thopas.

22. This section of a pamphlet published in February 1807, *Proposals for a Print after Stothard's Canterbury Pilgrims*, is quoted with additional context by Bennett, 96n25, and by Read, 172–73. On Blake's use of the Urry edition see note 6 above.

23. From 1803 to 1833 the manuscript now known as the Ellesmere was one in a multitude of art treasures owned by George Granville Leveson-Gower, second Marquis of Stafford and first Duke of Sutherland, who "deserves credit for having been one of the first owners of works of art in London to throw open his gallery to the public," a "courtesy [that] was extended much farther to artists." For the two quotations see respectively Ronald Gower, Lord Sutherland, *My Reminiscences*, 2 vols. (London: Kegan Paul, Trench, and Trübner, 1883), 1:82; and James Loch, *Memoir of George Granville, Late Duke of Sutherland* (London: privately printed, 1834), 10. From the manuscript the Chaucer figure was first reproduced in 1810, the other pilgrims later.

Blake and Stothard both lived close to Cleveland [Stafford] House, which as Bridgewater House is now international headquarters for an engineering firm. Evidence for the two artists' visits cannot be sought within records of the art collection itself, for none were kept. Leveson-Gower's grandson searched public and family archives in vain for private letters or papers on any subject whatsoever. See the *DNB* entry on Leveson-Gower, based largely on Gower and Loch. Blake's much-researched life history has revealed no visit by him; nor does Stothard's sole biographer Shelley Bennett know of one. I hope that someone with day-to-day access to London archives will take up the quest.

24. William Cavendish, Duke of Newcastle, *La Méthode et Invention Nouvelle de Dresser les Chevaux*, 1658, anon. transl. in *A General System of Horsemanship*, 2 vols. (London: J. Brindley, 1743), 1:30. The author was governor and riding master to the prince who became Charles II. Published from exile, the lavishly illustrated manual was frequently revised and reprinted and translated on the Continent and in England. For bibliography of this work and of other equine treatises available in England during the sixteenth through nineteenth centuries, see Betsy Bowden, "Before the Houyhnhmns: Rational Horses in the Late Seventeenth Century," *Notes and Queries* 237 (1992): 38–40.

25. On history of dressage see Anthony A. Dent, *The Horse through Fifty Centuries of Civilization* (New York: Holt, 1974), 142–52. Concerning equestrian statuary see [Laura Camins,] *Glorious Horsemen: Equestrian Art in Europe, 1500–1800* (Springfield, MA: Museum of Fine Arts, 1981), 30–31. For a summary of philosophical and psychological symbolism relating to horses, see Rolf P. Lessenich, *Aspects of English Preromanticism* (Cologne: Bohlau, 1989): 19–23.

26. Supposedly, also, one hoof raised means that the rider was wounded in battle, and four hooves on the ground means a natural death. On seriously held folk beliefs and the related narrative genre, see Jan H. Brunvand, *The Vanishing Hitchhiker: American Urban Legends and Their Meanings* (New York: Norton, 1981). Although no folklorist has traced this particular belief, journalist Ann Landers determined its falsehood and the extent of its historic-geographic distribution in a column that appeared 5 Sept. 1992 in *The Philadelphia Inquirer*, D2.

27. Bray, *Critical Description*, 136.

28. Cromek, "Procession," 40.

29. Carey, *Critical Description*, 31–32, quoting *GP* line 94. For the Sheridan quotation he apparently changed "off [i.e., right-hand] heel" to "left heel." Unless Carey knew a variant of "Prologue to *The Miniature Picture* [by the Countess of Craven]" differing from that in R. Crompton Rhodes, ed., *The Plays and Poems of Richard Brinsley Sheridan*, 3 vols. (New York: Macmillan, 1929), 3:278, the art critic's confusion about slightly technical vocabulary makes even more significant his detailed attention to Stothard's horses. Probably Carey did not ride, that is, but he readily recognized and described equine emotions and equestrian attitudes.

30. From an account by J.L. Adolphus included in John Gibson Lockhart, ed., *The Life of Sir Walter Scott*, 10 vols. (1902; rpt. New York: AMS, 1983), 9:121. I thank Mrs Maxwell-Scott for information about present-day Abbotsford (personal communication, 14 July 1992).

31. In "Artistic and Interpretive Context," 180–81 and passim, I propose as Holy Spirit their sullen, swinish black dog. That article's full-length commentary on visual details exclusive of equitation, for every pilgrim discussed in the

present article, is not repeated here. I have revised my interpretation of Parson and Poet.

32. Keynes, *Engravings by William Blake*, plates 31–33.

33. Carey, *Critical Description*, 26.

34. Carey, *Critical Description*, 49.

35. Concerning the Prioress's reputation through the centuries see Bowden, *Chaucer Aloud*, 21–49 (esp. 36–39 on Stothard's and Blake's depictions of her). On Blake's Prioress also see Mary Ellen Reisner, "William Blake and Westminster Abbey," *Man and Nature / Homme et Nature: Proceedings of the Canadian Society for Eighteenth-Century Studies* 1 (1982): 185–98 (esp. 191–94), as well as the two overviews Bowden, "Artistic and Interpretive Context," and Kiralis, "William Blake." The latter extensively compares Prioress to Wife of Bath.

36. Bray, *Life of Stothard*, 132.

37. On history and use of the sidesaddle – which was optional, not obligatory, for women before and after the Victorian era – see Dent, *Horse through Fifty Centuries*, 152–63; and Lida Fleitmann Bloodgood, *The Saddle of Queens: The Story of the Side-Saddle* (London: J.A. Allen, 1959).

38. Cavendish, *La Méthode*, 1:105.

39. E 536. At Blake's time and indeed today, the collected walk appears on equestrian statues partly because the most famous Greco-Roman statues, which display the gait, became models for later sculptors. See Camins, *Glorious Horsemen*; and Oliver Beckett, "Equine Sculpture," in *The Horse in Art and History*, ed. Michael Seth-Smith (New York: Mayflower, 1978), 34–41.

40. *GP* line 708, E 535. Concerning the Pardoner's reputation through the centuries see Bowden, *Chaucer Aloud*, 77–113 (esp. 100–103 on Stothard's and Blake's depictions of him). On Blake's Pardoner also see Mary Ellen Reisner, "Effigies of Power: Pitt and Fox as Canterbury Pilgrims," *Eighteenth-Century Studies* 12 (1978–79): 481–503; Reisner, "Westminster Abbey," 191; and the two overviews Bowden, "Artistic and Interpretive Context," and Kiralis, "William Blake."

41. Carey, *Critical Description*, 62.

42. Carey, *Critical Description*, 17.

43. Charles Thompson, *Rules for Bad Horsemen, Addressed to the Society for the Encouragement of Arts, &c.*, 3rd ed. (London: J. Robson, 1765), 22, 29–30.

44. The relationship of riding equipment to social class appears most consistently in reference to Chaucer illustration itself, because other early artwork is much likelier to show upper-class equestrians. See Bowden, "Visual Portraits of Canterbury Pilgrims"; and Edwin Ford Piper, "The Miniatures of the Ellesmere Chaucer," *Philological Quarterly* 3 (1924): 241–56. On pragmatic functions of riding equipment, unchanged across the centuries, see Ann Hyland, *Equus: The Horse in the Roman World* (New Haven: Yale University Press, 1990), esp. 136–40.

45. Carey, *Critical Description*, 45.

46. Neither Stothard's dazzling belle nor Blake's energy-exuding Whore of Babylon can be analyzed apart from contexts far too vast for an article. My book in progress treats visual and verbal interpretations of her just between 1665 and 1809.

47. Carey, *Critical Description*, 13–14.

48. Cromek, "Procession," 40.

49. Bray, *Life of Stothard*, 131.

50. Carey, *Critical Description*, 57–58.

51. Quotation from *Proposals for a Print*, cited in note 22 above. Frontispiece portraits of Chaucer appear in the editions of Thomas Speght (1598, 1602, 1687) and John Urry (1721). Concerning them see Hammond, *Bibliographical Manual*, 122–30; and Derek Pearsall, *The Life of Geoffrey Chaucer: A Critical Biography* (Oxford: Blackwell, 1992), 305–6.

52. Cromek, "Procession," 41n. As established artists, Stothard and Blake had access to British Museum materials including Harleian MS 4866, which is a copy of Hoccleve's *Regement of Princes* that fulfills one verse's promise to provide a picture of Chaucer in the margin (not actually painted by Hoccleve, of course). On Chaucer portraits see Hammond, *Bibliographical Manual*, 49; Pearsall, *Life of Chaucer*, 303–6; Bowden, "Canterbury Pilgrims and Their Horses," 31–34; and Lois Bragg, "Chaucer's Monogram and the 'Hoccleve Portrait' Tradition," *Word & Image* 12/1 (1996): 127–52. On access to the British Museum see Bowden, "Artistic and Interpretive Context," 189n13.

53. Carey, *Critical Description*, 69.

54. Carey, *Critical Description*, 59.

55. For reproductions of the horses illustrating Spenser and Hayley, see Martin Butlin, *The Paintings and Drawings of William Blake*, 2 vols. (New Haven: Yale University Press, for Paul Mellon Centre for British Art, 1981), vol. 2, plates 879 and 347, hereafter cited by plate number only. For discussion of the Spenser procession, see John E. Grant and Robert E. Brown, "Blake's Vision of Spenser's *Faerie Queene*: Report and an Anatomy," *Blake Newsletter* 8 (1974–75): 56–85. For Gray reproductions, see Geoffrey Keynes, ed., *Water-Colours Illustrating the Poems of Thomas Gray* (Chicago: J.P. O'Hara, 1972), designs 56, 61, 70, 73–76, 79–81, 85, 107. In this series, one underequipped horse even holds bitless reins in its own mouth, like a dog holding a leash to beg a walk (design 74).

56. Within Blake's original artwork I locate horses as follows, including horselike creatures such as donkeys and centaurs. These references are to books searched during preliminary research in 1990–91. Because Blake's visual art continues to be reproduced in ever more comprehensive formats, any revised list would itself be outdated by press time. I cite each item as reproduced in only one source. I do not repeat *Night Thoughts* plates for *Four Zoas*. I would welcome additions or corrections to this list: David Bindman with Deirdre Toomey, *The Complete Graphic Works of William Blake* (New York: Putnam's, 1978), plates 380, 385; Butlin, *Paintings and Drawings*, plates 98, 145, 164, 187–88, 198,

243, 347, 385–86, 390, 396, 410–16, 419, 440, 456, 504, 528, 543, 575, 578–79, 584, 587, 595, 878–81, 1115; *The Illuminated Blake*, ed. David V. Erdman (Garden City, NY: Anchor/Doubleday, 1974), index s.v. horse(s); David V. Erdman with Donald K. Moore, eds., *The Notebook of William Blake: A Photographic and Typographic Facsimile* (Oxford: Clarendon, 1973), emblem 3 (N18, 77); Essick, *Separate Plates*, figure 99 (a possible exception, if the tiny decorative equestrian has stirrups); John E. Grant, Edward J. Rose, and Michael Tolley with David V. Erdman, eds., *William Blake's Designs for Edward Young's Night Thoughts* (Oxford: Clarendon; New York: Oxford University Press, 1980), designs 68, 87, 125, 281, 480, 521; Keynes, *Water-Colours*, as listed in note 55 above; Milton Klonsky, ed., *Blake's Dante: The Complete Illustrations to the Divine Comedy* (New York: Harmony Books, 1980), plates 24, 53; and Bette Charlene Werner, *Blake's Vision of the Poetry of Milton: Illustrations to Six Poems* (Lewisburg, PA: Bucknell University Press, 1986), illustrations 28, 40, 49, 55.

57. The two battle scenes are reproduced respectively as Essick, *Separate Plates*, figure 106; and Butlin, *Paintings and Drawings*, plate 145.

58. Among the viewers John Flaxman, to his eternal credit, convinced Lord Elgin not to restore the marbles. Concerning him and other invited visitors see B.F. Cook, *The Elgin Marbles* (Cambridge: Harvard University Press, 1984), 60–63; David Irwin, *John Flaxman 1755–1826: Sculptor Illustrator Designer* (London: Studio Vista, 1979), 174–75; and Jacob Rothenberg, *"Descensus ad Terram": The Acquisition and Reception of the Elgin Marbles* (1967; rpt. New York: Garland, 1977), 212–356.

59. For the identity of Theseus killing a centaur, see James Stuart and Nicholas Revett, *The Antiquities of Athens, Measured and Delineated*, 5 vols. (1762–1830; rpt. of vols. 1–3, New York: B. Blom, 1968), 3:9. In vol. 2 (1787), chapter 1, plates 10–12 show the Centaurs and Lapithae, and plates 13–30 the Parthenon frieze (all engraved by James Newton). In vol. 3 (1794), chapter 1, Blake engraved plates 21–24 (dated 1792), including figure 8 here.

60. Quotations from Stuart and Revett, *Antiquities of Athens*, 2:14. Plate 17 refers to volume 2, chapter 1. On Greek equitation see J.K. Anderson, *Ancient Greek Horsemanship* (Berkeley: University of California Press, 1961).

61. E 270, 217, 491, 641; John Baskett, *The Horse in Art* (Boston: New York Graphic Society, 1980), 88.

62. Cromek, "Procession," 39.

63. No records show that Blake owned a copy of *Gulliver's Travels*. According to G.E. Bentley, Jr., *Blake Books* (Oxford: Clarendon, 1977), 598–601, his closest proven contact would be his three engravings after Stothard in the same volume of *The Novelist's Magazine* as a reprint of Swift's best-known work. Blake need not have owned or read the entire book to be aware of the Houyhnhnms, though, nor to derive inspiration from Swift's caustic characterization of them as creatures of pure Reason.

64. E 687; Cavendish, *La Méthode*, 1:13. On Swift's use of Cavendish see Bowden, "Before the Houyhnhnms."

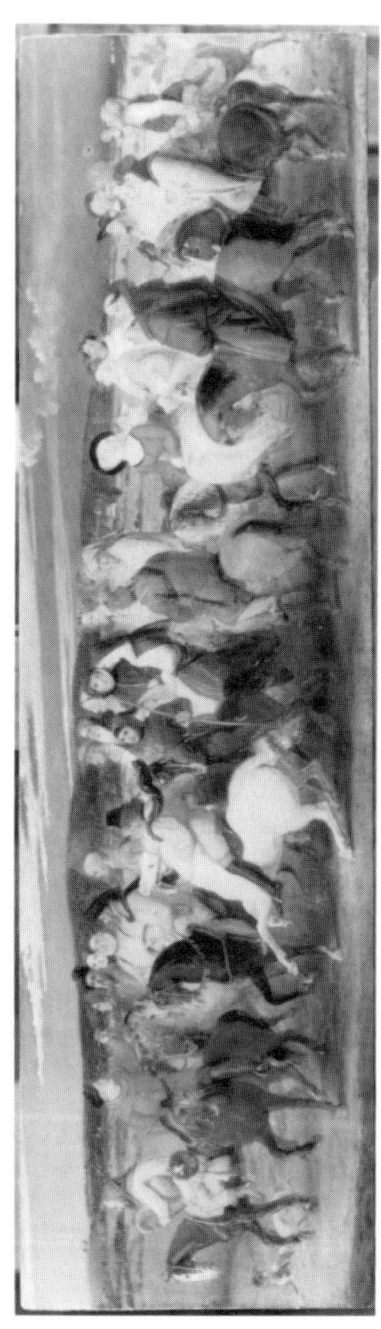

1. *The Pilgrimage to Canterbury*. Painted by Thomas Stothard, 1807. 92.5 cm × 31.8 cm. Tate Gallery, London.

2. *Chaucers Canterbury Pilgrims*. Drawn and engraved by William Blake. Fourth state, ca. 1820–23. Based on Blake's 1809 painting. 71 cm × 31 cm. The Huntington Library, San Marino, California.

3. The Squire. From the Ellesmere manuscript. Fifteenth century.
53 mm × 69 mm. The Huntington Library, San Marino,
California.

4. Segment of Parthenon frieze. Plate 14 of chapter 1 of volume 2 of *The Antiquities of Athens* (London, 1787). Drawn by James Stewart or Nicholas Revett, engraved by James Newton. 35.5 cm × 16 cm. Anne & Jerome Fisher Fine Arts Library, University of Pennsylvania.

5. The Squire. From page 59 of *The Works of Geoffrey Chaucer*, ed.
John Urry (London, 1721). 11 cm × 15 cm. Annenberg Rare Book
and Manuscript Library, University of Pennsylvania.

_Terre à terre, à Main gauche._

6. Horse and rider demonstrating a _terre à terre à main gauche._ From plate 18 (1:54/55) of William Cavendish, Duke of Newcastle, _A General System of Horsemanship_ (London, 1743). Drawn by Abr. a Diepenbeke, engraved by Petr. Clouwet. 12 cm × 16 cm. Fairman Rogers Collection, Veterinary School Library, University of Pennsylvania.

7. Horse and rider demonstrating a collected walk. From page 29 of
volume 1 of William Cavendish, Duke of Newcastle, *A General System of
Horsemanship* (London, 1743). Engraved by R. Parr. 21 cm × 13 cm.
Fairman Rogers Collection, Veterinary School Library, University of
Pennsylvania.

8. Segment from the Temple of Theseus frieze. Plate 21 of chapter 2 of volume 3 of *The Antiquities of Athens* (London, 1794). Plate 1792. Drawn by William Pars, engraved by William Blake. 37.5 cm × 20.5 cm. Anne & Jerome Fisher Fine Arts Library, University of Pennsylvania.

# Medieval Mozart: *König Garibald* and *La Clemenza di Tito*

## Werner Wunderlich

Ein hehres Fest bringt uns die neue Sonne,
Denn heute sind es fünfundzwanzig Jahre
Dass Garibald der Bayern Thron bestieg. . .
Er brachte seinen Völkern Heil,
Und jeden Tag bezeichnet eine Wohltat.–
Dem Titus gleich, der Römer edlen Kaiser,
Hielt Er den Augenblick verloren, den
Er nicht zum Glück der Menschheit angewendet. . .
Drum jauchzt das Volk, und sein sind alle Herzen;
Es füllet sich die weite Königsstadt
Mit Gästen, und aus weit entfernten Landen
Sieht man sie strömen zu dem Völkerfeste.

[The new sun brings us a noble celebration, / For today it is twenty-five years / Since Garibald ascended the Bavarian throne. . . He brought his people salvation, / And every day is marked by some good deed.– / Like Titus, the Romans' noble Emperor, / He counted as lost the moment, which / He did not dedicate to the happiness of mankind. . . For this the people rejoice, and all hearts are his; / The broad royal city fills / With guests, and from far-distant lands / One sees them streaming to the peoples' festival.][1]

Before the royal palace at Regensburg the seer Theodat calls upon the "Bavarian warriors and women" to remember the beneficent work of their sovereign. Well-versed in Roman historiography, he unctuously praises his illustrious lord as a second Titus. He quotes the famous sentence, "*Amici, diem perdidi*" ["Friends, I have lost a day"], which Suetonius put in the mouth of the first Titus, when the latter was said to have complained that he had not fulfilled a single person's wish for a whole day. Theodat is therefore laying it on rather thickly, in celebrating calculated displays of favour as imperial benefits for the whole of humanity. But his panegyrical exaggeration of course flatters the Bavarian king, who is equated with the Roman emperor. The full glory of the idealised historical exemplar is transferred to the one being honoured. This emotive homage on the occasion of the twenty-fifth anniversary of Garibald's rule illustrates for all the meaning and solemnity of the festivities.

The ingratiating expression of joy does demand, however, a slight revision of historical dates to suit the requirements of Providence:

> Der Krone Schmuck seh ich nun wieder glänzen,
> Erneuert ist das alte Königthum'.
> Und Max erweitert seiner Staaten Grenzen,
> Und giebt dem Volk' – Ihn lohnet ew'ger Ruhm. . .
> Es wird nach fünfundzwanzig-fünfzig Jahren
> Die Nation sich Ihres Herrschers freu'n,
> Und zweymal seh' ich das beglückte Bayern
> Des *Allgeliebten* Jubelfeste feyern.

[I see the crown jewels gleaming once again, / The ancient kingship is renewed, / And Max expands the borders of his lands, / And gives to the people – eternal fame is his reward. . . / After twenty-five times fifty years / The nation will rejoice in its ruler, / And two times over do I see fortunate Bavaria / Celebrate the jubilee of the all-beloved!][2]

This second jubilee of an "all-beloved" is the twenty-fifth anniversary of the ruler Maximilian Joseph I's ascendancy to the throne in 1824. If we subtract the prophetic multiplication $25 \times 50$, or 1250 years, we arrive at the date 574. The events described meanwhile belong historically to the year 588, but let us not be hindered by petty subtraction. Theodat's approximate mental arithmetic aims at a heavily symbolic play on numbers. As magisterial oracle he is less concerned with exact dating. From the retrospective of the jubilee year 1824, the past becomes a historical narrative whose dénouement is the present. In the light of Theodat's vision, history is raised to the symbolic level of an eternal truth. In their dramatic revelation, a character in a Mozart opera, memories of its model in antiquity, representation of Agilolfing rule, and the prophecy of Wittelsbachian history, combine to make many connections. This historically bold transference of the image of the Roman Emperor Titus Flavius Vespasianus (79–81) on to Garibald (555–590), the earliest known ruler of Bavaria, with its associated reflection of Max Joseph of Bavaria, "father of his country," was carried out by the Munich actor and dramatist Cäsar Max Heigel. Heigel accomplished this feat of revisionism in his *König Garibald*, an adaptation of Mozart and Caterino Mazzolà's *La Clemenza di Tito* (KV 621). The first performance was held the evening before the royal jubilee:

> In the Royal Hoftheater, on the 15th, Mozart's *Titus* was presented in an illuminated hall with great splendour and artistic extravagance as a festival piece, entry being free, with an entirely altered text drawing an analogy with the Bavarian Titus.[3]

The opera was greeted with resounding applause as an "allegorical celebration in two acts", and a repeat performance was given on the 20th of February, "for that portion of the public who did not have the opportunity to revel in its splendour at the first performance."[4] Shortened to two acts for Mozart by Mazzolà,[6] Pietro Metastasio's three-act libretto[5] had been by far the most popular of the operas of courtly tribute in the *ancien régime*. Ritual theatre presented the good prince personified in the stage-hero as an eternal exemplar, under the cloak of an antiquity transformed by the present. By 1824, Metastasio's work had been adapted to the musical stage at least sixty times, most recently in 1816 by Heinrich August Marschner. Granted, until that time the text had been revised only by Mazzolà,[7] and a complete reworking was as yet unrealised. Heigel's "Germanic" adaptation, written in the patriotic fervour of the Romantic period, was the first of these.[8] In 1837 a second "medieval" version followed, penned by Anton Wilhelm Florentin von Zuccalmaglio, alias Waldbrühl, who had already furnished *Idomeneo*, *Die Entführung aus dem Serail* and *Die Zauberflöte* with new librettos. His adaptation of *Tito*, *Karl in Pavia*, picks up the thread of Frankish-Lombard history present in Heigel's piece, dramatising the conquest of Pavia in 784 – the end of the Lombard kingdom under Desiderius – and the coronation of Charlemagne, the "Carolingian Titus," as king of the Lombard people.

Until about 1850, the continuing interest in Mozart's *Tito*[9] was considerable. The popularity of individual numbers in both public and private recitals is evident in the many arrangements for piano, wind instrument and household chamber ensemble; concerto presentations in musical academies,[10] and pasticcios, or performances with added musical interludes, by Domenico Cimarosa, Joseph Weigl, Peter von Winter and Johann Simon Mayr[11] offer further proof. Beethoven is said to have played in 1798 in Prague a variation of the Annio-Servilia duet *"Ah perdona al primo affetto"* (Nr. 7) for piano.[12] The public debacle at the opening performance in Prague – the coronation opera commemorating Leopold II's Bohemian enthronement on the evening of September 6, 1791 – clearly had no repercussions, for the opera was performed many times afterwards in the Moldavian capital. Years later, after the first performances in Vienna on December 29, 1794 in the Kärntnertor Theater and March 31, 1795 in the Burg Theater, *La Clemenza di Tito* achieved success on many stages. Especially in German-language versions, such as *Titus der Gütige*, the work was able to establish itself in repertoires.[13] German librettos were written by, among others, Joseph von Seyfried,[14] and by Leopold Anton Kozeluch, Friedrich Rochlitz, Johann Jakob Ihlee and Christian August Vulpius.

On June 26, 1802, for example, the theatre at Lauchstädt, newly renovated according to plans drawn by Heinrich Gentz and Friedrich Rabe – the Weimar Theater gave guest performances in the summer palace of the Saxon court – opened with a festival production of *Titus*, an adaptation believed to have been written by Goethe's brother-in-law, Vulpius.[15] In Goethe's mythological-allegorical prologue *"Was wir bringen"* the figure of Pathos, tragedy, makes a final entry after Phone, opera, with three stanzas of verse. The first two speak of tragedy in general, the last, of its cathartic effect. The idea of a redemptive balance between menacing horror and sublime morality, achieved aesthetically, can be understood as an allusion to Mozart's ensuing *opera seria*, whose last notes ring with a conciliatory *lieto fine*. The verses express that attitude of mind which, in Mozart's opera, honoured the harmonious and humanistic resolution of conflicts as a classical ideal:

> Doch senkt sich spät ein heiliges Verschonen
> In der Beklemmung allzu dichte Nacht,
> Am holden Blick in höhre Regionen
> Fühlt nun sich jedes edles Herz erwacht,
> Dort drängt's euch hin, dort hoffet ihr zu wohnen,
> Auf einmal wird ein Himmel euch gebracht;
> Vom Reimen lässt das Schicksal sich versöhnen,
> Und alles löst sich auf im Guten und im Schönen.

[Yet in the end a holy compassion pierces / The too-dark night of apprehension, / Every noble heart feels itself awakened / By the sweet glimpse of higher realms. / There it impels you, there you hope to live, / At once a heaven is laid before you; / By rhyme fate lets itself be reconciled, / And all is resolved in what is good and fair.][16]

Mozart's opera, however, posits quite problematic, indeed provocative political questions concerning both restoration and liberalism: is the loving kindness of a sovereign an appropriate basis on which to build civil society? May private interests rob the separation of powers of its force? What meaning does legitimate clemency have when opposed to legal justice as the right of all people? How can an absolutist and capricious mercy be in harmony with efforts to establish constitutional rights? Despite such thorny questions, Mozart's opera was highly regarded by the bourgeois public of 1800, and its title hero was considered a model of that middle-class consciousness shaped by humanism. The ideals of modern humanism and a classicist interpretation of form derived from German adaptations of antique models encouraged critics and audience alike to perceive in *Titus* an "apex of classicism,"[17] a master work, whose initial purpose as a coronation opera for absolutism[18] had slipped from public memory. Republican ideas of the French Revolution had freed the forms and ideals, materials and figures of classical antiquity from the *ancien régime*'s intepretation of antiquity, and broken with the antiquarian pomp of baroque. Mozart's music was seen in any case as privileged art, full of harmony and a source of profound thought.[19] Friedrich Rochlitz, one of the first translators of the *Tito* libretto, and also the first Mozart biographer, Franz Xaver Niemetschek, praise the composer's operas and their title heroes:

> With a touch peculiar to himself Mozart took in the simplicity, the still sublimity of the character of Titus and of the whole plot, and transferred them in entirety to his own composition. Every aspect, even the moderation of the instrumental parts, carries this stamp, integrated into the beauty and unity of the whole.[20]

Contributing not a little to this spreading perception was the performance style of the Empire's antiquarianising classicism, evident, for example, in the monumental Roman splendor of the Frankfurt performance of 1799. Moreover, the almost Biedermeier outlook of the early nineteenth century saw Titus as a person who suppressed his own wishes for the good of others and was satisfied with what he had been given. As a figure of valiant resignation, Titus fitted to a certain extent into a hero cult not confined to the rebel or the genius. Such were the conditions – albeit self-contradictory – under which the *opera seria* appeared after the French Revolution not as anachronistic, but thoroughly acceptable to bourgeois society.

Along with the bourgeois reception, however, there persisted an aristocratic custom originating in the princely tradition of magnificent musical performance established under the Austro-Hungarian Empire and other German states of the period. Again and again in the first half of the nineteenth century, *Titus der Gütige* was put on at royal processions, marriages, Saints' days, birthdays, coronations and other official celebrations.[21] "You beautiful day, you who gave us the compassionate ruler. . ."[22] exults a ceremonial song commemorating the twenty-five year reign of the "father of the fatherland,"[23] Duke Maximilian Joseph von Pfalz-Zweibrücken, who in expectation of inheriting the Bavarian throne converted from Protestantism to Catholicism, and acceded on February 16, 1799 following the death of the Bavarian Elector Karl Theodor; leaving his Palatinate court in Mannheim, he entered Munich as Maximilian Joseph IV. One of the many pamphlets celebrating the anniversary of this ruler (who with Napoleon's elevation of Bavaria to a kingdom in 1806, had become King Maximilian Joseph I) celebrates his deeds with the words, "From his sceptre sprinkles blessed dew."[24] Known affectionately in both political and familiar contexts as Max Joseph, he was honoured by his subordinates during his lifetime[25] for his governmental reforms, his tolerance and liberalism, charity and charisma, and at his death in 1825 was mourned as "the best ruler among all who have ever graced a throne," as one of the "most noble people of all time" and "the good King, the favourite of God and men."[26] In reality, Bavaria was transformed during Max Joseph's reign by the hand of his directing minister Count Montgelas; through increasing secularisation and territorial consolidation, he was to help it become a unified and modern state without privileges of rank. Legal reforms such as the humanisation of the penal code,[27] constitutional guarantees for such civil rights as religious freedom, and a competent administration, brought harmony, peace and increased middle-class prosperity.[28] As a promoter of the arts and sciences, music and theatre, Max Joseph also made a name for himself.[29] It was because of the King, himself a music connoisseur, that the Munich Court Orchestra (already strengthened under Karl Theodor by musicians of the then world-famous Mannheim Kapelle) became one of the most respected of its day.[30] Karl Theodor's plan "to construct a national theatre for the development of German music and performance"[31] was also realised by Max Joseph. Built by Karl von Fischer, the National Theatre was dedicated in 1818. Destroyed by fire in 1823, it was immediately rebuilt by Leo von Klenze under royal commission, and opened with celebratory fanfare in 1825. It was accordingly the Hoftheater designed by François de Cuvilliés and opened in 1753 – and actually reserved for Italian opera – which served as performance hall for the "Bavarian" opera of homage:

> Tonight at six a celebratory performance was given in the royal theater. The whole playhouse was bedecked in inviting white and blue colors. One of the ceiling panels, luminously radiant in its aspect, filled the theatre with a magical light. The invited guests were attired in the most splendid dress. The royal couple were received by the assembled with friendly jubilation to the sound of trumpets and timpanis. The curtain was drawn to reveal the most ethereal stage decoration. To the soft strains of a new instrument – the Aeolian harp – there gradually appeared twenty-five brightly glowing stars, each one containing a praying angel representing a great wish for the fatherland. In the middle of these there last appeared the name of Max Joseph, magnificently lit, eliciting a general outburst of approval, an enthusiastic cheer from the whole house, who, with deep emotion began chanting "Hail to the King!" Hereafter followed the opera, *König Garibald*, written by C.M. Heigel. In times long past, Garibald was Bavaria's great benefactor, as Maximilian Joseph now is.[32]

Sentimental and mindful of tradition, the many cultural spectacles and royal patriotic hymns of the anniversary proceedings exploited the initial period of Bavarian history for the purposes of honoring Max Joseph. Heigel's nationalistic adaptation of *Tito* must be viewed in this context. The contemporary audience was not content simply with a new staging of Mozart's festival opera, but wanted to see in it the reflection of Max Joseph. The Munich jubilee sought to reflect the well-respected ruler in the celebrated virtues of the Titus figure, to applaud him publicly in the tradition of elegant opera performance, and to glorify his person through Mozart's majestic music. Above all, however, Heigel's "new" text wanted to express homage for the ruling King by honouring the historical continuity of the Bavarian line and his embodiment of it. A somewhat naive historicism understood the past as a legitimating force of state and country, as a condition of the extant ruling lineage, as well as a process of organic fusion between the "father of the country" and its "children." Heigel's reconfiguration had thus to turn its face from the strikingly antiquarian décor of Mozart's opera in order to discover in Bavaria's history material which in itself testified to an elevated past and acted also as a "distant mirror" of the glorious present. In this naive understanding of history, "the good old days" became a conventional self-fashioning. Against the background of the German wars of liberation, and following the Romantic discovery of "old Germanic antiquity" (combined with technological-economic crises and socio-political decay on many levels), a historically-derived idealisation and patriotic preoccupation with the past had been made manifest since the 1800s in countless literary and artistic products dramatising medieval themes (these often seen as a better alternative to the present). Works such as Franz Grillparzer's *König Ottokars Glück und Ende* (1825) or Christian Dietrich Grabbe's *Hermannsschlacht* (1836) testify, like countless other (mostly trivial) historical dramas using "the Germanic Heroic Age" or the "romantic Age of Chivalry" as their setting, to the desire to use history for both a traditionally-oriented self-creation and a topically-relevant self-awareness.

The literary fashion of "Germanicism" and "Medievalism" also seized the opera, where suitable materials and themes were adapted from newly revived and updated productions. Irrational and supernatural accounts drawn from mythology, heroes and adventures from the epic, motifs from legends or fairy tales, historical figures and events taken from the migration and Stauffenberg periods, conventional images of courtly chivalry and stout citizenship, pastoral harmony and Catholic piety, joined with serene, joyful or sombre refrains to form operetta-style or heroic-romantic works of music.[33] Carl Maria von Weber's *Silvana* (1810) and *Euryanthe* (1823), Louis Spohr's *Faust* (1816), E.T.A. Hoffman's *Undine* (1816), Heinrich August Marschner's *Kyffhäuserberg* (1820) and *Der Templer und die Jüdin* (1828), and Franz Schubert's *Fierrabras* (1823) are (all close in time to Heigel's *König Garibald*) the outstanding examples of "medieval opera." This latter became eventually a phenomenon of the period, marked increasingly by hack-work librettos. In addition to Wagner's musical dramas, Konradin Kreutzer's *Melusine* (1833), Otto Nicolai's *Il templario* (1840; *Der Tempelritter*, 1845), Louis Spohr's *Die Kreuzfahrer* (1845), Heinrich Marschner's *Kaiser Adolph von Nassau* (1845), Albert Lortzing's *Undine* (1845), *Der Waffenschmid* (1846) and *Rolands Knappen* (1849), Robert Schumann's *Genoveva* (1847), Felix Draeske's *König Sigurd* (1857), *Gudrun* (1885) and *Herrat* (1892), Peter Cornelius' *Der Cid* (1865) and *Gunlöd* (1891), Richard Metzdorff's *Der*

*Fall des Gepidenreiches* (1875; also, *Rosamunde*), Johann Josef Abert's *König Enzio* (1862; *Enzio von Hohenstaufen*, 1875) and *Ekkehard* (1878); August Klughardt's *Iwein* (1879), Karl von Perfall's *Raimondin* (1881), Karl Goldmark's *Merlin* (1886), Richard Strauss's *Guntram* (1894), Hans Pfitzner's *Der arme Heinrich* (1895), Otto Feller's *Die Albingenser* (1895), Eugen d'Albert's *Gernot* (1897), and Victor Gluth's *Horrand und Hilde* (1899) were in nineteenth-century Germany among the most popular works of this branch of opera,[34] of which only a very few were able to establish themselves lastingly in the repertoire: a fate shared with most of these operas by *König Garibald*, apparently staged only on the two occasions mentioned in connection with the anniversary celebrations. This musical homage is an anomaly, though, among the "medieval operas" in so far as its score was borrowed nearly in full from a previously successful work, and then infused with a pseudo-medieval subject. Such a method of revision – integrating a new libretto into an extant score – was however also attempted in the 1800s with *Idomeneo* and *Così fan tutte* as well as others among Mozart's Italian operas.[35]

In a letter to his father in Salzburg dated September 29, 1777, the young Mozart wrote "I am glad to be here; and I am of the opinion, as are many of my good friends, that if I were to stay here but one or two years, I could make myself worthy and well-respected. . .".[36] Mozart was invited to the Bavarian Residenz eight times in all; there his music was recognised and popular.[37] In January or February of 1775 he is said to have composed the *Missa brevis* C-Major, the *Spatzenmesse* (KV 220), in Munich. During this time he also agreed to a piano competition against the famous musician Ignaz Franz von Beecke to be held in the well-known inn "Zum Schwarzen Adler." In October of 1777, he gave a concert at this same tavern consisting of several of his piano pieces and divertimenti. Still in Munich, he composed in the winter of 1778–79 the "Dürnitz-Sonata" for piano (KV 284a), several concert-arias (KV 300b, 365a, 368, 369) and songs (KV 367a, 367b), as well as a series of violin sonatas (KV 301–6) dedicated to Princess Maria Elisabeth. He performed a number of his piano concertos, serenades and divertimenti at the residence of the Countess of Salerno and in association with the academies, and was present at other concerts containing arias from his early *opere serie*. Mozart's church music – pieces such as *Litaniae de venerabili altaris sacramento* (KV 125) composed for New Year's Day, 1775 – were played in the Munich Frauenkirche. His *opera buffa La finta giardiniera* was performed on January 13, 1775 in the Salvatortheater, while the *opera seria Idomeneo re di Creta*, commissioned by Karl Theodor as a "carnival opera," was lavishly staged on January 29, 1781 in the Residenztheater.

Mozart's great operas – *Die Entführung aus dem Serail* (1785), *Don Giovanni* (1791), *Die Zauberflöte* (1793), *Figaro* (1794) and *Così fan tutte* (1795) in its German version, *Die Wette* – enjoyed their opening performances in Munich, while his last *opera seria* was first presented in its German adaptation, *Titus*, on February 10, 1801. On July 21, 1805 *Titus* was again performed with interludes written by the Munich choir director and composer Carl August Cannabich and Peter von Winter, the Lower Bavaria-born opera composer Giovanni Simone Mayr and Salieri's pupil Joseph Weigl, the last having collaborated on the Viennese productions of *Figaro* (1786) and *Don Giovanni* (1788). In contrast to his predecessor, Karl Theodor, who patronised the German opera in Mannheim and Munich, Max Joseph favored the Italian, especially those in the style of Gioacchino Rossini, Luigi Cherubini and Gasparo Spontini, and the French, as represented by Giacomo Meyerbeer. In addition, operettas and folk pieces of both a devotional and entertaining nature were staged, mainly as a result of their popularity in the local Viennese theaters, "for the Munich audiences were charmed by Viennese farce."[38] In the newly renovated Isartor Theater, opened in 1812 under the musical direction of Peter Joseph von Lindpaintner and general leadership of Carl Bernbrunn, such expectations came to the fore: "Our public wants to see knightly romances."[39] The German opera of the National Theater was again revived in 1822 with the success of Weber's *Freischütz*.

Viewed against this historical backdrop, *König Garibald*, its score borrowed from *opera seria*, represents the theatrical intersection between German operetta and Italian opera:

> The text was supposedly written by Cäsar Max Heigel. In reality, he used an extant *Titus* libretto translated by Rochlitz, altering it in an ad hoc manner as was necessary. The only newly composed parts are the dialogue which comes in in the passage of Secco's recitative, and the second finale, which – while everywhere else Mozart's music was retained – like the introduction was composed by Stuntz.[40]

Cäsar Max Heigel, born in Munich on June 25, 1783, came from a family of actors.[41] He led a truly colourful and adventurous life, of which his autobiographical works – the anonymous *Bruchstücke aus den Ruinen meines Lebens* published in Aarau in 1820, and the *Skizzen aus dem Münchner Leben* and *Skizzen aus dem Nürnberger Leben*, which appeared in the twenties and thirties – offer some indication. Heigel was a political hothead and enthusiastic supporter of egalitarian freedom. He was sympathetic to the ideals of the French Revolution and to liberal notions of equality without affiliating himself to a particular political organisation. He enlisted in Napoleon's army, was severely injured, returned to his fatherland as an officer on the general staff, was then pursued by the French Governor for writing an incendiary pamphlet, fled through Switzerland and southern Germany to Tirol, and was finally captured and incarcerated by French authorities in 1807. Having escaped a penal batallion, he made his way to the Ile de France. He returned under obscure circumstances, and was again imprisoned in Munich in 1813 on unknown charges, though shortly released. Thereafter Heigel appeared as an actor on various stages in Switzerland, Bavaria, Karlsruhe and Vienna, and wrote pieces of a style befitting the demands of the contemporary theatre and directed no doubt at its particular audience. He was engaged twice before marrying Karoline Margarethe Stäb of Karlsruhe. In 1824 Heigel became director Bernbrunn's chief deputy and a writer and actor at the Isartor Theater, later serving in the thirties as director and dramatist in Bamberg and Nuremburg. In 1836, Odilon Barrot, leader of an opposition group against Louis Philippe, recommended him as a correspondent to several Parisian journals. Beginning in 1847, Heigel's family was to receive no more news of "fortune's favorite,"[42] and all trace of him was lost, according to his nephew, Karl Theodor,[43] in the tumult of 1848.

In addition to his autobiographical writings, poems and librettos, Heigel also composed a whole series of emotive, fantastic and farcical plays and "patriotic dramas." Clearly, he was gifted with a great talent for fantasy: "No actor who performed under the direction of Heigel (composer of the *Zeiträume*, the *Narrenhaus* and many other well-received pieces) in Munich, Innsbruck etc., and became acquainted with him during his stay in Vienna, could – and that includes the author of this book – give a sufficient account of his genuinely Münchhausen-like escapades. . .".[44] A whole series of his dramatic presentations – like for example the comedies *Das war dein Glück*, performed at the Viennese Burgtheater in 1804, and *Die Tollköpfe* (Hamburg, 1811), the drama *Ludwig von Ingolstadt*, staged in Frankfurt am Main in 1805, and *Hans von Dreisporn*, a "chivalric comedy" rehearsed at the Isartor Theater in 1824 – have never been printed.[45] Among those published were a brief homage *Zur Genesung Ihrer Durchlaucht der Kurfürstin Friderike Karoline* (1799), various popular pieces such as *Die Zeitalter* (1812, reissued 1832), farces of a local colour (the two *Fasching in München*, 1828 and 1829) and a few historical dramas like *Die Schlacht bei St. Jakob* (1822) and *Max Emanuels erste Waffentat* (1833). In Germany and Austria, regional patriotism and enthusiasm encouraged these "dramas of the fatherland" to borrow heroes and rulers from the aristocratic tableaux of the Hapsburg, Guelph and Hohenstauffen families. In fashion since the last third of the eighteenth century, this genre was popularised by works like the "national drama," *Ludwig der Vierte, genannt der Bayer* by Johann Nepomuk Lengenfelder (1780), or Joseph Marius von Babo's *Otto von Wittelsbach* (1781), and, under Max Joseph, became almost compulsory with the announcement of a prize by the directorate of the Bavarian Hoftheater in 1819.[46]

As a librettist, Heigel was involved in diverse opera productions. He translated Benoit-Joseph Marsollier's text *Léhéman ou la tour de Neustadt* for the opera *Macdonald* by Nicolas-Marie Dalayrac (Munich, 1803), Rouget de Lille's libretto for Hippolyte-André-Baptiste Chelard's heroic opera *Macbeth* (Munich, 1828), as well as arias and hymns from the Italian libretto by Guiseppe Maria Foppa for Fernando Paër's comic opera *Sargines oder Der Zögling der Liebe* (Munich 1804). In addition to *König Garibald*, he also adapted the operatic texts for *Die Zauberfackel oder Die Siebenschläfer* (Munich, 1825), from Leopold Huber's *Die Todtenfackel*; for Peter Joseph von Lindpaintner's *Der Vampyr* (Stuttgart, 1828), based on Lord Byron's story *The Vampyr*; and Aloys Schmitt's *Das Oktoberfest zu Paderborn* (Frankfurt am Main, 1843), from historical sources of the Carolingian period. Heigel's practical stage experience, his authorial handling of patriotic themes and his conspicuous inclination to musical theatre seemed to predestine him to the role of Mazzolà's "translator." Textual similarities indicate that Rochlitz's "Songs for the opera: *Titus der Grossmüthige*, in two acts, put to music by Mozart after the Italian of Metastasio"[47] may have served as a model.

For *König Garibald*, Vice-Kapellmeister Joseph Hartmann Stuntz (1793–1859)[48] composed an introduction to the first act, a new finale to the second. As prologue and epilogue, the additions to a certain extent provide the context and reference point for the tribute paid to Max Joseph and the Wittelsbachian ruling house. Stuntz was a student of the Viennese court composer (and rival of Mozart) Antonio Salieri, as well as the Munich opera composer and Hofkapellmeister, Peter de Winter. From his hand came, among other works, several successful Italian-language operas: *La rappresaglia* (Milan, 1819), *Costantino* (Venice, 1821), *Dalmiro ed Argone* (Turin, 1822) and *Elvira et Lucinde* (Milan, 1823). For performance in Munich he wrote *Heinrich IV zu Givry* (1820), *Charlot* (1821) and *Maria Rosa* (1846). The same year that *König Garibald* opened, Stuntz became opera director at the Hoftheater and one year later succeeded de Winter as Hofkapellmeister. After the appointment of conductor Franz Lachner in 1836, Stuntz dedicated himself primarily to the composition of church music and men's choral music appropriate to the many patriotic festivals held by Ludwig I. Because of his own Italian operas, based as they were in part on medieval subjects, and his intimacy with the Viennese classics, Stuntz was seen as the ideal candidate to compose fitting musical addenda to Mozart's opera. The score of the two new pieces survives as autograph;[49] here and there the written text differs a little from the printed libretto.

The more specific circumstances of its composition, details as to its commission, production time and royalties paid, its sources and models, staging and production, its critical reception and the opinion of those select individuals whom it addressed, these have as far as is known been lost to posterity. Heigel himself, who otherwise spared no detail of his personal life, recorded next to nothing concerning his work in the theatre. His nephew, Karl Theodor, conjectured as to why his uncle may have written the libretto:

> The author of this extravagant and enthusiastically laudatory poetry may have been incited by a desire to display convincingly his recently doubtful loyalty.[50]

In fact, Heigel was – by his own account, unjustly – pursued and imprisoned several times on political grounds. His autobiographical sketches are marked by these experiences. After his release from imprisonment in Switzerland in 1818, Heigel had bewailed pathetically:

> Den mächt'gen Gang des Herrschers lenkt
> Des Bürgers leise Stimme nicht.

> [The citizen's quiet voice does not affect / The sovereign's powerful step.][51]

It may be that his permanent appointment to the theatre in 1824 affected a change of heart, and that he thus undertook his patriotic task with enthusiasm. In any case, his text expresses similar sentiment. In the "Preface," Heigel elucidates the historical reasons for his choice of subject matter – "the present does not fill up the whole of time"[52] – and justifies his retention of the original score:

> Should one still ask, why choose the figure of Garibald? – If he does not match the greater descendant whose anniversary celebration we undertake today, still, the learned Scots, whom he

called to his court to spread Christianity, called him 'the Titus of Bavaria.'

It was this title which determined the choice of accompanying music. Mozart's masterpiece should recall at every moment through its familiar notes the delicate allusion to our new Titus, and no-one will dispute this judicious blending.[53]

Whether traveling monks of the early Irish-Scottish or Anglo-Saxon Continental missions did in fact give the Bavarian ruler the name of the Roman Emperor as an honorary title is, however, completely unconfirmed; just as the same form of address for Max Joseph was in no way in common use, but appears to have been employed only by Heigel with regard to his adaptation of the *Titus* opera and the Garibald story.

The opera relates the courtship of the Lombard King Autharis. Enraptured by "the fame of her great virtue,"[54] he wishes to pay court to Garibald's fair daughter Theodolinde, for she has appeared to him in a "sweet-golden" dream,[55] and made captive of his heart. For her part, Theodolinde recognises in him the ideal which her future spouse must epitomise in order to be worthy of her. Autharis presents himself in Regensburg incognito under the pseudonym Udo; for if he were to be rebuffed, he would not wish to be exposed to this humiliation at Garibald's court as the king of his people. As the couple however mutually confess their love, overwhelmed by their feelings at first sight, Autharis reveals his true identity to Theodolinde under an oath of silence. Challenged by the arrogant behaviour of the heathen priests, Autharis – a follower of Christian teaching – destroys a heathen cult-site. To his delight, Theodolinde supports him in this furious act: "I do not know how to win you more worthily."[56] Garibald tolerates this show of devotion out of consideration for the foreigner's customs and morals. Although Autharis's violent abuse of hospitality ought to be punished by death, Garibald allows clemency to prevail. Theodolinde at once then reveals herself as the true instigator of the impiety and declares her love for this stranger whose life Garibald has spared, while expelling him from the land. When Garibald learns from Theodolinde the identity of his guest, who has been moved by his mildness, he is thankful and happy to have practised restraint: "It is the heart that brings us higher joys."[57] At the Bavarian border, Autharis reveals his true identity, and the opera ends with a glorious vision: in the rule and person of the Wittelsbachian Max Joseph, the famous history of Bavaria which began with the Agilolfing Garibald will be fulfilled.

Heigel's libretto is based on historical materials confirmed by original sources. The figure of Garibald had been made accessible for epic
representation and reproduction by Johann Nepomuk Mederer's Bavarian
history of 1777[58] and Vinzenz von Pallhausen's 1810 investigation of the
first Agilolfing and his daughter.[59] These works idealise both the people
and their king, but describe also – like Heigel's later work – the dangers of
creating such unity and harmony out of religious contrasts:

> . . . the Bavarians, remembering their good reputation gained
> by acts of courage – bold, honest and faithful, strong; men like
> oak trees, tall and slim in build, physically worthy in every way
> and humane in disposition, by nature willing and good-hearted.
> Garibald ruled as a father, still without written law, but through
> his word, according to the custom of the people and old tradi-
> tion. He and his family were inclined to Catholic teaching; but
> some of his people still clung to the heathen yoke, some were
> misled by deceitful priests.[60]

By 1806, a "patriotic drama" had already appeared, *Garibald, der erste
König in Bojarien*, by the actor August Wülfing.[61] This play of intrigue
tells the story of Garibald's elevation to the Bavarian throne by the
Frankish king Chlotar, and his subsequent marriage to Walatrud, Clotar's
former wife. Heigel's work by contrast has as its centre events that fall
chronologically about forty years later.

The legendary twilight of early Bavarian history allows only an
obscure image of Garibald's personality, his rule, and the political background of his daughter's marriage.[62] There is little certain knowledge
about the origin[63] and rise to power of the Bavarian line,[64] the Bavarian
dukedom,[65] the name and descent of the Agilolfings[66] as the first ruling
dynasty, Garibald's relationship to this family and his rank as ruler; the
state of research is correspondingly disputed. Despite such unresolved
issues, a brief outline of historical events – at least those necessary to an
understanding of Heigel's work – should be outlined.

The title page of the libretto says "König Garibald," the title on the
inside page "Garibald der Agilolfinger." Gregory of Tours, whose *Historia
francorum* first mentions Garibald in 555, refers to him as "duke,"[67]
whereas the *Historia langobardorum* of Paul the Deacon refers to him in
787–99 as "king."[68] The uncertainty of Garibald's title and position
points to the fickle nature of alliances and oppositions determined by
dynastic interests which in general characterised the relationship among
the Franks, Bavarians, Lombards, Visigoths and Byzantines in the sixth

century.[69] It was the Austrasian Merovingians who according to the *Lex Baiuvariorum* of 550 installed the Agilolfings as rulers of Bavaria, until Tassilo III was deposed by Charlemagne in 788 because he had rebelled against the law according to which the Agilolfing who had proved his loyalty to the Frankish king should be raised to the throne. This proviso effectually assured the Agilolfings an hereditary claim to the throne, while providing the Frankish kings with a means to remove any ruler deemed unfavorable. The ducal seat of the settled territories – the old Roman province of Noricum – was the ancient Praetorium in Regensburg.

Garibald owed his position as king to one of these familial alliances. The Merovingian King Theudebald of Austrasia married the Lething-born Princess Waldarada, daughter of King Wacho, of the Langobardian family. Following Theudebald's untimely death, his successor and great-uncle, Chlotar I, married the widow to increase his legitimacy to the title. When the Lethings were forced from the Lombard throne by Audoin, Chlotar I divorced his wife on political grounds, giving her, according to the account of Paul the Deacon, in marriage to "one of his own"[70] – namely, Garibald. With his marriage to Waldarada, the Lombard King's daughter and twice Frankish queen, Garibald, to whom the dukedom had already been promised, secured himself an enviable position. This prestigious prize may have led Paul the Deacon to refer to Garibald as "rex," though he was, in reality, little more than a Frankish vassal and ally of Austrasia. Garibald in fact used the turmoil ensuing from Chlotar I's death and the renewed division of the Frankish Empire into Neustria, Austrasia and Burgundy in 561 to carve out a powerful quasi-regal role for himself, releasing Bavaria from its Merovingian dependency and establishing it as an independent dukedom. To revive the Christian faith, Garibald next sent for the Frankish bishops Emmeranus, Corbinianus and Ruppert. Viewed in its historical context, the title "rex" accorded by Paul the Deacon was more a mark of recognition than an actual political rank. Meanwhile the inclusion of the church in the Frankish coronation was first introduced by the Carolingians in 751, sixty-four years after the seizure of power by the Austrasian *major domo* Pippin II, as a clever means of legitimating and blessing the contemporary reign. The mention of his official sanctioning no doubt lent the first Bavarian ruler a certain aura of Christian authority, one that Heigel's piece exploits in its portrayal of Max Joseph as the fulfillment of this royal succession.

The libretto is based on events of the year 587–88. Under the rule of Austrasian King Childibert II since 576, the Franks, in alliance with the Byzantine Emperor Maurice, had initiated a military invasion of northern

Italy; repelled by Duke Eoin von Trient, a relative of Garibald, Childibert was forced to seek other means of achieving his political aim. Desiring to renew familial alliances with the Agilolfing dukes and Lombard kings, he thus became engaged in 585 to Garibald's fifteen-year-old daughter, Theodolinde, and promised his sister, Chlodeswinde, in marriage to King Authari ("Autharis" in Heigel's libretto), who had worn the "Iron Crown"[71] since 584. A strong Austrasian-Bavarian-Lombard alliance seemed certain, but collapsed before fully solidified. When, in 587, the possibility of an Austrasian connection with the Visigoth ruler Reccared – and the attendant Frankish influence in Spain this promised – presented itself, the engagement to the Lombard King was abruptly dissolved. The rejected Authari – caught in a difficult position between Byzantium and the expanding Frankish kingdom of the Merovingians – now began to woo Theodolinde himself, became engaged in 588, and thus effectively changed fronts. The Lombard kings had meanwhile taken the epithet Flavius from their familial ancestor Titus in order to legitimise their claim as successors to the Roman throne in Italy. As a supporter, Authari not only represented a gain in prestige for Garibald, but also a strong ally in the Bavarian politics of autonomy. In 589, Childibert began a new offensive against this alliance; thereafter, all trace of Garibald is lost in the muddle of history. Whether he was killed, deposed, or forced to flee, no further mention is made of him. His successor (and perhaps, his son) Tassilo I allied himself more strongly with the Franks in 591 after the Frankish-Lombard reconcilliation.

Theodolinde and her brother Gundoald, the future Duke of Asti, fled before the advancing Franks to Authari. On the 15th May 589, the marriage of Garibald's daughter and the Lombard King was held in Verona. In the midst of a renewed Frankish offensive, Authari died so suddenly that – as with the unexpected death of Titus and later, Leopold II – rumours of poisoning surfaced. In 591 Theodolinde married in Milan the successor to the Lombard throne, Duke Agilulf of Turin – according to Fredegar's *Chronicae*, Ago, the son of Authari.[72] Theodolinde, who chose Monza as her residence, was an exceptional woman; she maintained a regular correspondence with Pope Gregory the Great, successfully converted the Arian Lombards to the Catholic faith and, from Agilulf's death until the maturity of her son, Adalwald, ruled the throne alone. She died in 626 shortly after her son was deposed.

Heigel's libretto borrowed its historical material from chapter 30 of the third volume of Paul the Deacon' *Historia Langobardorum*, his operatic plot developing the young hero's courtship. In Paul's Lombard history, King Authari would, in the words of Theodolinde's nurse, become king and marry the princess:

> 'For truly his person is worthy of one who should hold the kingdom and be linked to you in marriage.' For Authari was at this time in the first bloom of manhood, of proper stature, fair-haired and in every way good to look at.[73]

One could hardly tell from Paul's account that marriage during the Merovingian period was an integral part of the contemporary politics of alliance, less determined by personal affections than by practical ends such as the consolidation of dynastic relations and social power. The chapter indicated of the *Historia Langobardorum* contains all the usual elements of the popular courtship narrative:[74] the test of courage, the avowal of love, the surmounting of hardship, the disguised suitor and predestined wife. For his part, the suitor desires that his wife possess beauty, be of admirable quality and irreproachable conduct, while she hopes her future husband is powerfully built, of good character and high intellectual quality, courageous and generous. Yet it is also made clear that suitability of birth and equality of rank are preconditions which must be properly fulfilled if the marriage is to take place. There is no doubt as to the exceptional standing of the Agilolfing and Authari's aristocratic lineage. That the couple do not belong to the same faith – Authari is Arian, Theodolinde Catholic – is obviously of little importance to Paul, especially given the Bavarian princess's conversion, imminent in retrospect, of the Lombard people.

The narrative motif of the secret testing of the bride's suitability for her future duties as wife and queen by her disguised suitor[75] assumes especial importance in Paul's work. Authari arrives at Garibald's court in Regensburg incognito, supposedly looking for a wife for his king. This circumstance gives the narrator opportunity to make an exceptionally effective point. Authari first reveals himself at his departure through a heavily symbolic test of his manhood and abilities as a ruler:[76]

> As Authari approached the Italian border still surrounded by the Bavarians who had accompanied him, he raised himself in his saddle as high as he could and drove the battle-axe he carried in his hand with all his force into a nearby tree. Leaving it thus embedded, he said: 'Such blows does Authari strike.'[77]

The battle axe in particular demands especial strength and dexterity in its handling.[78] With his awesome blow, the Lombard King thus proved himself a great hero and powerful ally, the future progenitor of a strong people: his axe, male symbol of strength and dignity, is embedded in a tree, the female image of life and fertility. Heigel skilfully incorporates this anecdote in his finale. His Autharis plants his axe in an oak, revered by the Germans as a holy tree, an emblem of power and heroic virtue, as well as victory. The scene becomes a significant ritualisation of a fertile and powerful union from which the Bavarian ruling house will descend. The split oak is transformed into the genealogical tree of the glorious Bavarian ruler. The scene apparently made a great impression, for "their royal Majesties and the royal family left the hall amid the most joyful feelings of the assembly."[79]

The line-up of the original *Tito*-roles – that is to say their character, appearance, social environment, political position and relationship to one another – all had to be altered to suit the historical adaptation and the take-over of motifs from Paul the Deacon, as also the image of patriotic history and the celebratory purpose made clear in prologue and finale. Certain conflicts and contradictions with Mozart's plot and characters were unavoidable. Heigel was compelled in his piece to expand the cast of characters while reworking their various attributes; he was further able to use only thirteen of the score's twenty-six musical pieces, as follows:

| Act 1 *Tito* | Act 1 *Garibald* |
| --- | --- |
| Nr. 1 Duet Sesto/Vitellia "Come ti piace imponi" | Duet Autharis/ Theodolinde "Ford're, befiehl – ich folge" |
| Nr. 2 Aria Vitellia "Deh se piacer mi vuoi" | Aria Theodolinde "Schlägt mir dein Herz voll Liebe" |
| Nr. 4 March | |
| Nr. 5 Chorus "Serbate, oh Dei custodi" | Chorus "Dem König jauchzet, ihr Völker" |
| Nr. 6 Aria Tito "Del più sublime soglio" | Aria Garibald "Glänzend am Himmelspole" |
| Nr. 5 (repeated) | |
| Nr. 9 Aria Sesto "Parto, ma tu ben mio" | Aria Autharis "Feurig ich eil' zu Thaten!" |

| Act 1 *Tito* | Act 1 *Garibald* |
|---|---|
| Nr. 10 Tercet Vitellia/ Publio/Annio "Vengo. . . aspettate" | Tercet Theodolinde/ Widomar/Branor "Folget ihm! Nein verweilet" |
| Nr. 12 Quintet Vitellia/ Servilia/Sesto/Annio/ Publio with chorus "Deh, conservate, oh Dei" | Finale Autharis/Branor/ Sunnhilde/Widomar/ Theodolinde and chorus "Verstummet eitle Klagen" |

| Act 2 *Tito* | Act 2 *Garibald* |
|---|---|
| Nr. 14 Tercet Sesto/Vitellia/Publio "Se al volto mai ti senti" | Tercet Autharis/ Theodolinde/Widomar "Wird bald ein schauernd Lüftchen um deine Wange beben" |
| Nr. 15 Chorus with Tito "A grazie si rendano" | Chorus with Garibald "Erhebet die Seelen" |
| Nr. 19 Rondo Sesto "Deh per questo istante solo" | Aria Autharis "Ach nur einmal noch im Leben" |
| Nr. 23 Rondo Vitellia "Non più di fiori" | Aria Theodolinde "Nie wird mich Hymen lächelnd entzücken" |
| Nr. 24 Chorus "Che del cie, che degli Dei" | Chorus "Herr der Meere, Herr der Blitze!" |

In addition, Heigel was compelled to construct a meaningful framework for the time-bridging historical allegory of the Bavarian dynasty. He accordingly prepared a prologue for the opera, and introduced a kind of prelude to the plot, while a coda makes direct reference to Max Joseph's anniversary. "To our modern view, it does indeed appear strange enough. . ."[80] remarked the chronicler of the Hoftheater, referring to the roles and characterisations which result, again as follows:

| GARIBALD-ROLES | TITO-ROLES | VOICE-RANGE | CAST |
|---|---|---|---|
| Garibald | Tito | Tenor | Mittermayer |
| Walrade | | | Fries |
| Grimoald | | | Hölken |
| Gundoald | | | Urban |
| Theodolinde | Vitellia | Soprano | Siegl |
| Autharis (Udo) | Sesto | Soprano | Verspermann |
| Branor | Annio | Soprano | |
| Sunnehild | Servilia | Soprano | Pesl |
| Widomar | Publio | Bass | Schechner |
| | | | Hannmüller |
| | | | |
| Asprant (Druid) | | | Vespermann |
| Theodat (Scottish seer) | | | Esslair |
| Ganfried (Scottish seer) | | | Staudacher |

The appearance of a powerful Germanic warrior like Autharis or Branor singing a male role soprano – a voice-range which may have had more dramatic justification with the characters of Sesto and Annio – is not without comic effect. More significant, however, is the shift of focus within the main area of conflict. This is particularly evident in the case of Theodolinde and Autharis. In the Mozart/Mazzolà version, Sesto's burning love provides a rational motive for Vitellia's attempt to seize power, to overthrow the usurper Tito and gain the throne by conspiracy and betrayal, rebellion and assassination, deposition and coup. By contrast, Heigel's Theodolinde and Autharis are inflamed by a selfless passion for one another. Their conflict is also the result of tensions between duty and love, but is free of political ambition, private hopes of revenge and blind pride. This romantic emphasis certainly stems from a firm vision of a story with a "happy ending," and is not convincing from the standpoint of the characters and their feelings; it does not develop its oppositions with a sense of fate, but through artificial and unmotivated difficulties. Theodolinde, convinced of the genuine nature of Autharis's love, gives his violent outburst against the pagan temple her blessing, and shares his furious sense of mission. Autharis intreprets this as a proof of great affection, believes his suit thereby strengthened, and thus perpetrates the act of aggression against the heathen shrine in the interests of the true faith. He does not need to be prodded, as was Sesto by Vitellia; Theodolinde's immediate pious agreement transforms his militant fundamentalism into a kind of courting ritual. Autharis is not compelled by Theodolinde to an act of rash revenge. When he reveals his identity to her, she, deeply moved, asks for some proof of affection before consenting to marry – a request he gladly heeds: "Your nod is my command – I follow."[82] This joyful obedience is not submissive acquiescence, but a demonstration of noble convictions and deep respect. By contrast, Sesto sees in his oath only a means to secure personal happiness. His unquestioning love accepts as part of the bargain the murderous death of a friend and ruler as well as his own execution. It is Tito's unconditional kindness – a product of his own unfulfilled desires – which alone protects him from the judicial authority of the state. Individual interests are placed above those of society and country, and private morality supersedes *raison d'état* dedicated to the common good.

Like Tito, the title character Garibald embodies ethical principles of course intended to recall those of Max Joseph. Certainly Heigel's title-character, by virtue of his role as a kind-hearted and politically subtle mediator, is deprived of the sort of tortuous inner conflict which plagues Tito. The Bavarian prince acts out of a compassion based on Christian ideals; his foregiveness is not motivated by private interests – he does not know who Autharis is nor in what relationship he stands to Theodolinde. Garibald establishes a public standard of clemency intended as a model for the resolution of religious conflict in his territory. The political principle of his leadership is reminiscent of the "mild law" in *Witiko*, Adalbert Stifter's late novel (1865–7), in which the title character maintains Bohemia's integrity against the resistance of his irascible and vengeful peers by thoughtful honesty and kindness. This basic posture also distinguished Max Joseph, and directed his successful policy of religious tolerance. The opera's title character is a promulgator of ideas who embodies a sense and aim of history in keeping with Heigel's contemporary society. Motivated by religious conviction, Garibald acts in consonance with political necessity, not against it as does Tito. A conflict between private freedom of action and public demand never arises, and Garibald accordingly endures no inner conflict. For this reason, the music of the Tito arias does not match the texts of Garibald's, nor the character's mood. What in Mozart's opera corresponds musically and psychologically to the expression of feeling and the state of inner torment becomes, in Heigel's piece, mere musical decoration.

This disparity between text and music is especially evident, both aurally and visually, in the two rondos. The parts for solo instruments – the clarinet in Autharis's "Full of fire, I hurry to the deed!" and the basset horn in Theodolinde's "Never will Hymen charm me" – lose their dramatic function and meaning in the context of Heigel's revision. In the original, voice and instrument communicate as partners. In their dialogue, the conditions of conflict unfold and the soul's misgivings are articulated, to particular effect in Sesto's "Parto ma tu ben mio" (Nr. 9) and Vitellia's "Non più di fiori" (Nr. 23). In Autharis's and Theodolinde's pieces, however, the melodies of the solo instruments become meaningless arrangements with no contrast or discord to express in sound.

Branor and Sunnehild are likewise disassociated from their original roles, resembling more the second couple in a lyrical drama, and have little in common with *Tito*'s Annio and Servilia. Widomar, Garibald's general, is much like his Italian counterpart, Publio, in his advocacy of the use of state powers, but remains a comparatively bland character of only peripheral interest. The remaining newly-created characters are stylised embodiments of plot function without independent motivation: unpleasant opponents like the Druid Asprant, pious protagonists such as the seer Ganfried, paternal pastors like Theodat, youthful heroes like Garibald's sons Grimoald and Gundoald, a caring maternal figure in Garibald's wife, Waldrade.

The Italian text of the *Tito* opera – as is typical of the *opera seria* – takes the form of metrically and rhythmically regular verse. This form is both prerequisite and basis for the musical articulation and verbal formulation of emotion. The *seria* verse allows for great plasticity in individual expression and character development. In *König Garibald*, however, the music only vaguely corresponds to the text. Heigel's German libretto finds almost no reflection in Mozart's music, and the intellectual state of the characters is poorly articulated. The music serves only as a medium of joyous celebration, a pleasant background divorced from the theatrical and dramatic experience of the opera. This is particularly the case with the recitatives. Lengthy passages are sung, as in operetta, without musical accompaniment. Only a few bars of the Tito/Publio recitation in Act I: iv are borrowed directly, albeit in greatly abbreviated form. In Mozart's opera, the decisive twists of plot and dramatic heightening of action occur in the context of these recitatives, most definitively in Tito's struggle over conflicts between love and sacrifice, mercy and justice, as well as in his own inner turmoil over the resolution to exercise clemency.

*König Garibald* mediates the past in the prophetic light of a dawning era, such that the opera's vision is at once oriented toward past and future. The apotheosis of the concluding tableau almost recalls Goethe's later poem *Vermächtnis* (1827):

> Das Wahre war schon längst gefunden,
> Hat edle Geisterschaft verbunden,
> Das alte Wahre fass' es an. . .
> Dann ist Vergangenheit beständig,
> Das künftige voraus lebendig,
> Der Augenblick ist Ewigkeit.

> [The Truth had long since been found, / has united a noble company of spirits / Let the old truth embrace it. . . / So the past continues, / The future is still alive, / The moment is all eternity.][83]

The baroque and the classicist use of Roman times in *La Clemenza di Tito* are transformed by Heigel into a romantic and patriotic appropriation of Germanic times. In its connections between past and present, the opera anticipates a certain vision of the future, expressed in the homage to Max Joseph. In keeping with a nationalist view of the past, the Bavarian State Opera was eager for the piece to establish the state's origins within the historical time-frame of early Christianity, maintaining both the mythical tradition of its founder and the ethnic character of the Bavarian people. The end of the opera points auspiciously to Max Joseph's rule, as well as to the state and nation of Bavaria as the fulfillment of history. Heigel's work represents a vision of the past, not actual historical events. His view of history is moreover medieval in that it pays homage to the notion of typology.[84] Cultural myth is interpreted as fact through the meaningful coupling of the past with the new by a present which considers itself in full possession of history's purpose and aim. The romantic understanding of history thus perceives the figures, events and structures of its own period as an enhanced recurrence, a historical completion. Such a perspective on history observes epochs and events from whatever standpoint has been reached, from their fulfilment in the present, taking over the past and re-aligning ancient times unhesitatingly on the contemporary. *König Garibald* achieves this coupling of past and present through the imaginative powers of a modernity that erroneously believes that history has a goal.

By means of its historical subject, and with the aid of Mozart's uplifting music, Heigel's piece binds past and present in a theatrical alliance which can only be understood in terms of its historical context. What the recluse in Novalis's *Heinrich von Ofterdingen* says to Friedrich and Marie von Hohenzollern about the real meaning of history is an appropriate description of Heigel's aspirations, in terms of plot and effect, for his *König Garibald*:

> only then, when man is in a position to see the whole progression, neither taking everything literally nor confusing with wilful dreams the actual order of events will he notice the secret links between past and present, and learn to construct history from both hope and remembrance. Only for him to whom the past remains present may it be possible to uncover the simple rule of history.[85]

## NOTES

1. The quotation is from *König Garibald: Oper in zwei Aufzügen. Zur Jubelfeyer der fünfundzwanzigjährigen Regierung Sr. Majestät des Königs von Baiern Maximilian Joseph, den 16ten Februar 1824 gedichtet von Cäsar Max Heigel. Musik von Mozart. Introduction und zweites Finale von J[oseph] H[artmann] Stunz* (Munich: Lentner, 1824), 13. Werner Wunderlich's article has been translated by Susan Mintz and the editor. Only verse quotations are given in both original and translated form.

2. *König Garibald*, 59.

3. *Eos* (Munich, 1824), vol. 27, 108.

4. *Eos*, vol. 28, 110.

5. Pietro Metastasio, *La Clemenza di Tito. Dramma per musica* (Vienna: Schönfeld, 1734).

6. Caterino Mazzolà, *La Clemenza di Tito. Dramma serio per musica in due atti da rappresentarsi nel Teatro nazionale di Praga nel settembre 1791. In occasione di sollennizzare il giorno dell'incoronazione di Sua Maestà l'Imperatore Leopoldo II* (Vienna, 1791); and Franz Giegling, ed., *La Clemenza di Tito* (Kassel: Bärenreiter, 1970), in Wolfgang Amadeus Mozart, *Neue Ausgabe sämtlicher Werke, Serie II: Bühnenwerke, Werkgruppe 5: Opern und Singspiele*, vol. 20, KV 621).

7. The entry in Mozart's autograph catalogue asserts that Mazzolà had by request reworked Metastasio's *Tito* into a proper opera, see Wilhelm A. Bauer und Otto Erich Deutsch, eds., *Mozart: Briefe und Aufzeichnungen* (Kassel: Bärenreiter, 1963), 4: 154.

8. See August Scharnagl, "*König Garibald*, Oper in zwei Aufzügen. Gedichtet von Cäsar Max Heigel. Musik von Mozart," *Mozart-Jahrbuch* (1980–83), 392–8.

9. See Ludwig Finscher, "*La Clemenza di Tito*," in Carl Dahlhause, ed., *Pipers Enzyklopädie des Musiktheaters: Oper – Operette – Musical – Ballett* (Munich and Zürich: Piper, 1991), 4: 334–41; Stefan Kunze, *Mozarts Opern*, 2nd ed. (Stuttgart: Reclam, 1995) 523–53; John A. Rice, *W.A. Mozart: La Clemenza di Tito* (Cambridge: Cambridge University Press, 1991); Julian Rushton, *Clemenza di Tito*, in Stanley Sadie, ed., *The New Grove Dictionary of Opera* (London and New York: Norton & Co., 1992), 4: 881–3; Wolfgang Willaschek, *Mozart-Theater: Vom Idomeneo bis zur Zauberflöte* (Stuttgart and Weimar: Metzler, 1995), 358–419.

10. See Rudolf Angermüller, *Mozart im XIX Jahrhundert* (Munich: Internationale Stiftung Mozarteum/Bayerische Vereinsbank, 1985), 6, 42.

11. See Karl Gustav Fellerer, "Mozartbearbeitungen im frühen 19. Jahrhundert," *Neues Mozart-Jahrbuch* 2 (1942), 224–230; and Fellerer, "Zur Rezeption von Mozarts Oper um die Wende des 18./19. Jahrhunderts," *Mozart-Jahrbuch* 1965/66 (1967), 39–49 (41ff.); Rudolf Angermüller, *Mozart: Die Opern von der Uraufführung bis heute* (Frankfurt a.m., Berlin, Zürich: NZZ Verlag, 1988), 261–275 (269 ff.).

12. Jaroslav Bužga, "Einige Gedanken über die Uraufführung und über die Rezeptionsgeschichte der Oper *La Clemenza di Tito*," in Rudolph Angermüller et al., eds., *Bericht über den Internationalen Mozart-Kongress Salzburg 1991* (Kassel: Bärenreiter, 1992), 2: 773–6 (773).

13. Beate Hiltner, *La Clemenza di Tito von Wolfgang Amadé Mozart im Spiegel der musikalischen Fachpresse zwischen 1800 und 1850: Rezeptionsgeschichtliche Untersuchungen unter besonderer Berücksichtigung der Wiener Quellen und Verhältnisse* (Europäische Hochschulschriften, series 36: Musikwissenschaft, vol. 128, Frankfurt a.m.: Lang, 1994), 39ff.; and Hiltner, "*La Clemenza di Tito* von Wolfgang Amadeus Mozart: Wiederentdeckung des 19. Jahrhunderts," *Musica* 48 (1994), part 4, 211–214.

14. *Titus: Eine ernsthafte Oper in zwey Aufzügen; nach dem Italienischen der Clemenza di Tito des Metastasio frey bearbeitet, und in Music gesetzt von W.A. Mozart* (Kassel: Hampe, 1797).

15. *Gesänge aus der Oper Titus, nach La Clemenza di Tito frei bearbeitet, in zwei Aufzügen. Die Musik ist von Mozart* (Weimar: n.p., 1799).

16. *Was wir bringen: Vorspiel bei Eröffnung des neuen Schauspielhauses zu Lauchstädt*, in Dieter Borchmeyer and Peter Huber, eds., Johann Wolfgang Goethe, *Sämtliche Werke*, Part I, vol. 6 (Bibliothek deutscher Klassiker, vol. 97, Frankfurt a.m.: Deutscher Klassiker Verlag, 1993), 265–300, (300).

17. *Wiener Theaterzeitung*, no. 29 (1836), 354.

18. See Harm Klueting, "Der aufgeklärte Fürst," in Wolfgang Weber, ed., *Der Fürst: Ideen und Wirklichkeiten in der europäischen Geschichte* (Cologne, Weimar, Vienna: Bühlau, 1998), 137–67.

19. See Gernot Gruber, *Mozart und die Nachwelt* (Salzburg and Vienna: Residenz, 1985), 99ff.

20. Jost Perfahl, ed., Franz Neimetschek, *Ich kannte Mozart: Leben des K.K.*

Kapellmeisters Wolfgang Gottlieb Mozart nach Originalquellen beschrieben: Mit einem Nachwort, Berichtigungen und Ergänzungen von Peter Krause, 3rd ed. (Leipzig: 1984), 73.
21. See especially Hiltner, note 13 above, 76 ff.
22. Prolog und Gesang zur Feier der fünfundzwanzigjährigen Regierung Sr. königl. Majestät Maximilian I (Würzburg: n.p., 1824), 2.
23. Zur Jubelfeyer des Fünf und zwanzigsten Allerhöchsten Regierungsjahres Seiner Königlichen Majestät, Maximilian Joseph, Königs von Baiern etc. etc. (Wurzburg: Dorbath, 1824), 11.
24. Das fünf und zwanzigjährige Regierungs-Jubiläum Maximilian Josephs Königs von Baiern gefeiert am 15. und 16. Februar 1824 von den Bewohnern Bambergs (Bamberg: Drausnick, 1824), 14.
25. See especially Johann Michael von Söltl, Maximilian Joseph, König von Bayern: Sein Leben und Wirken (Stuttgart: Scheible, 1837); Hans Reidelbach, Charakterzüge und Anekdoten als Bilder der Güte und Wohlthätigkeit aus dem Leben der bayerischen Könige Max Joseph I., Ludwig I. und Max II (Munich: Keller, 1895).
26. Adam Joseph Onymus, Trauerrede zur Todenfeyer für seine Majestät den verewigten König von Baiern Maximilian I. gehalten am 21. October 1825 in der Domkirche zu Würzburg (Würzburg: Bonitos, 1825), 15.
27. See Walter Deml, "Die Entwicklung der Gesetzgebung in Bayern unter Max I. Joseph," in "Wittelsbach und Bayern: Krone und Verfassung, König Max I Joseph und der neue Staat," in Hubert Gläser, ed., Beiträge zur Bayerischen Geschichte und Kunst 1799–1825 (Munich and Zürich: Piper/Hirmer, 1980), 72–82. The humanising of criminal law received special attention, an area of reform in which Leopold II had a half-century previously been prominent as Archduke of Tuscany. His labours in the cause of legal reform and further as successor to Joseph II as Kaiser were not least in gaining him the respectful nickname of "the German Titus," see Werner Wunderlich, " 'Der Genuss dieses Kunstwerks erfordert eine reingestimmte Seele. . .': Tradition und Rezeption der Herrscherethik in Mozarts Oper La Clemenza di Tito," in Ingo Schneider, ed., Europäische Ethnologie und Folklore im internationalen Kontext: Festschrift für Leander Petzoldt (Frankfurt: Lang, 1999), 581–604.
28. Eberhard Weis, "Die Begründung des modernen bayerischen Staates unter König Max I (1799–1825)," in Max Spindler, ed., Handbuch der bayerischen Geschichte, vol. 4/1, rev. ed. (Munich: C.H. Beck, 1979) 3–86; and Weis, "Das neue Bayern – Max I Joseph, Montgelas und die Entstehung und Ausgestaltung des Königreichs 1799 bis 1825," in "Wittelsbach und Bayern," see note 27, 49–64.
29. See Hubert Gläser, ed., "Krone und Verfassung. König Max I Joseph und der neue Staat," Beiträge zur bayerischen Geschichte und Kunst, 1799–1825 (Munich: Hirmer, 1992).
30. See Hans Schmid, "Musik," in Spindler, ed., Handbuch der bayerischen

*Geschichte*, see note 28, 1212–33; Robert Münster, "Das Musikleben in der Max-Joseph-Zeit," in "Wittelsbach und Bayern," see note 27, 456–471.

31. Oswald Hederer, "Karl von Fischers Nationaltheater in München," in "Wittelsbach und Bayern," see note 27, 395–402, (395).

32. *Feier des fünfundzwanzigjährigen Regierungs-Jubiläums seiner Majestät Maximilian Joseph I, Königs von Bayern in allerhöchstdesselben Residenzstadt München* (Munich, 1824), 3.

33. See Jens Malte Fischer, "Singende Recken und blitzende Schwerter: Die Mittelalteroper neben und nach Wagner – ein Überblick," in Peter Wapnewski, ed., *Mittelalter-Rezeption: Ein Symposion* (Germanistische Symposien Berichtsbände, vol. 6, Stuttgart: Metzler, 1986), 511–30; Hans-Ulrich Schäfer-Lembeck, "Die Darstellung des Altdeutschen in den Opern des 19. Jahrhunderts" (Deutsche Hochschulschriften, vol. 1050, Egelsbach: Hänsel-Hohenhausen, 1995).

34. The list is derived from the chronological and thematic compilations of Fischer, see note 33, 525–530.

35. See Angermüller, *Mozart im XIX. Jahrhundert*, note 10, 32ff.; Werner Wunderlich, *Mozarts Così fan tutte. Wahlverwandtschaften und Liebesspiele* (Facetten der Literatur, vol. 6, Bern, Stuttgart, Wien: Haupt, 1996), 66ff.

36. Stefan Kunze, ed., *Wolfgang Amadeus Mozart: Briefe* (Universal-Bibliothek Nr. 8430, Stuttgart: Reclam, 1987), 58.

37. See Robert Münster, " 'Ich bin hier sehr beliebt': Mozart und das kurfürstliche Bayern," in *Eine Auswahl von Aufsätzen zum 65. Geburtstag des Autors hrsg. von einem Kollegenkreis* (Tutzing: Schneider, 1993).

38. Adolf Johann Bäuerle, *Director Carl: Roman und Wirklichkeit* (Wien: Hartleben, 1856), 237.

39. Bäuerle, *Director Carl*, 211.

40. Franz Grandaur, *Chronik des Königlichen Hof- und National-Theaters in Munich zur Feier seines hundert-jährigen Bestehens* (Munich: Ackermann, 1878), 100.

41. See Wilhelm Kosch, *Deutsches Theater-Lexikon. Biographisches und bibliographisches Handbuch* (Klagenfurt, Wien: Kleinmayer, 1953), 1: 732; "Heigel, M[üller] R[einhard]," in *Deutsches Literatur-Lexikon*, 3rd ed. (Bern, Munich: Francke, 1979), 7: col. 666.

42. [Cäsar Max Heigel], *Bruchstücke aus den Ruinen meines Lebens: Von H\*\*\** (Aarau: Sauerländer, 1820), 85.

43. Heigel, Karl Theodor, "Das Leben des Schauspielers und Schriftstellers Cäsar Max Heigel," in *Süddeutsche Monatshefte* 10/2 (1913), 1–10, 183–193 (193).

44. Bäuerle, *Director Carl*, 267.

45. Carl Diesch, ed., *Grundrisz zur Geschichte der deutschen Dichtung, aus den Quellen von Karl Goedeke*, 2nd ed. (Düsseldorf: Ehlermann, 1951), 11/1: 171ff.

46. See Friedrich Sengle, *Das historische Drama in Deutschland: Geschichte eines literarischen Mythos* (Stuttgart: Metzler, 1974), 110ff.

47. Friedrich Rochlitz, *Gesänge zu der Oper: Titus der Grossmüthige, in zwey Aufzügen, nach dem Italiänischen des Metastasio von M. Rochlitz. In Musik gesetzt von Mozart* (Dresden: n.p., 1796). Rochlitz does not seem to have been aware of the fact that Mazzolà had reworked Metastasio's libretto. His version was intended for a production by the Joseph II Actors' Company: the first production was on 26th May 1796 in the Linekisches Bad theatre in Dresden.

48. See Edgar Refardt, *Historisch-Biographisches Musikerlexikon der Schweiz* (Leipzig and Zürich: Hug, 1928), 305; Rolf Gross, "Joseph Hartmann Stunz als Opernkomponist," Munich Dissertation (Würzburg: Tiltsch, 1936); and Gross, "Joseph Hartmann Stunz," in *Die Musik in Geschichte und Gegenwart: Allgemeine Enzyklopädie der Musik* (Kassel: Bärenreiter, 1965), 12: col. 1645–6.

49. *Garribald der Agilolfinger: Allegorisches Fest in zwey Abtheilungen, gedichtet von Cäsar] M[ax] Heigel. Musik von Mozart. Introduction und zweytes Finale von J[oseph] H[artmann] Stuntz. (Garibald der Agilolfinger. Fato nel mese di febrajo 1824)*, autograph score, Bayerische Staatsbibliothek Munich: Sign. Mus. Mss. 4050/2.

50. Karl Theodor Heigel, "Aus dem Leben...," see note 43, 190.

51. Cäsar Max Heigel, *Bruchstücke*, see note 42, 95.

52. Heigel, *Bruchstücke*, 95.

53. *König Garibald*, see note 1, "Vorbericht," v.

54. *König Garibald*, I iii, 15.

55. *König Garibald*, I iv, 19.

56. *König Garibald*, I x, 32.

57. *König Garibald*, II ix, 55.

58. J[ohann] N[epomuk] Mederer, *Beyträge zur Geschichte von Baiern*, vol. 1 (Regensburg: Montag, 1777).

59. Vincenz von Pallhausen, *Garibald, ersten König Bojoariens und seiner Tochter Theodelinde, erste Königinn in Italien: Oder die Urgeschichte der Baiern entworfen und mit Beweisstellen, kritischen Bemerkungen und mehreren bisher noch unbekannten Notizen beleuchtet* (Munich: Lentner, [1810]).

60. von Pallhausen, *Garibald*, 2.

61. August Wölfing, *Garibald, der erste König in Bojarien: Ein vaterländisches Schauspiel in fünf Aufzügen*, in *Neuste deutsche Schaubühne für 1806* (Frankfurt a.M., Leipzig: n.p., 1806), 5: 1–148.

62. See Nikolaus Orlop, *Von Garibald bis Ludwig III: Herzöge, Kurfürsten und Könige in Bayern* (Munich: Hugendubel, 1979), 16ff.; Wilhelm Stürmer, "Garibald," in *Lexikon des Mittelalters* (Munich and Zürich: Artemis, 1989), 4: col. 1116; and Stürmer, "Garibald," in *Reallexikon der germanischen Altertumskunde*, 2nd ed. (Berlin, New York: de Gruyter, 1998), 10: 446–7.

63. It is disputed whether the ethnogenesis of the Bavarians stems from a race native to the land or has been affected by immigrant "Bajuvarii" from "Baia," i.e. Bohemia. See Norbert Wagner, "Zur Herkunft der Agilulfinger,"

*Zeitschrift für Bayerische Landesgeschichte* 41 (1971), 19–48; R[einhard] Wenskus, R[einhard], "Agilofinger," in *Reallexikon der Germanischen Altertumskunde*, 96–98; and Wagner et al., "Bajuwaren," in *Reallexikon*, 601–627.

64. Kurt Reindel, "Das Zeitalter der Agilofinger: Politische Entwicklung," in Spindler, ed., *Handbuch der bayerischen Geschichte*, 2nd rev. ed. (Munich: C.H. Beck, 1981), 1: 140–151; Rudolf Reiser, *Agilolf oder Die Herkunft der Bayern* (Munich: Ehrenwirth, 1977), 44ff.; and Reiser, *Die Agilolfinger* (Pfaffenhofen: Ludwig, 1985).

65. Joachim Jahn, *Ducatus Baiuvariorum: Das bairische Herzogtum der Agilolfinger* (Monographien zur Geschichte des Mittelalters, vol. 35, Stuttgart: Hiersemann, 1991).

66. It is disputed whether this early medieval noble family is of Frankish, Burgundian, Lombard or Visigothic origin, or whether the family name of this *genus ducale* derives for instance from a Bishop of Metz, Agiulf, in office around 600, or from Theudolind's second husband, the Lombard king Agilulf, who may well have come from the Thuringian family of the Anawas. See Erich Zöllner, *Die Herkunft der Agilulfinger: Zur Geschichte der Bayern* (1965); Wenskus, "Agilolfinger," in *Reallexikon*, see note 63; Jörg Jarnut, *Agilolfingerstudien: Untersuchungen zur Geschichte einer adeligen Familie im 6. und 7. Jahrhundert*. (Monographien zur Geschichte des Mittelalters, vol. 32, Stuttgart: Hiersemann, 1986), 12ff.

67. *Gregorii episcopi turonensis historia francorum*, IV/9, in *MGH SS rer. Mer.* I/1, 147.

68. *Pauli historia langobardorum*, III/30, in *MGH SS rer. Lang. saec. VI.–IX*, 109.

69. Ludo Moritz Hartmann, *Geschichte Italiens im Mittelmeer*, vol. 2/1, "Römer und Langobarden bis zur Theilung Italiens" (Gotha: Perthes, 1900), 56ff.; Erich Zöllner, *Geschichte der Franken bis zur Mitte des sechsten Jahrhunderts* (Munich: C.H. Beck, 1970), 101ff.; Reinhard Schneider, *Königswahl und Königserhebung im Frühmittelalter: Untersuchungen zur Herrschaftsnachfolge bei den Langobarden und Merowingern* (Monographien zur Geschichte des Mittelalters, vol. 3, Stuttgart: Hiersemann, 1972), 21ff.; Eduard Hlawitchka, "Studien zur Genealogie und Geschichte der Merowinger und der frühen Karolinger," *Rheinische Vierteljahrsblätter* 43 (1979), 1–99; Jörg Jarnut, *Geschichte der Langobarden* (Urban-Taschenbücher, vol. 339, Stuttgart: Kohlmeyer, 1982), 39ff.; Wilfried Menghin, *Frühgeschichte Bayerns: Römer und Germanen, Baiern und Schwaben, Franken und Slawen* (Stuttgart: Theiss, 1990).

70. See *Historia langobardorum*, III/60.

71. So called because the golden crown set with jewels had in it an iron ring, which according to legend the Empress Helena had had made from the nails of the True Cross for her son, the Emperor Constantine.

72. See *Chronicarum quae dicuntur Fredegarii scholastici*, IV/34, in *MGH SS rer, Mer.*, 2: 133.

73. *Historia langobardorum*, III/30, 109.

74. Cf. H1381.3.1, "Quest for bride," in Stith Thompson, *Motif-Index of Folk-Literature. A Classification of Narrative Elements in Folktales [etc.]*, rev. ed., (Bloomington, Indianapolis: Indiana University Press, 1989), 3: 499.

75. Cf. H300–499, "Marriage tests," in *Motif-Index*, 3: 398–411.

76. Cf. H131, "Identification by an axe," in *Motif-Index*, 3: 386.

77. *Historia langobardorum*, III/ 30, 109 ff., (129).

78. Cf. F666, "Skillful axe-man," in *Motif-Index*, 3: 192.

79. *Flora: Ein Unterhaltungs-Blatt* (1824), Nr. 28 (17th February), 112.

80. Grandaur, see note 40, 100.

81. The parts and cast-list are given by the theatre programme of 15th February 1824.

82. *König Garibald*, I iv, 18.

83. Goethe, *Sämtliche Werke*, I/2, "Gedichte 1800–1832," see note 18, 685 f.

84. See Friedrich Ohly, "Typologische Figuren aus Natur und Typus," in *Formen und Funktionen der Allegorie: Symposion Wolfenbüttel 1978* (Stuttgart: Metzler, 1979), 126–166, (126ff.).

85. In Paul Kluckhohn, Richard Samuel et al., eds., *Novalis: Schriften* 3rd rev. ed. (Stuttgart: Kohlhammer, 1977), 1: 257.

# Victorian Appropriations: Lady Charlotte Guest translates *The Mabinogion*

## Judith Johnston

In this article I will address both the issue of cultural appropriation and the role of gender in such appropriation via women's translation into English in the nineteenth century. Such translation I read as part of an imperialist enterprise because translation gives access not only to prevailing ideas and philosophies, but also to myths, tales, legends and songs; a form of cultural colonisation. Stephen Copley and Peter Garside in their work on the politics of the picturesque have commented on the way in which "the discourse of the Picturesque intersects with and is shaped by the discourses of colonialism at various points," using the sentimentalisation of the Scottish landscape as an example.[1] As they have read the Picturesque as helping to shape colonial discourse, so I wish now to consider translation as an enterprise also helping to shape colonial discourse. I should make clear at the outset that it is not the act of translation per se that is appropriative, rather, it is that translation in time forwards the colonial project.

The colonial project is forwarded in part because translation assists appropriation and the downgrading of colonised language and culture. Language, as Lefevere has shown, is not the main problem in translation, the problem lies in ideology, poetics and "cultural elements that are not immediately clear, or seen as completely 'misplaced' in what would be the target culture version of the text to be translated."[2] The target language, shifted out of its culturally significant context, reappears in another form: in the case of tales and legends, for instance, that form is most often locked into a particular mode: quaint, noble savage, child-like. I am using the term "appropriation" here as defined by David Spurr in *The Rhetoric of Empire*. Spurr describes appropriation as a two-fold process in which the coloniser, as if by natural inheritance, takes over a territory and its products/productions, and at the same time disguises this act of appropriation by pretending to be acting "on the part of the colonised land and people."[3]

I first started thinking about this issue when I came across a translation of Australian Aboriginal legends by Katherine Langloh Parker published in 1896. Langloh Parker defines herself as a "Collector" of the folk-lore of the Noongahburrahs and in the Preface acknowledges "my great indebtedness to the blacks, who, . . . were most ready to repeat to me the legends," naming in particular Peter Hippi, Hippitha, Matah, Barahgurrie, and Beemunny. The work is dedicated to Peter Hippi, "in grateful recognition of his long and faithful service."[4] Her target audience is, however, white children, "the children of their white supplanters"[5] as she terms it. In 1953 the translations were re-issued. The names of the local collaborators do not appear in this edition, instead the authority is Professor A.P. Elkin. The drawings by an aboriginal man from Corowa illustrating the 1896 text have also disappeared, to be replaced by pseudo-aboriginal drawings supplied by Elizabeth Durack. Langloh Parker had translated the tales of a local people she knew well, intending to make known a culture which, in the mistaken parlance of the day, was dying out. In the intervening half-century, the tales had been appropriated as entertainment for an audience no longer acknowledged as colonisers, the names of the tales' Aboriginal translators listed above expunged, and with them the cultural significance of the work.

I wondered to what extent this particular scenario might be applied to other translations, particularly by women, which had taken place across the nineteenth century, and decided to begin with the translation, by Lady Charlotte Guest, of the Welsh *Mabinogion*, and other tales, from *The Red Book of Hergest*.[6] Lady Guest's translation, while not precisely a colonising project in itself, is nevertheless part of the rise of English nationalism. At first celebrated in contemporary reviews for giving access to a "Welsh national literature,"[7] it is clear from reading the various reviews which appeared between 1838 and 1844, that this nationalism shifts from Welsh to English. A review of "Kilhwch and Olwen" in the *Monthly Review* in 1842 declares the tale to be "strictly and purely British"[8] and from then on a case is consistently made that Welsh literature "was not confined to the mountains of Wales."[9] This indeed is Lady Guest's own position, writing in the Introduction to the 1849 three-volume edition:

The Mabinogion however, though thus early recorded in the Welsh tongue, are in their existing form by no means wholly Welsh. They are of two tolerably distinct classes. Of these, the older contains few allusions to Norman customs, manners, arts, and luxuries. The other, and less ancient, are full of such allusions, and of ecclesiastical terms. Both classes, no doubt, are equally of Welsh root, but the former are not more overlaid or corrupted, than might have been expected.[10]

As early as 1840, when Part 3, "Gereint the Son of Erbin" was issued, the shifting of cultural significance had already begun. The *Monthly Review* in its "Notices" announces the publication and quotes from a speech by Dr Thirlwell, Bishop of St. David's at the Abergavenny Cymreigyddion meeting, 8 October 1840: "I am inclined to believe, that there must be some particular charm in that literature which has found grace in ladies' eyes."[11] In an age when the current ideology maintained a rigid separation of male and female spheres of activity, literature for ladies carries very particular implications: less challenging, less erudite, simple, charming and other such epithets.

Earlier, the same London journal, the *Monthly Review*, in noticing "Part 2, Peredur the Son of Evrawc" had celebrated Lady Guest's considerable achievement in terms that suggest some measure of supremacy over "the principality" as Wales is termed:

> The tale, according to the agreeably quaint translation, is even more interesting than its predecessor. Lady Charlotte Guest is doing more to popularise and make the English reader acquainted with the old Welsh National literature than all the other living antiquaries in the principality, boastful as some of them are of its treasures.[12]

The issue of local nationalism as a failed enterprise in Wales itself, as hinted at here, is interesting. Linda Colley remarks that English nationalists "were much less repelled by their union with Wales, partly because this connexion was so much older, but primarily because the Welsh seemed so much less threatening."[13] Colley goes on to note particularly that what distinguished the Welsh from the Scots was the retention of their language which three out of four still spoke by choice as late as the 1880s. The review of Part 3, already quoted from the *Monthly Review* in 1840 praises in particular Lady Guest's "liberality and patriotism in this grand undertaking" (p. 610). It seems clear to me that the "patriotism" being celebrated here is not a Welsh one, but her work as contributing to English Nationalism. If this is so, then reception of the translation is confirmed as appropriation.

The earliest reviews (1838–9) note that for the last 12 years, the special Society for the Publication of Ancient Welsh Manuscripts had failed to achieve anything towards their aims, having "neither money nor Welsh"[14] and the review in the *Athenaeum* remarks that when

> the Cymreigyddion, from the difficulties in the way, (a whole nation find difficulties in translating and publishing what might easily be compressed into a couple of octavos!) and from past disappointments, were about to abandon the enterprise, Lady Charlotte Guest at once declared that she would both translate the book and publish it at her own expense.[15]

The *Monthly Review*, noticing "Part 1, The Lady of the Fountain," also remarks on the Society's failure "owing either to a want of knowledge of the Welsh language, the want of money, or the want of manuscripts" and continues:

> At length to rescue the province from the disgrace which apathy or deficiency of one sort or another entailed, and also to circulate the "Llyfr Coch o Hergest", or "Red Book of Hergest", which contains a collection of Welsh legendary tales, Lady Charlotte Guest of Dowlais volunteered her talent and her purse.[16]

It should be clear from these examples that the London-based periodical press celebrated the translation of the Welsh legends in terms both nationalistic and acquisitive, fulfilling Spurr's definition of appropriation to a nicety. While at times the reviews blur national boundaries, neverthe-less a very particular prejudice develops, notably when the scorn of the *Athenaeum* is so palpable, emphasised both by parentheses and exclama-tion, "(a whole nation find difficulties . . .!)." Clearly the Welsh nation is intended here, while the *Monthly Review* believes the "province" has been rescued from "disgrace."

While each tale in Lady Guest's *Mabinogion* is presented in modern Welsh orthography up front, followed by the English translation and then the copious notes, also in English, the presence of the Welsh is not specif-ically commented upon in the English press until 1843. The *Monthly Review* notes only that the work is "curiously illustrated with fac-similes,"[17] or as the *Spectator* puts it:

The getting-up of the work is magnificent; and in its typography, its vellum-like paper, and the different fac-similes of
manuscripts, as well as the wood-cut vignettes, reflects the
highest credit upon its provincial publisher.[18]

In 1843, however, the *Monthly Review* produced a long article titled
"Welsh Fiction,"[19] which considers the first four parts, 1838–1842, of
Lady Guest's translation and draws attention to the fact that to

> the Welsh text has been added a literal English translation,
> some few explanatory notes, and fac-similes of the oldest manu-
> scripts in this and other countries, of the romances corre-
> sponding to each Mabinogi.[20]

It should be noted that the Welsh text is missing from later editions such
as that of 1902 edited by Owen Edwards and published by Fisher Unwin.

While it can be argued that Charlotte Guest made these medieval
manuscripts available to the Welsh, it is difficult to estimate how many
people in 1838 could read and write Welsh, or for that matter how many
people could actually read and write at all. The London-based Welsh
school teacher William Owen Pughe had produced the two-volume
*Dictionary of the Welsh Language* (1832) and his translation of "Pwyll"
along with the text was serialised in the first Welsh periodical, the
*Cambrian Register*, from 1796. Both his *Dictionary* and his *Cambrian
Biography* (n.d.) were used by Lady Charlotte for her Notes accompanying the translations.[21] Guest and John in their 1989 biography also
provide, as Appendix 4B, a list of the books in Lady Guest's possession in
1852 relevant to the Mabinogion. The list includes another *English and
Welsh Dictionary 1798–1805* by Richard. The knowledge of Middle
Welsh in the period is less easily determined but appears not to have been
wide-spread if we go by Charlotte Guest's own evidence. It seems the
scholar Elijah Waring "provided the initial impulse for her particular
project" and when he visited Dowlais in October 1835 Lady Guest noted
"he is somewhat acquainted with ancient literature. . . . He is the only
person I have found so in this country except George Clark."[22]

Guest and John suggest that the four branches of the Mabinogion,
"Pwyll," "Branwen," "Manawyddan" and "Math" may have existed in
manuscript form since about 1200 "but they were most probably relayed
orally over several generations before ever assuming written form" (p. 97).
In oral cultures, such as the Australian Aboriginal one with which I
began, a translation's reception, as much as the work of the translator,

effects a form of appropriation such that the culture subjected to the imperialism of another is brought to a standstill, locked, in this case by the printed English, into a time-frame and a category from which it is difficult to escape. In the case of Lady Guest's translations from written medieval sources, publication into English naturally does not have this effect, the written tales are already locked into their medieval time-frame. However, the categorisation of the work is a different matter. To begin with, as I have already mentioned, the translation was critiqued as woman's work. The *Spectator* writes of the "fair translator," and the *Athenaeum* believes the "translation is a good one, – clear, simple – preserving much of the quaintness so apparent in the original" while the *Monthly Review* also remarks the "agreeably quaint translation" and elsewhere calls it "a translation quaint and happy."[23] A later *Spectator* review believes the tales will have considerable attraction "not only for the most childish vulgar but for persons perfectly competent to detect their critical faults."[24] All of these remarks might be considered qualified to some degree, and reductive.

Women had a particular part to play in cultural colonisation via translation: the female translator is like the female colonist, not only does she participate in the enterprise, she contributes to its effectiveness, even if she sees herself as at one with her new land. The *Monthly Review* remarks in 1843 that "Lady C. Guest could not have bestowed a more acceptable gift upon her adopted countrymen than the collection of the Mabinogion."[25] It is thus clear that the English periodical press saw her relationship with Wales in that light. Rita Kranidis has commented on emigrant women's roles in imperialism that

> emigrant women are neither coloniser nor colonised, yet they may be said to be both. Insofar as they manifest the nation's perpetually expanding cultural borders, they are national subjects who are simultaneously not integral, legitimated parts of the empire.[26]

Translation expands cultural borders, and might be likened to colonial botanising, an activity undertaken more by women than men. Once you name, and transcribe, you acquire. Frederic Will raises questions "about naming and meaning and indirectly suggests that translation can be viewed as a form of naming, fiction-making, and knowing."[27]

But there is another facet to the process. It is a woman's sense of exile, or displacement. Edward Said defines exile as a "discontinuous state of being" but he elaborates this by suggesting that the exile creates "a new world to rule."[28] Charlotte Guest's class and wealth permitted her an opportunity to dominate ("unfair domination" is Said's term in *Culture and Imperialism*)[29] and her elaborate production of a translated *Mabinogion* represents her own attempt to locate a place for herself that was different from her husband's world yet well within the acceptable parameters of the ideology of the day: the woman's sphere. If John Guest, the ironmaster, dominated industrial production in Wales in the 1830s, his wife discovered a role for herself in dominating cultural production, a domination the reviews of her day, to which I have already referred, make very clear.

Other spheres existed of course, apart from the ideologically gendered ones I have just described. Edward Said writes of an "isolated cultural sphere" and a "debased political sphere," pointing out that these are not separate at all, but rather that "the two are not only connected but ultimately the same." He goes on to show that culture is mistakenly regarded as separate from power, adding:

> representations are considered only as apolitical images to be parsed and construed as so many grammars of exchange, and the divorce of the present from the past is assumed to be complete.[30]

It was, of course, Said's metaphorical language which attracted my attention to this statement because "parsing," "construing," "grammars of exchange" are terms so intimately connected with the act of translation. Thus while we might view Lady Guest's translation as isolated to the cultural sphere, in practice her activity is as much a part of the political sphere as her husband's activities as a Whig member of parliament for the pocket borough of Honiton in Devonshire were.

As Janet Wolff shows in *Feminine Sentences*, women found a place in cultural production as "artists, authors, patrons, and members of cultural institutions"[31] and certainly Charlotte Guest's translation came about partly as a result of her sense of herself as a patron both of the Welsh and of Welsh National literature, for instance by attending the Eisteddfod in Cardiff and by appearing at the Cambrian Ball "in my regular Welsh peasant's dress which I had worn at Abergavenny. Such a thing I believe had never been seen before in London and it caused quite a sensation."[32] In a trip that same year to Scotland she records an ongoing antipathy "to the Scotch" but adds that the highlander "is a man of a different race and reminds me forcibly of my own Welsh."[33] There is very little difference between such a statement and titles like *Our Maoris* by Lady Martin

(1884) in which the possessives "my" or "our" are so significant, used much as parents would say "my son" or "our children." This characteristic also occurs in the *Athenaeum* review of Guest's Part IV, "Kilhwch and Olwen," which suggests that

> it would be difficult to find in the whole range of English fiction a tale of equal antiquity, and one which places the rude, warlike, and imaginative character of our Celtic aborigines so vividly before us.[34]

The foregoing is in part my response to the key standing questions I confronted when beginning this article, that is, why Lady Charlotte Guest took this project on and what prompted her to learn Welsh in the first place and to become involved in Welsh culture. Rhys Phillips, posing this identical question in 1921, attributes her incentive merely to a life-long habit of self-education and study, noting from her son's publication of her Journals that "with the aid of her brother's tutor, she studied Greek, Latin, Hebrew, and Persian, for all things oriental appealed to her."[35] Of course this may have been *part* of the reason, but in considering my own answers to these questions, my response is indebted in particular to Janet Wolff's book *Resident Alien*. In its opening chapter Wolff offers an examination of the condition of dislocation through the writing of twentieth-century women, insights which are also applicable to nineteenth-century women as Wolff herself shows.[36]

Lady Charlotte Guest was indeed a stranger in town, a young 21-year-old escaping from an unhappy home-life through marriage, in July 1833, to a man of 48, a dissenter, a man in "trade," but also, redeemingly, extremely wealthy and a Member of Parliament. After the honeymoon the pair set off to visit their Welsh home at Dowlais, an event she dramatises in her diary suggesting the extent to which a sense of displacement preoccupies her mind:

> the country *did* smile as we started on our route and I could not have entered my new abode under more favourable circumstances. . . . By the time we reached the house it was quite dark and the prevailing gloom gave full effect to the light of the blazing furnaces, which was quite unlike all I had ever before seen or even imagined. . . . My first impulse was to establish myself in the library, by far the pleasantest room in the house. From the very moment I entered it I felt quite settled and at home.[37]

What strikes me about the language Charlotte Guest uses, the way the furnaces dominate the landscape, is its similarity to the travel-writing of women in Canada or Australia in the 1830s and 1840s, that mixture of seeking "home" and at the same time the celebration of difference, the exotic, for instance, native figures lit by firelight are a common motif in travel writing from this period.[38] Linda Colley also makes a strong case for the distinctness of Wales at this time, quoting an English writer on tourism in 1831: "if nothing can please him but what is *foreign*, he will find the language, manners, and dress of the inhabitants [of Wales], . . . as completely foreign as those of France and Switzerland."[39]

Oddly enough in 1839 the reviewer in the *Spectator*, discussing Part II of Charlotte Guest's translation, the tale of Peredur, calls on analogies associated with exotic travel to explicate the translated tale itself. The reviewer is exercised about the "impossibilities" of the tale, citing giants and dragons, the sudden acquisition of skills, and in particular the class issues: sudden intimacy between people, perfect strangers recounting family troubles and concerns, easy access to princes, and the familiar treatment of princes. The reviewer discovers a parallel however:

> in the narratives of American and African travellers, or even amongst the petty potentates of the East. The still more strange facility, shocking to our sense of moral feeling, with which a substitute is found for the dearest ties, also obtains amongst nations in an early stage of society, where necessity and hourly hazard prevent the growth of refined sentiment. When the Red Indians have slaughtered part of a family, they think they make full reparation, should mercy touch them, by finding the survivors with husbands or wives; and stranger still, this sort of recompense seems admitted.[40]

Lady Charlotte was a displaced woman both in regard to locality and to class, and it is significant that she almost immediately set about learning the local language. Within two months she was taking lessons in modern Welsh from the rector, Evan Jenkins and in November 1833 writes in her diary: "Welsh my study, and Ariosto and Chaucer once again my relaxation." A year later, September 3, 1834 she records "Baby leaves but little time for anything, and that time must be spent on Welsh."[41] As Wolff remarks, in discussing contemporary accounts by women who have found themselves outsiders, some women "have stressed the crucial importance of. . . foreign language as a catalyst in change, in development, and often, in literary and other forms of creativity."[42] Guest's relationship with the working people through language is marked once again as typically colonial in its limitations as can be located in this brief vignette from her diary dated 17 July 1837 when she went to hear her husband speak at a political meeting:

> Far from the incivility they talked of at Dowlais the crowd was quite obliging to me; when first I came up there was a buzz of one asking another to make room for me, and when I put my finger to my lips and said "goshey goshey," they smiled at my Welsh and were as quiet as possible.[43]

Janet Wolff's reading of Caren Kaplan's article on deterritorialisation highlights the way in which "the position of outsider enables a special vision," relating both to the idea of home, and to the idea of exile.[44] Although marginalised socially in Wales by her upper-class rank, and by her husband's powerful position as the ironmaster, a reversal of the usual process, Guest's mobility of class and geography gave her both intellectual and critical advantage. But throughout the published sections of her diary which I have been able to examine, the reader gains an overwhelming sense that Charlotte Guest's was indeed both an imperialist and a feminist project, although never expressed in either of those terms. As a feminist project she sought for both identity and position, "in opposition," as Wolff puts it, "to linear narratives of the self and essentialist conceptions of gender and place."[45]

The following long extract from Charlotte Guest's diary, dated 27 April 1839, I have put together from two separate sources. It gives, I think, a sense of Lady Guest fulfilling exactly this style of feminist project and it is important to note her use of the possessive yet again: "my house," "my works," "my blood." The extract is written in triumph at being "complimented" (her term) with her own room at the new offices of her husband's firm in London, a room of one's own having, as we know, particular feminist significance:

> I think it is a retreat that I shall often be tempted to resort to from the gaieties and interruptions of Grosvenor Square. I have so schooled myself into habits of business that it is more congenial to me to calculate the advantage of half per cent. commission on a cargo of iron than to go to the finest Ball in the world. But whatever I undertake I must reach an eminence in. I cannot endure anything in a second grade. I am happy to see we are at the head of the iron trade. Otherwise I could not take pride in

my house in the City, and my works at Dowlais, and glory (playfully) in being (in some sort) a tradeswoman. Then again, my blood is of the noblest and most princely in the Kingdom, and if I go into Society, it must be the very best and first. I can brook no other. If I occupy myself in writing, my book must be splendidly got up and must be as far, at least, as decoration and typography are concerned, at the head of literature, and I delight in the contrast of the musty antiquarian researches and the brilliant fetes and plodding counting house, from all of which I seem to derive almost equal amusement. And then I can sit and laugh at the gravest of them all as vanities, and moralise upon the thought of how soon the most important of them will cease to be of any avail or interest to me. Yet while they last and while there is youth and health to enjoy them, surely it cannot be wrong to take pleasure in the various blessings of this life.[46]

The note of triumph is at first undisguised but as the entry proceeds so Guest attempts to restore her sense of what is appropriate both to gender and to class by using parenthesis. If she glories in being a "tradeswoman," it is only "playfully" and she is only "in some sort" a tradeswoman as she remembers what is due to her rank. Lady Charlotte Guest's ambition for her book is clearly defined by herself in the foregoing extract more in terms of book-making, of appearance, than in terms of literary quality, which might seem to narrow the intellectual significance of the enterprise considerably, except that she put extraordinary work into both the translation and the notes as almost every contemporary reviewer comments.

Charlotte Guest's translation of these Welsh tales is a tale in itself of cultural appropriation that remains to the present a considerable success story. She would never have understood her process in that way however and in 1837, attending a Cymreigyddion Meeting, she laments that it seemed:

there was not the same display of genuine and native enthusiasm among the lower order of Welsh Literati themselves, which had been so animating and gratifying in 1835. I am afraid the Society is beginning to be tamed down to the conventional rules of English taste.[47]

It is clear that Wales, and its language, dress and customs, represents for her an exotic location.

Perhaps not surprisingly, Charlotte Guest's actual moment of decision to translate the *Mabinogion* is not included in the edited version of her Journal produced by her grandson, the Earl of Bessborough in 1950, from which many entries are omitted. Moreover, a subsequent family biographer, Revel Guest, with Angela John, has commented on the numerous errors of transcription in this publication, particularly of Welsh words.[48] They also pinpoint more accurately the project's timeline. On 17 October 1837 Charlotte Guest records in her Journal that there will be an attempt to obtain Owen Pughe's manuscripts and notes but this is never mentioned again and appears to have been unsuccessful.[49] Guest and John name the particular scholars linked with Lady Guest's translation as Tegid (Rev. John Jones) and Carnhuanawc (Rev. Thomas Price) and in fact declare that these two men were "crucial to the success" of the project.[50] Charlotte Guest's Journal entry for 30 November 1837 records that

> Mr. Justice Bosanquet, has, through Tegid kindly lent me his copy of the Llyfr Goch y Hugest,[51] the Mabinogion, which I hope to publish with an English Translation, notes, pictorial illustrations. Price of Crickhowel and Tegid have promised their assistance, and by God's blessing I hope I may accomplish the undertaking.[52]

It is easy to misread the extracts from the Journal which come hard upon this one. She writes on 4 December 1837 of reading "part of the Tale of Kilhwch and Olwen translated by Justice Bosanquet from the Mabinogion. It pleases me much. There is a great field for annotation."[53] I believe this translation is from medieval Welsh into modern Welsh because on 8 December she writes of needing "some plan for translating Justice Bosanquet's Copy, as I do not feel inclined to give up my scheme of publishing it myself." She then writes that Mr Jones (Tegid) "has taken Justice Bosanquet's M.S. and is to copy from it one story at a time in a fit manner to go to the Press, viz: in Modern Orthography which would be more generally useful, and send them to me to translate."[54]

Subsequent editors of the English versions of these tales insist that through lack of knowledge or poor instruction, sadly, Lady Guest mistitled the tales as *The Mabinogion*. Most subsequent editions or new translations, while doggedly pointing out her error of transmission, nevertheless appear under the very sobriquet she provided. All those editors and translators who are Lady Guest's successors, well into the twentieth century, explain with care and precision her "error," and invariably attribute it to misunderstanding of the Welsh term, offering very rational explanations as to how the mistake might have occurred. For instance, Jeffrey Gantz, translator of the current Penguin edition, writes:

> Each of the Four Branches ends with some form of the phrase, "So ends this Branch of the Mabinogi." Inasmuch as the Welsh word *mab* means "boy", Lady Charlotte concluded that *mabinogi* was a noun meaning "a story for children" and that *mabinogion* was the plural of the word. In fact, the word *mabinogion* does not exist in Welsh, though it appears once by mistake in "Pwyll." *Mabinogi* is a genuine Welsh word, but in these texts it applies only to the Four Branches in which it appears. Strictly speaking, this collection ought to be called "The Mabinogi and Other Early Welsh Tales," but that is cumbersome, while "The Mabinogion" is established and convenient.[55]

Jones and Jones believe the word is better interpreted as "a tale of youth" (a meaning gradually reduced to simply "a tale"), rather than "for children," and Rachel Bromwich has suggested "a tale of descendants."[56]

I should make it clear at this point that I have no quarrel with subsequent translators, nor with their translations. I know no Welsh myself, ancient or modern. My interest is solely in translation as an imperialist project, as a means of cultural colonisation and in the part women played in that project. Guest's real part in creating the title is in fact very minor. It is apparent from her journal that the name "Mabinogion" for some particular Welsh tales was in common parlance well before her first translated tale appeared in print. As Jones and Jones point out, her understanding that "mabinogion" was the plural of "mabinogi" was an error in common with most Welsh scholars of her time.[57] Few subsequent editors have been able to resist the title's usefulness as a neat package label. As Jeffrey Gantz so rightly sums up, it is "established and convenient."

Thus by accident, Lady Guest's mistake places her imprimatur both on the received English title of these early Welsh tales and therefore on the translation of them as a whole. Because of the title, every subsequent edition pays some form of acknowledgment to Charlotte Guest with a consistency that seems to me to be remarkable, if based solely on that error in the title. It is even more remarkable because of the difficulty in determining to what extent she fully translated from medieval Welsh the translated tales which appear under her name. Guest and John note that the early twentieth-century Welsh scholar W.J. Gruffydd believed "the main credit should go to the two scholars who "devilled" for her, Tegid and Price."[58] The Preface written for the first part in 1838, and republished for the 1849 edition, acknowledges the copy Tegid produced of Justice Bosanquet's manuscript but the expressed indebtedness is to the Justice for its use, rather than to Tegid for the work. She does however express her obligation to Tegid "for the trouble he has taken to forward my wishes with respect to publishing the MS. as correctly as possible."[59] There is no acknowledgement in the 1849 edition of the work of Thomas Price with whom Lady Guest worked so closely throughout the production of the Tales from 1838 to 1845. Meic Stephens believes the

> extent of Charlotte Guest's labours as a translator is an open question: she was certainly acquainted with Welsh and her children were taught the language, but it seems likely that her part in the venture was the rendering into graceful English of her collaborators' literal translation rather than any close involvement in the basic task of translating the original texts.[60]

Modern translators of the tales vary in the extent to which they address the question of Guest's translating ability. In 1977 Patrick Ford acknowledges Guest's translation as important because the earliest into English, noting tactfully that hers "is a graceful and romantic rendition. . . suited to the tastes of her mid-nineteenth-century audiences."[61] Jones and Jones in 1948 give a full translation history, carefully pointing out the names of Guest's Welsh collaborators and deciding that hers is "a charming and felicitous piece of English prose, and has been justly esteemed by every succeeding generation of readers as a classic in its own right."[62]

Although in 1929 Ellis and Lloyd praise her translation's "charm and literary qualities," they are far more severe regarding the translation project itself:

> Only one attempt has been made hitherto to render into English the whole of these romances, namely, that by Lady Charlotte Guest, with the assistance of Tegid, in 1838–49. The intention of Lady Charlotte Guest appears to have been to produce a version which could be used for the instruction and amusement of her own children, with the result that parts of her translation are either inaccurate or bowdlerised.[63]

The accusation that the work is "inaccurate or bowdlerised" appears to be unsubstantiated. It seems to me that subsequent editors, Jones and Jones for instance, would have commented on extensive inaccuracies and alterations had they existed and none of the subsequent translators do take issue with the translation itself. A random check of their translation of various tales against those of Charlotte Guest shows few variations. In "Pwyll Prince of Dyfed" for instance at the start:

> **Guest**: Once upon a time, Pwyll was at Narberth his chief palace. . .
> **Jones & Jones**: And once upon a time he was at Arberth, a chief court of his . . .;

and the ending is rendered by both as follows:

> **Guest**: And Pryderi ruled the seven Cantrevs of Dyved prosperously, and he was beloved by his people, and by all around him.
> **Jones & Jones**: And Pryderi ruled the seven cantrefs of Dyfed prosperously, beloved by his people and by all around him.

"Branwen the Daughter of Llyr" similarly reveals few variations, as did other tales I checked. The concluding lines of "Branwen" for instance:

> **Guest**: In Ireland none were left alive, except five pregnant women in a cave in the Irish wilderness; . . .
> **Jones & Jones**: In Ireland no person was left alive save five pregnant women in a cave in the Irish wilderness; . . .

The comment by Ellis and Lloyd that the work may have been produced merely to instruct and amuse her children is also unfounded. Lady Guest certainly dedicated the 1849 publication to her two eldest sons, but had no children when the project began. The dedication, "To Ivor and Merthyr," however, reinforces the notion that Wales was, for Charlotte Guest, a site of positive, rather than negative, displacement, which she invests with romantic and sentimental associations. She tells her sons, in the dedication, to cultivate the literature of the country "in whose beautiful language you are being initiated, and amongst whose free mountains you were born," adding in even more intensely romantic style:

> May you become early imbued with the chivalric and exalted sense of honour, and the fervent patriotism for which its sons have ever been celebrated.
> May you learn to emulate the noble qualities of Ivor Hael, and

the first attachment to your Native Country, which distinguished that Ivor Bach, after whom the elder of you was
named.[64]

In 1921 Rhys Phillips produced a short work titled *Lady Charlotte Guest
and the Mabinogion*, in which he defends Lady Charlotte from "unlettered
gossips and certain village writers" who had "found it difficult to believe
that an English lady could effectually surmount the difficulty of rendering
into English a series of texts written in early Medieval Welsh."[65] This
work carefully sets out Guest's due acknowledgment of any existing translations and her re-rendering of same, and cites her journals as evidence of
her participation in translation where none, or only partial ones, existed.
The book is, unfortunately, predominantly and least effectively argued
from a class position. The denigration implicit in "unlettered gossips" at
the beginning culminates in a citation from Burke's *Peerage* of Lady
Guest's pedigree at the conclusion.

The 1989 biography authored by Guest and John produces more
positive evidence of Lady Guest's exact role in the translation. Her Deed
Box, held in the National Library of Wales, was explored and they found
that the Welsh text is "presumably in Tegid's handwriting." They
conclude that Lady Guest translated into English from the copy in
modern Welsh supplied by Tegid and that then Price "worked with her
on this, improving it," a version thence turned into "the graceful and
elegant English which was her hallmark." Admitting that Price's role is
never acknowledged in the "Preface" of the 1849 edition, they suggest
this might be explained by his death before its publication.[66] However,
the Preface is actually to the first tale of 1838, as I have shown, and Price's
name appears nowhere in it. It is very clear that Lady Guest never properly acknowledged the extensive work of her two Welsh collaborators.
However, Guest and John note that Rachel Bromwich has done some
comparative work based on segments of translation of "Pwyll" and
"Math" and found that the Guest translation "clearly owes nothing to the
earlier versions and is in several instances more accurate than Owen
Pughe," despite the fact that it was probably "more of a collaborative
effort than she fully acknowledged."[67]

While not properly a Mabinogion tale, because it is the oldest of the
Welsh tales translated, I include here a comparison of Lady Guest's
[collaborative] translation of the first paragraph of "Kilhwch and Olwen"
as she titles the tale, with those of three later translations.[68] It is clear that
differences in the English translations anyway are minimal:

Kilydd, the son of Prince Kelyddon desired a wife as a help-mate, and the wife that he chose was Goleuddydd, the daughter of Prince Anlawdd. And after their union, the people put up prayers that they might have an heir. And they had a son through the prayers of the people. From the time of her pregnancy Goleuddydd became wild, and wandered about, without habitation; but when her delivery was at hand, her reason came back to her.

Kilydd, the son of Celyddon Wledig, wished for a wife to eat at the same table with him. This is the wife he wished for: Goleuddydd, the daughter of Anlawdd Wledig. After the wedding-feast with her, the country started to pray that they might have an heir; and they had a son through the prayers of the country. And from the time she became pregnant she roamed about madly, without trusting any dwelling. When the appointed time came to her, her reason returned to her.

Cilydd son of Cyleddon Wledig wished for a wife as wellborn as himself. The wife that he took was Goleuddydd daughter of Anlawdd Wledig. After his stay with her the country went to prayers whether they might have offspring, and they got a son through the prayers of the country. But from the time she grew with child, she went mad, without coming near a dwelling. When her time came upon her, her right sense came back to her.

Cilydd son of Celyddon Wledig desired a woman as well-born as himself. The woman he wanted was Goleuddydd daughter of Anlawdd Wledig. After his wedding feast with her, the country went to prayer to see whether they would have an heir. And through the country's prayers, they got a son. From the time she became pregnant she went mad and avoided civilised places. When her time came her senses returned to her.

Rhys Phillips makes much of the evidence of Lady Guest's own journals regarding the extent to which she actually translated the medieval Welsh into English, and the extent to which she used modern Welsh transcriptions provided for her. I wondered if she was using the word "translate" loosely for "transcribe" but that appears not to be the case. See for instance her very precise statement from 6 January 1838 that she finds translation "rather difficult for me, being so little conversant with the Welsh, and the *Mabinogion* being in such a cramped and ancient style."[69]

This might suggest medieval Welsh but could also simply mean that rendered into modern Welsh the ancient style made translating more difficult. On the 22 January 1838, five days after the birth of her fourth child, she had been given permission "to set to work with my dictionaries on a fresh sheet of the Mabinogion, which I finished":[70] this suggests translating from modern Welsh to English. However, by July she is pleased to discover she can understand *old* Welsh words (my emphasis) without a dictionary. In March 1839 she records that the *Dream of Ronabwy* "is very tiresome and difficult Welsh, and I did not get on much with it." Of *Peredur* she boasts "I have transcribed it, translated it, written the notes, provided the decorations, and brought it almost out of the printer's hands."[71] This last quotation does seem to suggest that the word "transcription" denotes rendering medieval Welsh into modern. The advantage she did possess was the money and the social position to command considerable assistance. For instance, someone she names Nethercliff is recorded by Lady Guest as having "made me a facsimile of Sir John Bosanquet's MS. of *Peredur*";[72] she notes that researches "are being made for me at the British Museum"; and comments that it "would be a great advantage if [Tegid] would correct the press of *Peredur*." Colonel Vaughan lent her MS fragments of *Gereint* and Lord Mostyn promised to lend his copies of the *Mabinogion*.[73]

Guest's introductory essay to the 1849 three-volume edition, however, deals not with translation at all, but with the question of antiquity and origins, of comparative philology, with in fact the wealth of information she had gathered along the way, writing:

> it is one thing to collect facts, and quite another to classify and draw from them their legitimate conclusions; and though I am loth that what has been collected with some pains, should be entirely thrown away, it is unwillingly, and with diffidence, that I trespass beyond the acknowledged province of the translator.[74]

It is clear, despite this disclaimer, that this is the area of the work in which she took the most interest and where she felt herself to be on very sure ground making comfortable comparisons with other romance texts in the by now very familiar style of other nationalising scholars like Joseph Ritson and Walter Scott.

Philological investigation was a popular field of intellectual activity at the time, linked to attempts to establish a common source of all languages, a study in part produced by colonial encounters. Guest determines that the Mabinogion, although "early recorded in the Welsh tongue" is "by no means wholly Welsh" but nevertheless although "mixed up, indeed, with various reflex additions from beyond the border, . . . still containing ample internal evidence of a Welsh original."[75] In our own day, Ceri Davies confirms that the "so-called *Mabinogion* . . . (The Four Branches of the Mabinogi) are tales which belong entirely to the Celtic world, largely unaffected by the legacy of classical writing."[76] Rachel Bromwich has shown that *Culhwch ac Olwen*, for instance, shows evidence of "having been shaped by an author familiar with Christian customs and practices."[77] One would imagine that this would also apply to the four Mabinogi tales as well.

Finally, and ironically for my reading of cultural appropriation, Charlotte Guest speculates that the Cymric nation may once have been invaders themselves who, driven out of their conquests by the later nations, the names and exploits of their heroes, and the compositions of their bards, spread far and wide among the invaders, and affected intimately their tastes and literature for many centuries.[78]

Certainly the *Monthly Review* could confidently assert in 1843 that while Charlotte Guest's collection of tales is a "valuable gift" to the Welsh, "the Mabinogion is undoubtedly an acquisition to English literature."[79]

## NOTES

1. See Stephen Copley and Peter Garside, eds., "Introduction," *The Politics of the Picturesque: Literature, Landscape and Aesthetics since 1770* (Cambridge: Cambridge University Press, 1994), 6–7.

2. André Lefevere, "Translation: Its Genealogy in the West," in Susan Bassnett and André Lefevere, eds., *Translation, History and Culture* (London: Pinter, 1990), 26.

3. David Spurr, *The Rhetoric of Empire: Colonial Discourse in Journalism, Travel Writing, and Imperial Administration* (Durham, NC & London: Duke University Press, 1993), 28.

4. Katherine Langloh Parker, *Australian Legendary Tales: Folk-lore of the Noongahburrahs as Told to the Piccaninnies* (London: Nutt, 1896), xi.

5. Parker, *Legendary Tales*, xii.

6. The translation (into modern Welsh and English) originally appeared in seven parts between 1838 and 1845. In 1849 it was published as a three-volume edition. In 1877 Quarich published a one-volume reprint which omits the modern Welsh text. Charlotte Guest's English translation was published by Dent (Everyman) in 1902, by Fisher Unwin in 1902, and by Nutt in 1902; and by the Folio Society in 1980. Everyman reprinted consistently until 1937.

7. "The Mabinogion, Part II," *Monthly Review* 150 (1839): 132.

8.  "The Mabinogion, Part IV," *Monthly Review* 158 (1842): 284–7 (284).

9.  "The Red Book of Hergest," *Saint Pauls* 3 (1868): 308–20 (310).

10.  Lady Charlotte Guest, *The Mabinogion from the Llyfr Coch o Hergest and other Ancient Welsh Manuscripts, with an English Translation and Notes*, 3 vols. (London: Longman, Brown, Green, and Longmans, 1849), xviii.

11.  "The Mabinogion, Part III," *Monthly Review* 153 (1840): 610.

12.  "The Mabinogion, Part II," 132.

13.  Linda Colley, *Britons: Forging the Nation 1707–1837* (New Haven and London: Yale University Press, 1992), 13.

14.  "The Mabinogion – Early Welsh Legends," *Spectator* 2 (1838): 1067–8 (1067).

15.  "The Mabinogion," *Athenaeum* (24 November 1838): 833–5 (833).

16.  "Mythology and Legends," *Monthly Review* 148 (1839): 20–29 (24)

17.  "The Mabinogion, Part II," 132.

18.  "The Mabinogion – Early Welsh Legends," 1068.

19.  Ironically, this particular article, "Welsh Fiction," *Monthly Review* 160 (1843): 431–68, addresses a further act of acquisition, Villemarqué's Paris edition of the *Mabinogion*, which claimed to be a direct translation from the Welsh into French but which Lady Guest, and the *Monthly Review*, insisted was in fact a rendering of her English translation into French – but that is another story.

20.  "Welsh Fiction," 453.

21.  See Revel Guest and Angela V. John, *Lady Charlotte: A Biography of the Nineteenth Century* (London: Weidenfeld & Nicolson, 1989), 96.

22.  Guest and John, *Lady Charlotte*, 99, 100.

23.  Citations are respectively from the reviews already cited in *Spectator* (1838), 1067; *Athenaeum* (1838), 835; *Monthly Review* (1839), 132; *Monthly Review* (1839), 29.

24.  "National Literature – The Mabinogion: Legends of the Rhine," *Spectator* 12 (1839): 760–1 (761).

25.  "Welsh Fiction," 453.

26.  Rita S. Kranidis, "Introduction: New Subjects, Familiar Grounds," in Kranidis, ed., *Imperial Objects: Essays on Victorian Women's Emigration and the Unauthorised Imperial Experience* (New York: Twayne, 1998), 1–18 (14).

27.  Will, *Literature Inside Out* (Cleveland, OH: Western Reserve University Press, 1966), cited in Edwin Gentzler, *Contemporary Translation Theories* (London: Routledge, 1993), 29.

28.  Said, "Reflections on Exile," *Granta* 13 (1984): 159–72 (163, 167).

29.  Said, *Culture and Imperialism* (London: Vintage, 1994), xxiii.

30.  Said, *Culture and Imperialism*, 67.

31.  Janet Wolff, *Feminine Sentences* (Cambridge: Polity, 1990), 12.

32.  The Earl of Bessborough, ed., *Lady Charlotte Guest: Extracts from her Journal 1833–1852* (London: John Murray, 1950), 69.

33.  *Journal 1833–1852*, 95.

34.  "The Mabinogion, Part IV," *Athenaeum* (30 April 1842): 379.

35. D. Rhys Phillips, *Lady Charlotte Guest and the Mabinogion: Some Notes on the Work and its Translator, with Extracts from her Journals* (Carmarthen: Spurrell, 1921), 13.

36. Janet Wolff, *Resident Alien: Feminist Cultural Criticism* (Cambridge: Polity, 1995).

37. *Journal 1833–1852*, 16.

38. Charlotte Guest was not alone in this. See Moira Dearnley, " 'I Came Hither, a Stranger': A View of Wales in the Novels of Anne Beale (1815–1900)," *New Welsh Review* 1 (1989): 27–32 in which Dearnley writes of the "new world" in which Beale found herself on taking a position as governess at Llwynhelig. Beale comments in her first prose work of 1844 set in Wales on the "language of its primitive inhabitants" (Dearnley, 27).

39. Colley, *Britons*, 373.

40. "National Literature," 761.

41. *Journal 1833–1852*, 20, 35.

42. Wolff, *Resident Alien*, 2–3.

43. *Journal 1833–1852*, 51.

44. Wolff, *Resident Alien*, 9.

45. Wolff, *Resident Alien*, 9.

46. *Journal 1833–1852*, 89, and quoted in Phillips, *Lady Charlotte Guest*, 15.

47. *Journal 1833–1852*, 61.

48. Guest and John, *Lady Charlotte*, 115.

49. Guest and John, *Lady Charlotte*, 101.

50. Guest and John, *Lady Charlotte*, 106.

51. Guest and John note (115) that Lady Guest actually wrote the correct title, "Llyfr Coch o Hergest," in her manuscript journal. The misspelling in the published journal, edited by the Earl of Bessborough, is a typographical error.

52. *Journal 1833–1852*, 63–4.

53. *Journal 1833–1852*, 64.

54. *Journal 1833–1852*, 64.

55. Jeffrey Gantz, trans., *The Mabinogion* (Harmondsworth, Middlesex: Penguin, 1976), 31.

56. Citations are respectively from Gwyn Jones and Thomas Jones, trans., *The Mabinogion* (London: Everyman, 1948, repr. 1974), xii; and Gantz, *Mabinogion*, 32.

57. Jones and Jones, *Mabinogion*, ix.

58. Guest and John, *Lady Charlotte*, 113.

59. Lady Charlotte Guest, *The Mabinogion*, vi.

60. Meic Stephens, ed., *The Oxford Companion to the Literature of Wales* (Oxford: Oxford University Press, 1986), 233.

61. Patrick K. Ford, trans., *The Mabinogi and other Medieval Welsh Tales* (London: University of Cardiff, 1977), ix.

62. Jones and Jones, *Mabinogion*, xxxi.

63. T.P. Ellis and John Lloyd, trans., *The Mabinogion: A New Translation* (Oxford: Clarendon, 1929), vii–viii.

64. Lady Charlotte Guest, *The Mabinogion*, n.p.

65. Phillips, *Lady Charlotte Guest*, 9.

66. Guest and John, *Lady Charlotte*, 115.

67. Guest and John, *Lady Charlotte*, 101, 116.

68. Quotations are from the *Mabinogion* translations already cited of, respectively, Lady Charlotte Guest; Ellis and Lloyd; Jones and Jones; and Ford.

69. Phillips, *Lady Charlotte Guest*, 19.

70. *Journal 1833–1852*, 65.

71. Phillips, *Lady Charlotte Guest*, 25.

72. The facsimiles of medieval manuscript material in the 1849 three-volume edition of her work are signed "J. Netherclift, lithog."

73. See Phillips, *Lady Charlotte Guest*, 24–25, 26.

74. Guest, *Mabinogion*, xii.

75. Guest, *Mabinogion*, xvii, xxii.

76. Ceri Davies, *Welsh Literature and the Classical Tradition* (Cardiff: University of Wales, 1995), 39.

77. Rachel Bromwich and D. Simon Evans, *Culhwch and Olwen: An Edition and Study of the Oldest Arthurian Tale* (Cardiff: University of Wales Press, 1992), lxxviii.

78. Guest, *Mabinogion*, xxiii.

79. "Welsh Fiction" (see note 19 above), 467.

# The Norse Discovery of America and the American Discovery of Norse (1828–1892)

## Geraldine Barnes

In 1779, in the course of the proposed revision of the constitution of his alma mater, the College of William and Mary, Thomas Jefferson, Governor of Virginia, put before the state legislature a bill to the effect that the College should have a professorship in "ancient languages, including Oriental (Hebrew, Chaldee, Syriac) and Northern Tongues (Mœso-Gothic, Anglo-Saxon, Old Icelandic)."[1] It would, he wrote a few years later, be proper to make such paedogogical recognition of the "ancient languages and literature of the north, on account of their connection with our own language, laws, customs, and history."[2] Jefferson's proposition was unsuccessful, although he eventually presided over the incorporation of Anglo-Saxon into the curriculum of the University of Virginia on its establishment in 1819; but the institutionalised teaching of Old Norse in America had to wait until 1869, when Willard Fiske became Professor of North European Languages at Cornell University. In the meantime, however, the study of Old Norse history, language, and literature flourished in the 1830s among a group of New England men of letters, of diverse professional backgrounds and scholarly interests.

Their attraction to the Scandinavian North was sparked by three stimuli: the belief, allied with the notion coined by seventeenth-century English parliamentarians that the "Goths" were the champions of liberty, that all the Germanic peoples shared common political and legal institutions; the challenge of a new field of linguistic enquiry; and the lure of the romanticised Scandinavian past, as propagated in late eighteenth- and early nineteenth-century English literature. Simultaneous with this burgeoning curiosity about medieval Scandinavia was the revelation to the American reading public, in a volume entitled *Antiquitates Americanæ* (1837),[3] of eleventh-century Norse voyages to lands west of Greenland. Largely authored by the Danish scholar, Carl Christian Rafn, and published under the aegis of the Royal Society of Northern Antiquaries in Copenhagen, *Antiquitates Americanæ* contained the first modern edition of the Old Norse "Vínland sagas," *Grænlendinga saga* ("The Saga of the Greenlanders") and *Eiríks saga rauða* ("The Saga of Eric the Red"). *Antiquitates Americanæ* was widely reviewed and discussed in nineteenth-century America, but it was not to be the catalyst for the widespread trans-Atlantic study of Old Icelandic which Rafn anticipated.

In the vanguard of those New Englanders who turned their attention to Scandinavia in the 1830s was Henry Wheaton (1785–1848), American *chargé d'affaires* in Copenhagen from 1827–35, who, in an essay published in 1828, restated Jefferson's position on the Germanic descent of English and English law: "we deduce our origin, our language, and our laws, from the Scandinavian and Teutonic races."[4] Wheaton was the author of the first book-length history of Scandinavia in English, *History of the Northmen* (1831), a work which received much attention in America,[5] and of the first articles in American journals on the subject of Old Norse literature. His "Scandinavian Literature" appeared in the *American Quarterly Review* in 1828 and "Scandinavian Mythology, Poetry and History" in *The North American Review* the following year (1829). Wheaton's essay on "Anglo-Saxon Language and Literature," published in *The North American Review* in 1831, has more to say about Old Norse than Old English. The piece is essentially, as Adolph Benson puts it, "an apotheosis of Old Norse"[6] in which Old English fares poorly by comparison:

> . . . the Anglo-Saxon literature. . . certainly cannot be considered as a rich literature in comparison with the Icelandic, or old Scandinavian. . . The expressions in the poetical language of Scandinavia far transcend in fullness, richness, and variety, those of the Anglo-Saxon.[7]

Although Wheaton's command of Danish was excellent, it is doubtful whether he was competent in Icelandic. It was, it seems, the idea of Old Norse rather than the language itself which captured his imagination.

Drawing upon the account of the Vínland voyages in Torfæus's *Historia Vinlandiæ Antiqvæ* (1705), Wheaton relates the story in *History of the Northmen*[8] but limits further comment to a footnote conjecture that

Vínland might have been in the vicinity of Boston.[9] In a foretaste of things to come after the publication of *Antiquitates Americanæ*, however, the *American Monthly Review* devoted almost half its review of *History of the Northmen* to Norse voyages to America.[10] By contrast, Washington Irving, who had little regard for the North and had published his quasi-hagiographic *The Life and Voyages of Christoper Columbus* in 1828, ignored them in his not unfavourable review of *History of the Northmen* in *The North American Review*. Nevertheless, to illustrate the principles of alliterative verse, Irving cited a few lines of Milton in Icelandic (from Ebenezer Henderson's *Iceland*), which appear to be the earliest quotation from that language, other than titles and individual terms, in an American publication:

> *V*íd that *V*íllu diup
> *V*árd annum slæga,
> *B*öloerk *B*ídleikat
> *B*arni vitis à.

> [Into this wild abyss the wary Fiend
> Stood on the brink of Hell and looked;][11]

Henry Wadsworth Longfellow's lifelong interest in Scandinavian literature, which is likely to have been sparked by works such as Thomas Gray's *The Fatal Sisters* and *The Descent of Odin* and Walter Scott's *Harold the Dauntless* and *The Pirate*,[12] extended, at least briefly, to the study of Old Icelandic. During the summer of 1835 Longfellow spent a fortnight in Copenhagen, where he took some lessons in the subject from Rafn himself.[13] Other New Englanders also undertook to learn the language during the 1830s. The "learned blacksmith" Elihu Burritt added Old Icelandic to his extensive linguistic repertoire during service as librarian of the American Antiquarian Society from 1837–39. He also published the first substantial piece of translation from Old Norse in America, in the form of an excerpt, "Translated from the Icelandic," from *Grœnlendinga saga*, which appeared, along with a brief introduction to Old Icelandic literature and a synopsis of the first five chapters of *Grœnlendinga saga*, in the inaugural issue of *The American Eclectic* (1841).[14] Others made direct appeals to Rafn for assistance in the matter of grammars and dictionaries.

Rafn had a number of American correspondents during the 1830s. His most extensive exchanges were those which he initiated in the course of his research for *Antiquitates Americanæ* with Thomas Webb, secretary of the Rhode Island Historical Society, to seek information about possible viking remains in New England.[15] Among Rafn's other New England correspondents there were three who expressed a desire to learn Old Norse: Joshua Toulmin Smith, the English constitutional lawyer, reformer, and phrenologist, who lived in the United States for five years between 1837 and 1842; John Russell Bartlett, New York merchant and member of the Committee of the Rhode Island Historical Society; and George Perkins Marsh, lawyer, diplomat, and scholar, of Vermont.

Smith, who published an English translation of a substantial portion of *Antiquitates Americanæ* under the title *The Discovery of America by the Northmen in the Tenth Century* (1839), wrote to Rafn, enclosing two copies of the work, to solicit his opinion and corrections. At the same time, he expressed a desire to learn more Icelandic and to achieve "a closer familiarity, than the more general knowledge of it which I at present possess" and requested information about the best dictionary of the language available in Latin or English and advice about editions of some famous works of Old Icelandic history and literature: *Heimskringla*, *Landnámabók*, and the poetic *Edda*.[16]

Bartlett, who appears to have worked tirelessly in the commercial cause of *Antiquitates Americanæ*, exchanged numerous letters with Rafn between 1836 and 1839. He secured several subscribers to the work, arranged for William Jackson to distribute it, sought reviewers, sent copies of the reviews to Rafn, and circulated its prospectus widely.[17] In 1838, Bartlett wrote that he was "Feeling desirous to become acquainted with the Danish and Icelandic Languages" and asked Rafn if he would send him "A Danish and English Grammar and Dictionary and also an Icelandic and English Grammar & Dictionary," both of which he had "tried in vain to find . . . in any of our principal shops."[18] Rafn promised to send a Danish-English dictionary and, without identifying its author (even though he enclosed a letter which Bartlett was asked to forward to the man himself), mentioned that "An Iceland Grammar in English will soon appear in America."[19]

This "Iceland Grammar" was the work of the most accomplished American Old Norse scholar in the first half of the nineteenth century, George Perkins Marsh (1801–1882). Like Wheaton, Marsh had wide-ranging interests in the literature and culture of Scandinavia. Old Norse literature, he declared:

> . . . in the opinion of those most competent to judge. . . has never been surpassed, if equalled, in all that gives value to that portion of history which consists in spirited delineations of

character, and faithful and lively pictures of events, among nations in a rude state of society.[20]

Marsh's contribution to the first issue of *The American Eclectic* was a translation from Danish to English of the first part of an article by Peter Erasmus Mueller, originally published in *Nordisk Tidsskrift*. Entitled "The Origin, Progress and Decline of Icelandic Historical Literature," the essay gives a broad overview of Iceland's history and energetically addresses the question: "Why it fell to the lot of Iceland to kindle the torch of the northern historic muse, and how the light thence diffused could illuminate regions so distant from that far isle?" (447).

As Bartlett was to do a few years later, Marsh lamented the unavailability in America of books on Old Norse in the first preserved of his letters to Rafn and, with a view to making purchases direct from Copenhagen, asked him for bibliographical assistance.[21] Rafn's enthusiastic response, which included a full account of the state of progress of the forthcoming *Antiqutiates Americanæ* and the information that a copy of an Old Norse grammar by Erasmus Rask (*Kortfattet Vejledning til det oldnordiske eller gamle islandske Sprog*) was already in the mail, led to Marsh's compilation of three of Rask's works,[22] which he called *A Compendious Grammar of the Old-Northern or Icelandic language, compiled and translated from the Grammars of Rask*.

The *Compendious Grammar* was published in 1838, five years before the appearance of George Webbe Dasent's better known *A Grammar of the Icelandic or Old Norse Tongue translated from the Swedish of Erasmus Rask* (London, 1843). Production difficulties delayed printing, but Marsh was galvanised into action by the appearance of *Antiquitates Americanæ*, which, he said in the Preface to the *Compendious Grammar*, he expected "to awaken the attention of American scholars to the remarkable language in which the ancient and curious memorials contained in that volume are embodied, and thereby to furnish a fit occasion for bringing out a manual designed to facilitate access to the literary treasures of which the Old-Northern tongue is the vehicle" (iii–iv). The Preface also announced Marsh's preparedness to compile a comparative English-Icelandic grammar, if "the subject shall be found to excite sufficient interest to warrant the undertaking" (vi).

Henry Schoolcraft (1793–1864), geologist and celebrated ethnologist of the Algonquian tribes, had no particular interest in Old Norse history or literature, found the notion of runic inscriptions in New England highly dubious,[23] and does not appear to have been moved by his election to the Royal Society of Northern Antiquaries.[24] Nevertheless, he favourably reviewed *Antiquitates Americanæ*,[25] read the *Compendious Grammar*, and declared himself personally impressed by its author.[26] Moreover, although on the two occasions on which he refers to the *Compendious Grammar* in his *Personal Memoirs* Schoolcraft confuses Rask either with Rusk ("His [Marsh's] translation of *Rusk's Icelandic Grammar* is a scholar-like performance, and every way indicative of the propensities of his mind for philological studies" [564]) or Rafn ("I have perused Rafn's Grammar by Marsh" [624]), he was actively intrigued by the evidence provided by the work of cognate forms in European languages:

> It is curious to observe, in this language, the roots of many English words, and it denotes through what lengths of mutations of history the stock words of a generic language may be traced. Lond, skip, flaska, sumar, hamar, ketill, dal, are clearly the radices respectively of land, ship, flask, summer, hammer, kettle, dale. This property of the endurance of orthographical forms gives one a definite illustration of the importance of language on history.               (*Personal Memoirs*, 564).

The interests of other scholars in the 1830s extended both to Old Norse and Native American languages. Rafn himself sought information from Longfellow about the availability of grammars and dictionaries of the language of the native people of Massachusetts, Rhode Island, and Connecticut.[27] When he sent a copy of the medieval Icelandic lawbook, *Grágás*, to the Rhode Island Historical Society, Rafn expressed the hope that the Museum of the Royal Society for Northern Antiquaries in Copenhagen might receive in return a "collection of Indian antiquities."[28] In *The Discovery of America by the Northmen*, Joshua Toulmin Smith – some of whose lectures on phrenology were attended by Schoolcraft, who presented him with the skull of a Native American[29] – digressed to condemn the dispossession of the Cherokees.[30] Bartlett, author of *The Progress of Ethnology, an account of recent archaeological researches in various parts of the globe, tending to elucidate the physical history of man* (1847), was as interested in Native American languages as he was in Old Norse. In August 1851 he wrote at some length to Rafn from the headquarters of the Mexican Boundary commission in New Mexico about his linguistic ("I have collected some vocabularies of interest; and intent [sic] collecting them from all the tribes I meet")[31] and ethnographic study of the Apaches. Rafn appears to have enjoyed Bartlett's letters from the West: he mentions the receipt of this letter and refers to his enjoyment of another, written from Texas in September 1852, in his correspondence with the young Willard Fiske.[32]

By the 1840s, Marsh, Wheaton, Burritt, and Smith were, like Bartlett, moving in other directions: Smith back to England, where he resumed his legal career and, like Schoolcraft before him, took up geology;[33] Wheaton to Berlin as ambassador extraordinary and minister plenipotentiary to Prussia; and Burritt to the work of international pacifism. Marsh's Scandinavian interests turned to translations of the nineteenth-century Swedish poet, Bishop Esaias Tegnér, and other modern writers. In 1861 he was appointed minster to Italy, where he spent the rest of his life, although a reference to Gudbrand Vigfusson's *Sturlunga Saga* (1878), in a letter which he wrote at the age of seventy-nine to Willard Fiske,[34] indicates that his interest in Old Icelandic literature never abated.[35]

What, then, halted the scholarly momentum of the American discovery of Norse, which had gathered such a head of steam in the 1830s? First, Longfellow's interest in medieval Scandinavia remained essentially on a poetic level. Although Rafn had suggested *Eiríks saga rauða* as an appropriate text for his proposed study of Old Norse,[36] Longfellow's real interest lay in the work of Tegnér. His poem, "The Skeleton in Armor" (1841), which relates the flight to distant shores west of Scandinavia – unnamed, but signalled as Rhode Island – of a viking and a Norwegian princess, takes its inspiration from Tegnér's *Frithjofs saga*, not from *Eiríks saga* or *Grœnlendinga saga*.[37] In reply to Rafn's letter requesting information about Native American languages, Longfellow promised to "do all in my power to make the Literature of the North better known to my countrymen."[38] But although he may have lectured at Harvard on Icelandic literary history during his tenure of the Smith Professorship of Modern Languages from 1836–54,[39] Longfellow proved neither an apt nor interested student of the language. Icelandic was, he wrote in the journal which he kept of the summer of 1835, "a tongue which has a harsh, sharp and disagreeable sound."[40]

Second, Marsh's high hopes for an upsurge of interest in Old Norse language were defeated in the short term by technology. Three hundred copies of the *Compendious Grammar* were printed, but the author's absence from Burlington during the book's production resulted in so many proofreading errors that he circulated copies only privately.[41] In a letter of 1874 to Willard Fiske, to thank him for his encouragement in his efforts to learn Old Norse, Rasmus Anderson (1846–1936), the first professor of Scandinavian at the University of Wisconsin, says that he "knew of . . . Prof. Marsh," but he was clearly unaware of the *Compendious Grammar*. Finding Dasent's *Grammar of the Icelandic* too difficult, Anderson deplored the unavailability of an

English language Old Norse grammar "adapted" to the needs of Americans:

> I thought there might possibly be text books in the English
> Language published in England, that would be adapted for
> American scholars. I know Dasent has published an Icelandic
> grammar, but I think it is a translation of Rask's, and that is by
> far too intricate for beginners.

He accordingly invited Fiske to write and publish a "suitable grammar and reader in the English language."[42]

In the longer term, the Norse-avid public which Marsh envisaged for his proposed comparative Norse-English grammar never materialised; and it was a generation before Willard Fiske, who had left Hamilton College in 1850 to pursue the study of Scandinavian at the Universities of Copenhagen and Uppsala, publicly attributed his fascination with the subject in part to "the influence of certain writings of our present honored minister to Italy."[43] Like Bartlett, Marsh had worked diligently to promote sales of and interest in *Antiquitates Americanæ*, because he saw the work as the means of awakening interest in the literature of medieval Scandinavia.[44] Ironically, however, the publication of *Antiquitates Americanæ* turned the majority of the reading public's concerns back to American history instead.

Rafn had, simply, overreached his aim of generating American interest in Old Norse. First, he "Americanised" the Vínland sagas. The very title, *Antiquitates Americanæ*, served to deflect interest from their Scandinavian context. Second, he initiated an historical controversy which, particularly in the second half of the century, generated a certain amount of actively anti-Norse sentiment. The evidence of the Vínland sagas that Europeans had set foot in America some 500 years before Columbus impinged upon fundamental questions of national history and identity. In its size, splendour, and confident although utterly unfounded assertions about actual Norse landing sites along the New England coast, *Antiquitates Americanæ* gave the Vínland voyages a substance and authority which constituted a potentially serious challenge to the image, so successfully promulgated by Washington Irving in the *Life and Voyages of Christopher Columbus* (1828), of America as a land unseen, unnamed, and otherwise without mortal creator before 1492. For many, particularly in the years leading up to the Columbus quincentenary in 1892, it became a case of Leif vs. Columbus. Whereas the Rhode Island Historical Society was hospitable to the notion of viking New England, the Boston historical establishment was less than enthusiastic. Pre-eminent amongst it, Henry Schoolcraft's friend, George Bancroft, steadfastly consigned the Vínland sagas to the realm of legend through the many editions, over several decades, of his *History of the United States*, the first volume of which appeared in 1834.

Moreover, as a direct result of some of the claims in *Antiquitates Americanæ* for the runic provenance of a number of stone carvings in Massachusetts and Rhode Island, and as an indirect manifestation of the racial Teutonism which was gathering momentum in the second half of the nineteenth century, the 1830s' interest in the "Gothic" roots of America's legal and political institutions and investigation of the relationships between the Germanic languages degenerated into an occasionally ludicrously literal quest for New England's "viking" lineage. In an 1843 lecture by Marsh entitled "The Goths in New England," the Goths are, explicitly, the Anglo-Saxon forefathers of the Pilgrims and "Northern" only in the most general terms:

> ... our forefathers belonged to that grand era in British history, when the English mind, under the impulse of the Reformation, was striving to recover its Gothic tendencies, by the elimination of the Roman element. . . . The founders of the first New England colony, and their brethren, who followed them to their new home in the course of the same century, belonged to the class most deeply tinctured with the moral and intellectual traits of their Northern ancestry.[45]

By 1849, however, J. Elliot Cabot was claiming that, particularly in its maritime ability, "we may confidently assert, that the modern New England character has in it much more of the Norse than of the Saxon."[46] Charles Kingsley, a fervent advocate of racial Teutonism and especially its Norse element,[47] fanned the flames on a speaking tour of America in 1874. Lecturing on "The First Discovery of America," he claimed the Pilgrims not only as the ethnic kin of the Norsemen but also as "in many cases, their actual descendants."[48] With the announcement by Eben Norton Horsford, a former Harvard Professor of Chemistry, that he had unearthed Vínland on the River Charles in Massachusetts and his ceremonial unveiling of the site in 1889,[49] the archaeological quest for America's Viking Age culminated in a piece of unabashed theatre.

In the broader context of nineteenth-century American medievalism which, in the main, idealised the Middle Ages[50] the vikings were problematic. In "The American Scholar," an oration delivered to the Phi Beta

Kappa Society in 1837, George Marsh's contemporary, Ralph Waldo Emerson, expressed admiration for the elemental, generative vigour of those to whom he elsewhere referred as "these atrocious ancestors of Englishmen – the Briton, Saxon, Northman, Berserkir":[51]

> out of handselled savage nature, out of terrible Druids and Berserkirs, come at last Alfred and Shakspear – [52]

James Russell Lowell, who commemorated the Vínland voyages in his poem, "The Voyage to Vinland," also admired the energy of the blood-thirsty but law-conscious characters in Dasent's translation of *Njáls saga* (1861), whom he likened to the Border Ruffians of the 1850s.[53]

For a number of American commentators, however, the vikings remained irredeemably barbarian. By extrapolation, their language and literature were also beyond the pale. In 1869, the year of Fiske's appointment at Cornell, the *Nation* reviewer of Benjamin De Costa's *The Pre-Columbian Discovery of America by the Northmen* (1868), an English translation of a large proportion of *Antiquitates Americanæ*, dismissed the Icelanders and Greenlanders as renegade Northmen, unworthy of the name:

> The white inhabitants of the arctic circle had, for more than a century, ceased to be a part of the primitive nation, and should not be spoken of as Northmen. They were a branch broken off with violence from the parent tree; they had been driven forth as outlaws or expatriated as outcasts, and exiled beyond the northern line of the supposed habitable globe. . . . Ignorant, heathen, barbarous, brutal, when banished from Scandinavia, they were equally debased when, long afterward, venturing westward, they reached the shores of Greenland and Vinland.[54]

Anti-viking pronouncements in the Leif-vs.-Columbus debate became even more intemperate in the years leading up to the Columbus quatercentenary. J.P. MacLean's somewhat misleading titled *A Critical Examination of the Evidences Adduced to Establish the Theory of the Norse Discovery of America* (1892) paints a grotesque picture of medieval Iceland:

> On the marriage day it was bad taste not to be drunk and find a bed on the rushes on the floor. Solid drinking continued from Wednesday until Saturday. Polygamy was also practiced. The

Vikings were lawless in a bad sense. . . . The women who accompanied these expeditions distinguished themselves by a fierce cruelty. . . . The older the records the darker the picture. They ate nothing but raw cured meat and slept out of doors.[55]

In the meantime, self-interestedly ranging himself with such anti-Columbus extremists as Aaron Goodrich,[56] Rasmus Anderson attempted to harness the Vínland sagas to the regional causes of promoting Scandinavian at the University of Wisconsin and validating the citizenship of Norwegian immigrants to America[57] by writing a book with the deliberately provocative title of *America Not Discovered by Columbus* (1874).[58] Anderson himself was not an Old Norse scholar. He was proficient in Norwegian, but, according to Einar Haugen, had "pitifully inadequate"[59] training in other Scandinavian languages. In his autobiography, he admits to knowing no Old or Modern Icelandic before 1871, when he was taught by an Icelandic immigrant.[60] Anderson's authorial purpose, as declared in the Preface to *America Not Discovered by Columbus*, was "to create some interest in the people, the literature, and the early institutions of Norway, and especially in Iceland." The scholarly establishment was not impressed by this self-confessedly unoriginal[61] and, in Einar Haugen's words, "pugnacious little book."[62] Willard Fiske's steadfast silence throughout 1875, in the face of Anderson's increasingly agitated pleas for a response[63] to his petulant and bitter outburst about the book's poor reception by *The North American Review* ("Let us Westerners not try to be oxen while we are but frogs. Let us tear up the stump out of this beautiful land and raise nice crops of wheat for the editor of the North American Review &c; but let us not aspire to authorship"),[64] suggests that Fiske may have regretted acceding to Anderson's request for a contribution of about "1½ to 2 pages"[65] to the string of endorsements "On the Historical, Linguistic, Literary and Scientific Value of the Scandinavian Languages" which constitute the book's Appendix. Anderson's *Norse Mythology* (1875) fared better with the academy and led, after some faculty opposition and controversy, to the conferral of the title "Professor of Scandinavian Languages" but not to the establishment of a chair of Scandinavian or a full professorial salary.[66]

Despite the assertion by a college president, cited by Francis B. Gummere in the first issue of *Publications of the Modern Language Association* (1884–85), that Icelandic and Anglo-Saxon were "intellectual luxuries,"[67] Old Norse was taught in a number of American institutions of higher learning from the last decades of the nineteenth century. The principal route by which the subject entered the curriculum was neither ethnic pride among the Scandinavian-Americans who had begun to settle in Minnesota and Wisconsin at the end of that decade,[68] nor the perceived common ancestry with medieval Scandinavia and admiration for its literature which had inspired the scholars of the 1830s, and which Fiske embraced in his 1874 piece for Rasmus Anderson:

> The religious belief of our remote ancestors, and very many of their primitive legal and social customs. . . find their clearest and often their only elucidation in the so-called *Eddic* and *Skaldic* lays, and in the Sagas. The same writings form the sole sources of Scandinavian history before the fourteenth century, and they not infrequently shed a welcome ray on the obscure annals of the British Islands, and of several continental nations. . . . The old Icelandic literature, which MOBIUS truly characterizes as "ein Phänomen vom Standpunkte der allegemeinen Cultur und Literaturgeschichte". . . developed itself out of the actual life of the people under little or no extraneous influence. . . . For the English-speaking races especially there is nowhere, so near home, a field promising to the scholar so rich a harvest.[69]

It was, instead, as a by-way of the new discipline, introduced to America by scholars trained in German and Scandinavian universities, of "Germanic philology" and the concomitant cultivation of Teutonic mythology that Old Norse shored up its position as a subject offering.

Whereas the study of modern Scandinavian languages and literature thrived in the 1880s and '90s at the newly established departments of Scandinavian at the universities of Minnesota (1883), North Dakota (1891), and Wisconsin, interest in medieval Scandinavian was, with the notable exception of Harvard, the province of Germanic philology.[70] According to Einar Haugen's account of the history of Scandinavian Studies at Wisconsin, where, in 1874–75, "there appeared for the first time a sophomore course entitled Icelandic,"[71] the subject fared less well there than Norwegian, and only "its importance in philological training"[72] kept it on the curriculum (Anderson's class records suggest that the Icelandic course was not offered in 1878–79).[73] In 1883 Anderson and Fiske resigned from their positions at Wisconsin and Cornell: Anderson to serve as minister to Denmark during the first administration of Grover Cleveland, and Fiske to retirement in Florence, in the villa which had been George Marsh's home.

Anderson was succeeded as Professor of the Scandinavian Languages by his brother-in-law Julius Olson, who, as Flom puts it, "stressed more especially the modern literature."[74] After a course in 1891–92 which "did not prove especially popular,"[75] Old Norse was not taught again at Wisconsin until 1911, when Lee Hollander offered it to graduate students in the Department of German.[76] On Fiske's resignation from Cornell, the professorship of North European Languages was discontinued in favour of a chair of German Language and Literature, and, from 1891, the Göttingen-trained James Morgan Hart taught Old Norse there as an object of primarily philological interest.[77]

The career of Fiske's student, W.H. Carpenter, is a case in point. Carpenter wrote his Freiburg University thesis on the early fifteenth-century Icelandic *Nikolásdrápa Halls Prests*, and his published scholarship extends from medieval to modern Scandinavian literature and language. Although his review in the *American Journal of Philology* (1882) of Old Norse scholarship from 1860–1880 opens with the statement that

> With the continually growing interest in the comparatively new study of *Germanistik*, Old Norse like every other Germanic dialect has received in the last decade increased attention, and Old Norse philology has made most gratifying advances in lexicography, grammar and text criticism,[78]

the article gives a balanced account of work on language; editions of literary, legal, and historical texts; and literary criticism. Elsewhere, Carpenter laments the ransacking of Iceland's medieval manuscripts:

> Thanks to the indefatigability of early collectors, Árni Magnússon at their head, Iceland has been as thoroughly stripped of her early vellums, and even of their paper transcripts, as though they had never existed; and beyond those preserved in the archives in Reykjavik and the few fragments possibly in the hands of some private individuals who know their value, there are absolutely no parchments of any size, sort, or condition, left in the country.[79]

Carpenter's original appointment as "Instructor in Icelandic, Danish and Swedish" (1884) at Columbia University was retitled "Instructor in German and the Scandinavian Languages" two years later; and, in 1895, he became "Professor in Germanic Philology."[80] His publications nevertheless continued to embrace articles on Scandinavian literature and a substantial entry in *The Library of the World's Best Literature* (1887) on "The Eddas."

Flom's account of the teaching of Old Norse at American universities from 1869 to 1907 shows that eddic poetry and courses in mythology were popular, but that "[i]n the study of the prose the work has been practically limited to the Prose Edda, *Gunnlaugs saga*, *Laxdölsaga* and *Njálssaga*."[81] If an Old Norse class at Columbia, proposed in 1880 by one of Gudbrandur Vigfusson's former students, Charles Sprague Smith, ever eventuated, and if it used the several copies of the translation of *Eiríks saga rauða* by the English Norse scholar, John Sephton, which Vigfusson despatched to New York for the purpose,[82] Flom does not record it.[83] Benjamin De Costa's claim, in 1890, that "the study of the Icelandic Sagas has resulted in the erection of a statue to Leif Ericson in the City of Boston"[84] had nothing to do with it. The statue was conceived as another promotional venture by Rasmus Anderson, this time in a bid "to make the University of Wisconsin the chief center of Scandinavian study in the United States."[85] Anderson had intended the statue to stand in the front of the main building of the Madison campus of the University of Wisconsin,[86] but, when subscriptions from the mid-west Norwegian community proved unforthcoming, a fundraising committee was formed in Boston,[87] and the work was eventually unveiled there on October 29, 1887.[88]

Probably the most significant piece of nineteenth-century Norse scholarship in America, *The Finding of Wineland the Good* (1890),[89] an edition of *Grænlendinga saga* and *Eiríks saga rauða*, with extensive commentary and English translation, by Arthur Reeves, another of Fiske's students, was published in England and widely ignored by the American periodicals which had devoted so much attention to *Antiquitates Americanæ*. Fiske reviewed it for *The Nation*, and a short notice appeared in *The Saturday Review*, but the major focus of attention was from scholarly journals in the United Kingdom, Germany, and Scandinavia.[90] The *Proceedings of the Royal Geographical Society* called it "on the whole, the most valuable contribution that has yet been published in the literature of the Norse discovery of America."[91] Reeves was killed in a train accident in 1891, at the age of thirty-five. In his bibliography of American Scandinavian scholarship to 1907, Flom does not list either *The Finding of Wineland the Good* – presumably because it was not published in America – or, more surprisingly, Charles Sprague Smith's article on the historicity of the Vínland sagas, *Íslendingabók*, and the *Íslendingasögur*, which appeared in the *Journal of the American Geographic Society* for 1892.[92] Nor does Flom nominate a text of either *Grænlendinga saga* or *Eiríks saga rauða* among the pedagogical desiderata – "an annotated text edition of one of the Icelandic sagas, perhaps preferably *Gunnlaugs Saga* or an abridged form of the *Njáls Saga*, as also of the lays of the *Elder Edda*"[93] – with which he concludes his study.

Although Marsh and Anderson strove, by different means, to have it otherwise, the fate in nineteenth-century America of Old Norse accounts of the settlement of Greenland and landfalls west was to be read primarily as American "discovery" narrative. For most of those who regarded the "Vínland sagas" as historically unreliable, they, the language in which they were written, and the culture which produced them were of no account. The ascendancy of Germanic philology amongst professional educators in the latter part of the nineteenth century did not encourage the study of medieval Scandinavian history and literature for their own sake; nor was there any institutional accommodation for that combination of amateur "ethnological, philological and antiquarian" research, embracing both Native American and Scandinavian, to which Bartlett confirmed his continued commitment in his letter to Rafn of August 1851.[94] The Vínland voyages were commemorated in statuary, in the decorative arts,[95] in popular histories,[96] and amongst the more eccentric fringes of scholarship in nineteenth-century America, but not in university departments of Scandinavian, German, or English. Paradoxically, but, it seems, undeniably, the Norse "discovery" of America did little to promote, and as much, if not more, to impede the American discovery of Norse.[97]

## NOTES

1. Cited by Herbert Baxter Adams, *Thomas Jefferson and the University of Virginia*, U.S. Bureau of Education, Circular of Information No. 1 (Washington, 1888), 42 (from *Sundry Documents on the Subject of a System of Public Education for the State of Virginia* [Richmond, 1817], 60). See also Roy J. Honeywell, *The Educational Work of Thomas Jefferson* (Cambridge, MA: Harvard University Press, 1931), 112–13.

2. *Notes on the State of Virginia*, introd. by Thomas Perkins Abernethy (New York: Harper & Row, 1964), 145. Jefferson finished this book, which was written and revised between 1781–84, in 1785 (Abernethy, "Introduction," *Notes on the State of Virginia*, x). On Jefferson's interest in Anglo-Saxon, see, for example, Reginald Horsman, *Race and Manifest Destiny: The Origins of American Racial Anglo-Saxonism* (Cambridge, MA, and London: Harvard University Press, 1981), 18–23; Stanley R. Hauer, Thomas Jefferson and the Anglo-Saxon Language, *PMLA* 98 (1983): 879–98; Allen J. Frantzen, *Desire for Origins: New*

*Language, Old English, and Teaching the Tradition* (New Brunswick and London: Rutgers University Press, 1990), 15–19, 203–07.

3. *Antiqvitates Americanæ sive scriptores septentrionales rerum ante-Columbianarum in America* (Hafniæ [Copenhagen]: Societas Regia Antiqvariorum Septentrionalium, 1837).

4. Henry Wheaton, "Scandinavian Literature," *American Quarterly Review* 3/6 (1828): 481–90 (490).

5. For an account of the reviews of *History of the Northmen*, see Adolph B. Benson, "Henry Wheaton's Writings on Scandinavia," *JEGP* 29 (1930): 546–61 (558–9).

6. Benson, "Henry Wheaton's Writings on Scandinavia," 551.

7. Henry Wheaton, "Anglo-Saxon Language and Literature," *The North American Review* 33 (1831): 325–50 (326, 331).

8. *History of the Northmen, or Danes and Normans, from the earliest times to the Conquest of England by William of Normandy* (London, 1831), 22–31.

9. *History of the Northmen*, 24. Following the publication of *Antiquitates Americanæ*, Wheaton expanded this section in the second edition of *History of the Northmen, Histoire des peuples du Nord* (Paris, 1844).

10. *American Monthly Review* 1/3 (1832): 245–56 (246–50).

11. Washington Irving, rev. Henry Wheaton, *History of the Northmen*, in *The North American Review* 35 (1832): 342–71 (348). The Icelandic lines and English translation cited are from Ebenezer Henderson, *Iceland; or the journal of a residence in that island during the years 1814 and 1815*, 2nd edn. (Edinburgh, 1819), 545.

12. See Andrew Hilen, *Longfellow and Scandinavia: A Study of the Poet's Relationship with the Northern Languages and Literature*, Yale Studies in English 107 (New Haven: Yale University Press, 1947), 1–2.

13. See Samuel Longfellow, ed., *Life of Henry Wadsworth Longfellow, with extracts from his journals and correspondence*, 3 vols. (Boston and New York, 1891) 1, 209–16 [Vol. 12 of *The Works of Henry Wadsworth Longfellow, with Bibliographical and Critical Notes and His Life, with extracts from his journals and correspondence*, 14 vols., 1891–2.]; Hilen, *Longfellow and Scandinavia*, 11–27, 141.

14. See *The American Eclectic: or Selections from the Periodical Literature of all Foreign Countries* 1 (1841): 99–101, 107–11.

15. See *Antiquitates Americanæ*, 356–72, 397–404; Benedict Grøndal, ed., *Breve fra og til Carl Christian Rafn, med en Biographi* (Copenhagen: Gyldendalske Boghandel, 1869), 130–75.

16. Smith to Rafn, 6 May 1839, Fiske Icelandic Collection, Cornell University Library. See Þórunn Sigurðaróttir, *Manuscript Material, Correspondence, and Graphic Material in the Fiske Icelandic Collection: A Descriptive Catalogue*, Islandica XLVIII (Ithaca and London: Cornell University Press, 1994), Item 81, 34.

17. In a letter to Rafn of 4 June 1839, Bartlett says that he is about to circulate 2,000 copies. Fiske Icelandic Collection, Cornell University Library; Þórunn Sigurðardóttir, *Manuscript Material*, Item 81, 34.

18. Bartlett to Rafn, 9 April 1838, Fiske Icelandic Collection, Cornell University Library; Þórunn Sigurðardóttir, *Manuscript Material*, Item 81, 34.

19. Rafn to Bartlett, 1 June 1838, Fiske Icelandic Collection, Cornell University Library; Þórunn Sigurðardóttir, *Manuscript Material*, Item 81, 34.

20. George P. Marsh, *A Compendious Grammar of the Old-Northern or Icelandic language, compiled and translated from the Grammars of Rask* (Burlington, VT, 1838), ix.

21. Marsh to Rafn, 31 October 1833, Grøndal, *Breve*, 293–94. On Marsh's interest in Old Norse, see Richard Beck, "George P. Marsh and Old Icelandic Studies," *Scandinavian Studies* 17 (1943): 195–203; David Lowenthal, "G.P. Marsh and Scandinavian Studies," *Scandinavian Studies* 29 (1957): 41–52; and Lowenthal, *George Perkins Marsh, Versatile Vermonter* (New York: Columbia University Press, 1958), 52–55.

22. These, according to Marsh's Preface to the *Compendious Grammar* (iv), were *Vejledning til det Islandske eller gamle Nordiske Sprog* (1811); *Anvising till Isländskan eller Nordiska Fornspraaket* (1818); *Kortfattet Vejledning til det oldnordiske eller gamle islandske Sprog* (1832).

23. See Henry Schoolcraft, *Personal Memoirs of a Residence of Thirty Years with the Indian Tribes on the American Frontiers: with brief notices of passing events, facts and opinions, A.D. 1812 to A.D. 1842* (Philadelphia: Lippincott, Grambo and Co., 1851), 525–26.

24. As he comments in entries to his *Personal Memoirs* for 2 January 1839 ("I received a notice of my election as a member of the Royal Northern Antiquarian Society of Copenhagen, of which fact I had been previously notified by that Society. This Society shows us how the art of engraving may be brought in as an auxiliary to antiquarian letters; but it certainly undervalues American sagacity if it conjectures that such researches and speculations as those of Mr. Magnusen, on the Dighton Rock, and what it is fashionable now-a-days to call the NEWPORT RUIN, can satisfy the purposes of a sound investigation of the Anti-Columbian [sic] period of American history") and 21 February 21 1839 ("I wrote an article for Dr. Absalom Peter's Magazine, expressing my dissent from the very fanciful explanations of the Dighton Rock characters, as given by Mr. Magrusen [sic] in the first volume the Royal Society of Northern Antiquarians, published at Copenhagen"), *Personal Memoirs*, 630, 639.

25. "The Ante-Columbian History of America," *The American Biblical Repository* (April, 1839): 430–49.

26. "This gentleman has the quiet easy air of a man who has seen the world. His fine taste and acquirements have procured him a wide reputation." Schoolcraft, *Personal Memoirs*, 564.

27. Rafn to Longfellow, 26 November 1835, Grøndal, *Breve*, 176–77.

28. Rafn to Thomas Webb, 15 September 1838, Grøndal, *Breve*, 175.

29. "This gentleman lectured acceptably on this topic during the winter at Detroit. During these lectures, I gave him the skull of Etowigezhik, a Chippewa,

who was killed on Mr. Conner's farm about four or five years ago." *Personal Memoirs*, 594.

30. Joshua Toulmin Smith, *The Discovery of America by the Northmen in the Tenth Century* (London: Charles Tilt, 1839), 114–15.

31. Grøndal, *Breve*, 192.

32. Rafn to Fiske, November 10 1851; Rafn to Fiske, 8 June 1853. Fiske Icelandic Collection, Cornell University Library; Þórunn Sigurðardóttir, *Manuscript Material*, 98.

33. On the nineteenth-century perception that geology, philology, and jurisprudence were analogous disciplines, see Clare A. Simmons, " 'Iron-worded Proof': Victorian Identity and the Old English Language," in Leslie J. Workman, ed., *Medievalism in England, Studies in Medievalism* 4 (1992): 202–14 (209–10). See also Simmons, "Anglo-Saxonism, the Future, and the Franco-Prussian War," in Leslie J. Workman and Kathleen Verduin, eds., *Medievalism in England II, Studies in Medievalism* 7 (1996): 131–42 (133).

34. Marsh to Fiske, 3 April 1880, Fiske Icelandic Collection, Cornell University Library; Þórunn Sigurðardóttir, *Manuscript Material*, 92.

35. Lowenthal, "G.P. Marsh and Scandinavian Studies," 49–52.

36. Hilen, *Longfellow and Scandinavia*, 89.

37. See further Geraldine Barnes, "The Fireside Vikings and the 'Boy's Own' Vinland: Vinland in Popular English and American Literature (1841–1926)," in William F. Gentrup, ed., *Reinventing the Middle Ages and The Renaissance: Constructions of the Medieval and Early Modern Periods* (Turnhout: Brepols, 1998), 147–65 (149–52).

38. Longfellow to Rafn, 26 November 1835, Grøndal, *Breve*, 178.

39. Hilen, *Longfellow and Scandinavia*, 90.

40. Hilen, *Longfellow and Scandinavia*, "Longfellow's Journal" (15 September 1835), 141.

41. According to the entry in the *Catalogue of the Library of George Perkins Marsh* (Burlington: University of Vermont, 1892, 444) at the University of Vermont, the work was printed while Marsh was absent from Burlington, and "was disfigured by so many typographical errors that he never put it upon the market, though copies were freely given to scholars."

42. Anderson to Fiske, 22 May 1874, Fiske Icelandic Collection, Cornell University Library; Þórunn Sigurðardóttir, *Manuscript Material*, 68–9.

43. Horatio S. White, *Willard Fiske Life and Correspondence: A Biographical Study* (New York: Oxford University Press, 1925), 12.

44. See Lowenthal, "G.P. Marsh and Scandinavian Studies," 46–7.

45. George P. Marsh, *The Goths in New-England: A Discourse delivered at the anniversary of the Philomathesian Society of Middlebury College, August 15, 1843* (Middlebury, VT: Philomathesian Society, 1843), 11, 19. Despite Beck's claim to the contrary, the lecture itself reveals nothing of Marsh's "familiarity with Old Icelandic literature and his admiration for the Old Norse spirit" ("George P. Marsh and Old Icelandic Studies," 201).

46. J. Elliot Cabot, "Discovery of America by the Norsemen," *Massachusetts Quarterly Review* 6 (1849): 189–214 (189).

47. See Horsman, *Race and Manifest Destiny*, 75–6.

48. "The First Discovery of America," in *The Works of Charles Kingsley* (London, 1885), 237–62 (242).

49. See Eben Norton Horsford, *The Discovery of the Ancient City of Norumbega: A Communication to the President and Council of the American Geographical Society, at their special session in Watertown, November 21, 1889* (Cambridge, MA: n.p., n.d.).

50. See, for example, John Fraser, *America and the Patterns of Chivalry* (Cambridge: Cambridge University Press, 1982), 58–66, 78–83; Robin Fleming, "Picturesque History and the Medieval in Nineteenth-Century America," *The American Historical Review* 100 (1995): 1061–94.

51. Merton M. Sealts, Jr., ed., *The Journals and Miscellaneous Notebooks of Ralph Waldo Emerson* (Cambridge, MA: Belknap Press of Harvard University Press, 1965), 5:100; cf. 217, "Out of Druids & Berserkirs were Alfred & Shakspear made." On Emerson's ambivalent view of the Middle Ages, see Kathleen Verduin, "Medievalism and the Mind of Emerson," in Bernard Rosenthal and Paul E. Szarmach, eds., *Medievalism in American Culture: Papers of the Eighteenth Annual Conference of the Center for Medieval and Early Renaissance Studies* (Binghamton, NY: Medieval and Renaissance Texts and Studies, 1989), 129–50.

52. *The Collected Works of Ralph Waldo Emerson*, I, *Nature, Addresses, and Lectures*, introd. by Robert E. Spiller; text established by Alfred R. Ferguson (Cambridge, MA: Belknap Press of Harvard University Press, 1971), 61.

53. "Ideal border-ruffians those old Icelanders seem to have been – such hacking and hewing and killing, and such respect for all the forms of law!" James Russell Lowell, "To Charles Eliot Norton," 7 August 1861, in Charles Eliot Norton, ed., *Letters of James Russell Lowell*, 2 vols. (1893; repr. New York: Harper & Brothers, 1977), 1: 312.

54. Anonymous review of Benjamin De Costa, *The Pre-Columbian Discovery of America by the Northmen: Illustrated by Translations from the Icelandic Sagas* (Albany, NY, 1868), *The Nation* 8 (1869): 53.

55. J.P. Maclean, *A Critical Examination of the Evidences Adduced to Establish the Theory of the Norse Discovery of America* (Chicago: American Antiquarian Office, 1892), 52–3.

56. See Aaron Goodrich, *A History of the Character and Achievements of the So-Called Christopher Columbus* (New York: D. Appleton and Company, 1874).

57. On Anderson's lifelong championing of Norwegian-American culture, see Lloyd Hustvedt, *Rasmus Bjørn Anderson: Pioneer Scholar* (Northfield, MN: The Norwegian-American Historical Association, 1966).

58. Rasmus B. Anderson, *America Not Discovered by Columbus. An Historical Sketch of the Discovery of America by the Norsemen in the Tenth Century* (Chicago: S.C. Griggs and Company, 1874). In his autobiography, Anderson

says that he gave the work "a thoroughly sensational and defiant title. . . . not to detract in any way from the great honor to the Italian navigator, but to insist that he did not discover, but only rediscover the western world." *Life Story of Rasmus B. Anderson, written by himself, with assistance of Albert O. Barron*, 2nd edn., revised (Madison, WI: Rasmus B. Anderson, 1917), 210.

59. Einar Haugen, "Wisconsin Pioneers in Scandinavian Studies: Anderson and Olson, 1875–1931," *Wisconsin Magazine of History* (Autumn 1950): 29–36 (31).

60. *Life Story of Rasmus B. Anderson*, 276.

61. "There is nothing specifically original about it." Anderson to Fiske, 25 July 1874, Fiske Icelandic Collection, Cornell University Library; Þórunn Sigurðardóttir, *Manuscript Material*, 68–9.

62. Haugen, "Wisconsin Pioneers," 31.

63. "I am anxiously looking for a letter from you in reply to my last" (26 March 1875); "I suppose you are too busy" (30 April 1875); "And still I do not hear from you!" (14 May 1875); ". . . your profound silence during the present year" (23 October 1875). Anderson to Fiske, Fiske Icelandic Collection, Cornell University Library; Þórunn Sigurðardóttir, *Manuscript Material*, 68–9.

64. Anderson to Fiske, 15 January 1875, Fiske Icelandic Collection, Cornell University Library; Þórunn Sigurðardóttir, *Manuscript Material*, 68–9.

65. Anderson to Fiske, 25 July 1874, Fiske Icelandic Collection, Cornell University Library; Þórunn Sigurðardóttir, *Manuscript Material*, 68–9.

66. See Hustvedt, *Rasmus Bjørn Anderson*, 98–102.

67. Cited by Frantzen, *Desire for Origins*, 170.

68. To contradict the view, expressed in an 1887 article by D.K. Dodge, that Scandinavian immigrants were reluctant to assimilate, Albert E. Egge quotes the statement in the Minnesota newspaper, the *Northfield Independent* (February 9, 1888), that: "Of all from over the sea now coming to us they Americanize most quickly." See "Scandinavian Studies in the United States," *Modern Language Notes* 3 (1888): 131–35 (134).

69. Anderson, *America Not Discovered by Columbus*, 107.

70. See George T. Flom, *A History of Scandinavian Studies in American Universities, together with a bibliography*, Iowa Studies in Language and Literature 11 (Iowa City: The State University of Iowa, 1907), 15–20.

71. Haugen, "Wisconsin Pioneers," 31. Hustvedt notes that the course was optional and "open only to sophomores studying modern classics in the college of letters" (*Rasmus Bjørn Anderson*, 96).

72. Haugen, "Wisconsin Pioneers," 36.

73. Hustvedt, *Rasmus Bjørn Anderson*, 97.

74. Flom, *A History of Scandinavian Studies*, 6.

75. Haugen, "Wisconsin Pioneers," 31.

76. Haugen, "Wisconsin Pioneers," 36.

77. Flom, *A History of Scandinavian Studies*, 9.

78. W.H. Carpenter, "Recent Work in Old Norse," *American Journal of Philology* 3 (1882): 77–80 (77).

79. W.H. Carpenter, "A Fragment of Old Icelandic," *Modern Language Notes* 3 (1888): 118–23 (118).

80. Flom, *A History of Scandinavian Studies*, 10, 13.

81. *A History of Scandinavian Studies*, 39–40.

82. See Andrew Wawn, "The Spirit of 1892: Saga-Steads and Victorian Philology," *Saga-Book of the Viking Society* 23 (1992): 213–52 (217).

83. According to Flom's account of Scandinavian at Columbia, "The study of the Scandinavian languages was here introduced by Professor C. Sprague Smith, who gave a course in Danish in 1880–1881." *A History of Scandinavian Studies*, 10.

84. *The Pre-Columbian Discovery of America by the Northmen*, 2nd edn. (Albany, NY: Joel Munsell's Sons, 1890), 58.

85. *Life Story of Rasmus B. Anderson*, 190.

86. *Life Story of Rasmus B. Anderson*, 190.

87. On the "Norsemen Memorial" committee, see Rasmus Anderson, *America Not Discovered by Columbus*, 2nd edn. (Chicago: S.C. Griggs and Company, 1883), 31–32.

88. See *The Boston Evening Transcript*, 29 October 1887, 8.

89. Arthur Middleton Reeves, *The Finding of Wineland the Good. The History of the Icelandic Discovery of America, edited and translated from the earliest records* (London: Henry Frowde, 1890).

90. For a list of reviews of *The Finding of Wineland the Good*, see Halldór Hermannsson, *The Northmen in America*, Islandica II (Ithaca and New York: Cornell University Library, 1909), 68–9.

91. Review by "C.R.M.", *Proceedings of the Royal Geographical Society*, n.s. 13 (1891): 127–28 (128).

92. "The Vinland Voyages," *Journal of the American Geographic Society* 24 (1892): 510–35.

93. *A History of Scandinavian Studies*, 45.

94. "My interest in ethnological, philological and antiquarian subjects has not abated from my present position; on the contrary, I feel a greater desire than every to pursue my investigations in these sciences." Bartlett to Rafn, 1 August 1851, Grøndal, *Breve*, 190.

95. Catharine Lorillard Wolfe commissioned a stained glass window for "Vinland," her home in Newport, Rhode Island, from (William) Morris & Co. in the early 1880s. Its design is preserved in seven cartoons by Edward Burne-Jones. The one held by the Carlisle Art Gallery is entitled "The Voyage to Vinland the Good." See further *The Collected Letters of William Morris*, ed. by Norman Kelvin, 4 vols. (Princeton: Princeton University Press, 1984–1996), 2: 82–83, 422–45; *Burne-Jones: The paintings, graphic and decorative work of Sir Edward Burne-Jones 1833–98* (The Arts Council of Great Britain, 1975), 70.

96. For example, William Cullen Bryant and Sydney Howard Gay's *A*

*Popular History of the United States* (London: Sampson Low, Marston, Searle & Rivington, 1876), 35–63.

97. I am grateful for the constructive comments of Tom Shippey and Andrew Wawn during the writing of this paper; for the assistance, over many years, of Patrick Stevens, Curator of the Fiske Icelandic Collection at Cornell University; and to the staff in the Archives and Rare Book Collection of the University of Wisconsin at Madison.

# Enthusiast or Philologist? Professional Discourse and the Medievalism of Frederick James Furnivall[1]

## Richard Utz

In 1952, in a short but spirited essay for the journal *Essays and Studies*, Beatrice White begins her appreciation of Frederick James Furnivall's achievements with the following statement:

> I want to write about F. J. Furnivall's work for the best reason in the world, because I like it. I want to write about it because the glowing centre of his *literary enthusiasms* was his Elizabethan studies. I want to write about it particularly because I think it a pity that those qualities of *breadth, humility*, and *humanity*, characteristic of the more *genial and expansive scholarship* of his age, are, in these days of intensive *specialisation*, being danger-ously reduced to fit the increasingly limited scope of both field and vision.[2] (my emphases)

This introductory paragraph contains a commonplace complaint about the proverbially reductive specialisation of twentieth-century scholarship and yearns back to the Victorian days when someone like Furnivall would produce "genial" and "expansive" work. The paragraph also names as the basis for Furnivall's successes something vaguely termed "his literary enthusiasms." This essay will go back to the origins of the term "enthu-siasm" and confront it with what seems to be its eternal cognitive oppo-site, the professional discursive practice known as "philology." The goal of this return to the origins of both terms is to shed some light on the modern antagonism (deplored in White's statement) between a more broadly defined, not necessarily academic production and reception and the exclusively academic, objectivist study of fictional texts. In a final step, these observations will be linked to the different appreciations Frederick James Furnivall received by nineteenth- and twentieth-century German and Anglophone medievalists.

Alfred N. Whitehead once observed that the entire European philosophical tradition could be described as "a series of footnotes to Plato."[3] Whitehead's remark certainly applies to the origins of the antagonism between poetry and philosophy. Plato, much better known for his strict banning of poets from political responsibility in the *Republic*, orchestrates a discussion of this issue in his early dialogue, *Ion*, in a more conciliatory manner, as a disputation between philosopher and rhapsode.[4] Ion has just returned from Epidauros, where he has won first prize in the competition among the rhapsodes. Socrates first congratulates Ion on his exceptional skills (530b5–c6). Ion is pleased because he thinks of himself as the best rhapsode and therefore also as the best interpreter of Homer's texts. His authority is challenged, however, as soon as Socrates inquires if Ion can equally well interpret other poets. The rhapsode has to admit that his skills are limited to interpreting Homer alone. Socrates immediately proceeds to conclude that even Ion's understanding of Homer lacks the proper foundations. When Ion can speak about Homer at all, it is not an "Art," i.e. not knowledge of the subject matter (*techne*), which is responsible, but a divine power, which "magnet-like" captivates poet, rhapsode, and audience: Because the poets speak these beautiful texts as individuals "filled with the spirit" or "enthusiastic ones" (*entheoi ontes*) and "possessed ones" (*katechomenoi*) they are "not in a rational state of mind" (533c9–534a7).[5] Socrates's double-edged compliment, namely that the poets and rhapsodes speak from inspiration and delusion, makes Ion feel uncomfortable. He would prefer it if his talents could be viewed as a part of general rational thought. Homer, so he reasons, had depicted numerous areas of knowledge and techniques, such as chariot-racing, medicine, arithmetic, fishing, and warfare, so that the rhapsode was knowledgeable in these areas. Socrates rejects this. The chariot-racer knows most about chariot-racing, the doctor most about medicine, and the military strategist most about warfare, etc.; every discipline demanded knowledge only known to the specialist. Only that specialist was in a position to judge if anything could be learned from Homer about one of the *technai*. Consequently, Ion will have to be content with being looked upon as a "divine man" whose presentation of Homer's epics brings joy to everyone.

According to Heinz Schlaffer, Plato's dialogue confronts two ways of thinking each of which represents a distinctive period in Greek culture:

poetry, represented by the rhapsode Ion, is faced with knowledge, represented by Socrates the philosopher.[6] It is not personal vanity which makes Ion claim that as a rhapsode he knows everything, that he should even count as an army general because he had learned about military strategy from Homer (541b1–5). It was an accepted concept in Ancient Greece to believe that poetry taught knowledge. Socrates's ironic praise cites this *communis opinio* at the beginning of the dialogue in order to deconstruct it later. Knowledge contained in poetry had become questionable ever since a knowledge independent of poetry had gradually evolved. Plato demonstrates this in two steps:

1. For the various tasks and solutions of the *technai* a specific human skill is necessary, which would only be confused by the kind of enthusiasm which is the precondition of poetry. Thus, Plato distinguishes between the appearance of knowledge in poetry and the practical science on the basis of the same distinction which is still valid for the modern sciences.

2. The methodological progression of the Socratic questions and distinctions in *Ion* provides the best example to evidence the independence of theoretical knowledge (*episteme*), which searches for truth (*aletheia*), from the poetic knowledge which has its source in higher powers and operates through unconscious forces. Even if no knowledge can be gained from poetry, knowledge about poetry is possible. As rhapsodes are only interpreters of interpreters (535a9), it is the philosopher's task to explain the now unphilosophical essence of poetry. Exactly because he is not possessed by poetic enthusiasm, he is in a position to analyze it. The poet and his rhapsode are incapable of transmitting to others the special meaning of their works because they have only been inspired for one individual work and perceive others only dimly (532b8–c4). In the *Apology*, Plato has Socrates express his observation that poets are the least knowledgeable about poetry:

> [T]he poets did not compose their poems through wisdom, but by nature, and . . . they were inspired like seers and soothsayers. For these say many fine things, but know nothing of what they say. It seemed to me that poets experienced something similar; at the same time I noticed that because of their poetry, they regarded themselves as the wisest of men in other respects also, which they were not (22b8–c6).[7]

A special profession whose task it would have been to speak about poetry did not yet exist; however, the basis for such a profession is implicit in

Plato's judgment that non-poets, because rational thinkers, knew more about poetry than the poets whose enthusiasm had renderend them productive, but not wise and understanding. While the Greek genres of poetry could be experienced according to their specific occasions, themes, and forms, Plato's term of poetics (*poietike*) is a philosophical abstraction. "The whole" of poetry can only be illuminated by a non-poet. Plato never produces such a complete philosophical lore of poetics. He is only interested in demarcating his own, new discursive practice, philosophy, against the claims and incursions of poetry, an intention which he would later guarantee by banning poets and rhapsodes from his perfect state. Only his students, from Aristotle to the Alexandrian philologists, would elaborate Plato's theoretical positions on the rational explication of poetry to a discipline of its own.

The perspective which this new scientific discipline will have to take towards poetry is implied by the very circumstances governing the conversation between the philosopher and the rhapsode. Had Socrates actually seen Ion's performance of the Homeric songs at Epidauros, he, too, would have been fascinated. Now, however, they are in Athens, in the middle of prosaic and quotidian events, and speak in prose about poetry whose magic is ineffective. In this location epic narration does not possess and control the imagination, but the thoughts are allowed to roam freely and can be used for the exchange and examination of arguments: reflection about poetry demands a geographic and temporary distance from it. If one wanted to extrapolate, one could say that this scene already implies the ideal situation of the scientific treatment of poetry, as it was to become reality later in Alexandria; poetry then would no longer be performed by rhapsodes, in the theatre, as a processional song or during a feast but now existed in reified form, as a book, open to the distanced (and thus rational) view of the researcher. Poetry would become literature, to be encountered in, e.g., the great library of Alexandria, a building which still retained the metaphoric memory to poetic enthusiasm as its name, Museion, but which provided an institutional setting where disinterested, historical, philological, and thus unenthusiastic study of literature took place. In the late eighteenth and the nineteenth centuries, when philology in the Classical and Modern languages and literatures became institutionalised at the German universities, scholars would take this metaphoric distance one step further when they published their critical editions and interpretive essays in journals called *Deutsches Museum für Geschichte, Literatur, Kunst und Alterthumsforschung, Rheinisches Museum für Philologie,* or *Archiv für das Studium der neueren Sprachen und Literaturen.*[8]

Plato's confrontation of Greek philosophy and poetry paradigmatically foreshadows the altercation between poetry and science in later centuries and these centuries' specific cultural conditions. In a modified form a quite similar discussion would take place at the transition from the Middle Ages to Early Modernity, even if the critique then was not directed against the claims of poetry, but against the poetic carelessness of scholastic pseudo-science which venerated religious, poetic, and scientific texts as authorities of equal import.[9] And, in the second half of the nineteenth century, German philologists were to negotiate similar issues in their attempts to distinguish their own work as professional scholars from that of privateering colleagues in other countries.

Plato's *Ion* does not answer the anthropological question about the cultural functions of poetic discourse because such an answer would challenge his own contemporaries' prevalent religious convictions. Nevertheless, by intimately linking poetry to an enthusiasm which is divinely inspired, but nevertheless incapable of producing truth, Plato has opened a Pandora's box. Implicitly, the *Ion* contains exactly the questions the answers to which would bring about poetics and philology as disciplines of their own. More importantly, Plato's problematisations would only be answered when a knowledge of fictions had evolved so that a third element between truth and lie could be acknowledged and the licence for aesthetic experience would be given. That poetry is fictitious becomes obvious only since there is a definition of truth different from that which the poets pass off as true. In this respect, Plato's philosophy is a precondition for rendering conscious the relation between poetry and truth. Poetic enthusiasm was required to undergo philosophical critique so that its god-given irrationality could be revealed as the substance of aesthetic mimesis; of course with the consequence that the divine part of this enthusiasm was de-emphasised into a mere metaphor. Only in this humanised form could poetry become the subject of secular knowledge.[10]

The distinction between philosophical truth and poetic "truth" is also the logical version of a historical difference. Socrates, the philosopher, represents the most recent form of knowledge; Ion, the rhapsode, the oldest. Their dialogue is also to be understood as an altercation of the contemporary consciousness with its own cultural past. Because Homer's epics originated hundreds of years ago, their meaning has become strange so that the mere repetition of the words they contain (*epe*) no longer suffices, but the interpretation of the meaning (*dianoia*) has to help out (530b5–c6). Ion wants to be both singer and interpreter and does not notice that both capacities originate from different situations and demand different intellectual skills. As soon as the unreflected tradition of poetry becomes problematic and the historical distance between the origins and the later representation of poetry has become a conscious one, the productive poet and the reproductive singer will need as a third specialist the critically authenticating and interpreting philologist.

Anyone perusing current critical editions of Homer will realise that their lists of authentication and commentary still begin with the *grammatici antiqui*, indicating that the continuity between the first Greek philologists and their modern counterparts survived the rise and fall of countries and empires, in some cases even the destruction of the texts they were commenting. It is this very continuity of philological work through the centuries which allows us to relate the observations made so far to Frederick James Furnivall (1825–1910) and the reception of his work in different national and academic traditions.

Frederick James Furnivall was born at Egham, Surrey, in 1825. He was educated at a number of private schools near his home before spending a year of pre-university study (1841–42) at the recently founded University College, London. From there, he went on to Trinity Hall, Cambridge, where he received a B.A. in Mathematics in 1846. He then returned to London to study Law, was called to the bar at Gray's Inn in 1849, and established himself as a conveyancer. During this period of social and political upheaval in British history, Furnivall joined a group of passionate social reformers, the Christian Socialists led by John Malcolm Ludlow and Frederick Denison Maurice and, together with them, "[h]e threw himself with ardour into labour agitation, took the chair at public meetings, spoke in the streets, presided over a protest meeting in a railway arch, even sold his books to give a substantial sum to the strikers."[11] Like John Ruskin, he supported London's Working Men's College (founded in 1854), teaching English Grammar and Literature for five nights a week for the first ten years of the school's existence. Fascinated by the application of "scientific" methodologies in the humanities, Furnivall joined the Philological Society in 1847, became the society's secretary only six years later, and continued in this position throughout the rest of his life.

In 1858, he embarked upon the project which marked his entrance into the realm of scholarly endeavors: He convinced the Philological Society to undertake the publication of a "New English Dictionary" based on historical principles, held the editorship of the dictionary from 1861 to 1878, and remained one of the most indefatigable contributors after Sir James Murray had taken over as editor. The dictionary "was for him a mission that replaced the Christianity he had rejected (he had become an agnostic in the late 1850s), an act of reverence to the English nation and its history as embodied in its language."[12] In order to supply the dictionary project with reliable entries from historical sources as well as to render accessible to his contemporaries the original treasures of early English texts, Furnivall went on to found the Early English Text Society in 1864 (later followed by the Ballad Society and the Chaucer Society [1868], the New Shakspere Society [1873], the Browning Society and the Wyclif Society [1881], and the Shelley Society [1886]). For his encyclopaedic plan of the EETS he not only succeeded in enlisting many of the most famous national and international scholars, but – often assisted by students from the Working Men's College and other volunteers – edited 39 volumes himself, including *Hoccleve's Works*, *The Fifty Earliest English Wills in the Court of Probate*, *The Digby Plays*, the *Babees Book*, *Thynne's Animadversions*, the *Tale of Beryn*, the *Six-Text Print of Chaucer's Canterbury Tales*, and the posthumously published *Hali Meidenhad*.[13]

Recent Anglophone assessments of Furnivall's impressive foundational role in the development of English Studies agree that he should be thought of "more as a surveyor or engineer than as a scholar. He was like a Victorian explorer or empire builder, mapping out territories, building railways and bridges, improvising, facilitating access, preparing the way for others."[14] From the perspective of contemporary scholarship, he is said never to have "*edited* anything," but at the same time he is credited with making "all modern editions possible" and with being "the giant upon whose shoulders we all stand."[15] These current assessments mirror a conspicuous dichotomy of judgment which was first established by German Anglicists during Furnivall's own lifetime.

A comparison between the appreciation of Furnivall in German and Anglophone publications in the nineteenth and the early twentieth centuries yields revealing results. While most of the latter ones feel they can characterise Furnivall's efforts for the Early English Text Society and other projects as those of a "philologist," not a single German source employs the term. Although his German friends and colleagues praise him for facilitating access to manuscripts, for being a friendly host to them and to scholars from all over the world,[16] the title "philologist" is withheld from him. This is astonishing when one reviews the chorus of praise heaped upon Furnivall and his EETS by German scholars: indeed, German philologists were the first to take note of Furnivall's organisation. In a letter to Henry Bradshaw, written in 1868, Furnivall complains: "The master of the Charterhouse School said the other day to a boy, 'What is this Early English Text Society? I've never heard of it in England, but I see it in every German book I take up now. Ask your father if he can tell me anything about it.' "[17] Both Julius Zupitza, first professor (ordinarius) of English philology at the University of Vienna, and Richard Wülcker, the founding editor of *Anglia: Zeitschrift für englische Philologie*, underline the importance of the EETS for rendering possible the great increase in the scientific study of English in Germany in the final third of the nineteenth century.[18] Friedrich Kluge, Lorenz Morsbach, Franz Heinrich Stratmann, and Eduard Mätzner similarly acknowledge the influence of the EETS editions for their grammars, readers, and dictionaries.[19] And Bernhard ten Brink's *History of English Literature* (3 vols., 1877–93) could not have been written without the tireless labors of Furnivall and his collaborators, a fact which ten Brink acknowledges by dedicating the work to "Dr. Furnivall" who had received an honorary doctorate not from a British institution, but from the university of Berlin.[20] Furnivall's own love for everything German or Teutonic, from his studies of German at University College, London, to his rejection of the Latinate "Preface" in favor of the Germanic "Foreword," and his general admiration for German scholarship, made it even easier for his German colleagues to appreciate him.[21]

The reason why German scholars deny Furnivall the title of "philologist" has as much to do with their own, gradually narrowing national definition of this term as with the nature and motivations of Furnivall's work itself. In the course of the nineteenth century, and based upon (and in competition with) the successes of German Classical philologists, German scholars developed philology, the science-like study of historical texts in the national languages as a specifically German virtue, a research methodology at which Germans attempted to outshine their colleagues in any other country. This first comparative and patriotic and then increasingly nationalistic and narrowly formal process of "philologisation"[22] was coeval with Germany's late unification as a nation state, and the post-1871 German governments deliberately supported the institutionalisation of the new philologies to a point where, e.g., the contest for predominance between German and French Romance philologists or between German, British, and Danish philologists in the area of *Beowulf* studies evolved into veritable "arms races."[23] While the competition between German and British scholars was initially friendlier, German professors miss no occasion to stress the primacy and superiority of German philological scholarship on the one hand and the antiquarianism and amateurism of their English counterparts on the other.[24] In 1929, Arnold Schröer, professor of English Philology at Cologne University, described the relationship between both countries' medieval scholars from the 1840s on as one of close collaboration in what he calls the "spring of English literary and language science":

> How gratefully the English *enthusiasts* welcomed the old and young German academics and were ready to lend them a hand,[25] full of joy that the "learned doctors" copied and edited their manuscripts. The English did not yet have an organised science in this field; everything was private initiative; the most astonishing and admirable thing was, however, the idealism and the energy with which these *enthusiasts* were capable of influencing the public interest. Thus, they received the means to publish the literary and linguistic treasures of English history via the founding of "Societies".[26] (my emphases)

While Schröer acknowledges that the English commonsensical hesitancy to produce "doctored" or "sophisticated texts" had a conservative influence on the conjecture-loving efforts of German Anglicists, his statement also reveals the national pride of German philologists and the importance their philological training had for their professional identity. Even more interestingly, Schröer confronts German philology and the work of Zupitza and ten Brink with the enthusiasm of Furnivall. He quotes his own diary of the first encounter with Furnivall in 1881: "F. is not a philologist according to our strict, German terms, but an amiable man who seems to be independently wealthy, has texts printed, and is thus the right person to be founder and director of the New-Shakespere-Society and honorary secretary of the Philological Society, etc."[27] And concerning Richard Morris, who edited – often in collaboration with German scholars – a sizeable number of Old and Middle English texts for the EETS, Schröer muses "how lamentable it is that these Englishmen have no strict philological education; they are kind amateurs, often of astonishing versatility and considerable knowledge."[28] Schröer's binary opposition of an "enthusiastic" and a "philological" treatment of medieval texts underlines the work ethic of the professional German university scholar. He employs in his memoir the same specialised use of both terms which the Greek philosophers after Plato used to distinguish between the inspired but irrational poet or rhapsode and the distanced and rational philosopher, whose critique of enthusiasm prepares the way for the critical Alexandrian philologist. Conspicuously, Schröer uses "enthusiasts" once again in his essay when describing the efforts of a group of Furnivall's students in putting on a performance of *Hamlet*.[29] The German scholar has no trouble enjoying the performance and praising Furnivall and his players for their efforts. However, just as the philosopher Socrates distances himself from Ion, the possessed rhapsode, Schröer carefully dissociates his own critical knowledge and perspective of the written text of a play from the undistanced "enthusiasm" he witnesses among his English hosts. Quite obviously, the performance could never become part of his scholarly work.

The same distinction also informs Beatrice White's praise of Furnivall which was cited at the beginning of this essay. White, writing in 1952, when the Anglo-American academic community had abandoned the exclusively philological investigation of historical texts which it had borrowed from nineteenth-century German universities,[30] speaks of Furnivall's "genial" work, invoking just another term which implies a source of knowledge from beyond the realm of purely human rational thought. From White's vantage point, the too narrowly scientific and positivistic academic tradition of philology had brought about an undesirably disinterested methodology which left no room for observing the subjective, aesthetic, or socio-political meanings of literary texts. For German scholars in the late nineteenth and the early twentieth centuries, on the other hand, there was no doubt that Furnivall was lacking in the formal requirements for what they considered philological endeavors. Alois Brandl, who greatly appreciated Furnivall's work abstractly speaking, carefully avoids calling his fatherly friend a philologist when stating that "[a]ny one who wanted advice or an introduction, in order to do better work in the wide field of English philology, could command his knowledge, his time, and his influence with his friends." While he credits Furnivall with "the flame of. . . enthusiasm for the older literature," commends his "enthusiasm for. . . old writers," and praises him for "instinctively" guessing "the necessity for obtaining all available manuscripts of a given work, printing from the best, and carefully sifting the errors of the various groups" (and all of that without "having ever been to a seminar"), Brandl cannot bring himself – even in his contribution to the Festschrift for the English scholar – to co-opt Furnivall as a full member of his own discursive practice and profession: "Furnivall was not a philologist of thorough linguistic training, I should not even care to assert too positively that he could conjugate an Anglo-Saxon verb."[31]

However, the term "enthusiasm" as a characterisation of Furnivall's work is not exclusive to German philologists. While the latter tend to use it to distinguish their own objectivist approaches from that of the private English amateur, most of Furnivall's Anglo-American colleagues, even as recently as 1995 (!), also describe his work more often as that of an "enthusiast" than that of a philologist.[32] And Furnivall himself is reported to have said, to Roman Dyboski: "I never cared a bit for philology; my chief aim has been throughout to illustrate the social condition of the English people in the past."[33] This open admission of "guilt" to the man who was to become the founding father of English philology in Poland[34] and of the primarily social and national intentions of his Medievalism and Elizabethanism explains the true motivation of Furnivall's work. If Furnivall shared with German and other philologists many of the essential attitudes which were part of the archive of philological discourse in the late nineteenth century (tenacity, industry, self-denial, nationalism, painstaking care, orientation toward facts, etc.), for him the political and social functions of his work remained in the foreground. It is because of these extra-academic goals that Renate Haas has likened Furnivall to Jacob Grimm who, similarly, showed a "certain neglect of poetic refinement" and was "more interested in content than form."[35] Haas states:

> For Furnivall linguistic and literary studies remained – as they had been for Jacob Grimm, especially before 1848 – part of a broadly conceived history of culture. In this larger context, philology still revealed its old connections not only with history but other disciplines such as theology and jurisprudence. . . . It also more pronouncedly retained emancipatory functions, whereas under the harsh repressions of post-revolutionary Germany it was acceleratingly developing into a highly specialised and rigid pseudo-science.[36]

Thus, when Furnivall made conscious decisions to abandon quality control for some of his EETS editions because he was hastening to make more original texts available to the general public, especially the working classes and women, he could not have been more different from someone like his good German friend Julius Zupitza who was acceptable to the Austrian government precisely because "he is entirely dedicated to his philological studies" ("welcher. . . ausschließlich seinen philologischen Studien lebt"),[37] a characterisation in a letter of recommendation which was meant to assure the authorities that this candidate was not likely to exploit the newly created and thus greatly prestigious position as professor at the University of Vienna for the purpose of political agitation.[38] Furnivall believed that direct access to medieval texts such as *Piers Plowman's Creed*, "The Wife of Bath's Tale," or the *English Guilds*, and to these texts' alternative ways of living and thinking, might be powerful tools to bring about political and cultural change. Not unlike the rhapsode Ion, he held that the knowledge contained in historical texts had a cognitive immediacy and superior capacity to educate, in Furnivall's case to educate toward tolerance and fairness and against prejudice, selfish class-thinking and the overvaluing of external forms. Building on the now only metaphoric belief that the poet or rhapsode conveyed a higher truth, he was convinced that original poetic and historical texts were capable of producing superior insight and direction. By making these texts available to a large audience, he wholeheartedly embraced the role of the enthusiast, a role which – just like Jacob Grimm's "wild philology"[39] – was bound to meet with criticism in a modernist academic context where historical texts had become the objects of a supposedly politically disinterested, scientific investigation, but which transformed the lives of numerous non-academic readers and collaborators. Contemporary students of strictly philological research perusing the *OED*, for example, are rarely cognisant of the fact that students of the London Working Men's College had some part in it, including ordinary women such as "Lizzy" (Eleanor Nickel) Dalziel, first a "lady's maid," who became Furnivall's wife in 1862, or a young woman named Teena Rochfort-Smith. Similarly, only few medievalists consulting the volumes of the EETS or the old Chaucer Society will know that their secretary, W.A. Dalziel, came from the Working Men's College or that textual variants they may be examining were collated by the daughter of a German exile who would not only reinterpret the world but change it, Eleanor Marx.[40] And scarcely anyone will remember how Furnivall's enthusiastic encouragement assisted the lamentably few lady scholars, such as Caroline Spurgeon and Edith Rickert, who were struggling to gain admission to the male-dominated profession. As Beatrice White has stated, Furnivall was a forward-looking "feminist" who thought that Cambridge University was "preposterously antiquated in withholding degrees" from women "when they could beat men at their own game."[41] It would take German philologists more than four decades until they mustered – not always enthusiastically – some support for the women joining their field of specialty.[42]

White and Haas's fascination with Furnivall's refreshing educational, social, and political engagement and his unconventional lifestyle is in many ways a reaction against a heavily formalised and highly inflexible philological tradition which, after bringing about almost 100 years of unbroken progress in Classical and modern scholarship, had become "damningly unambitious,"[43] offered students, like Dante's Ulysses, "only the mountain of Purgatory – Grimm's Law, Verner's Law, Grassmann's Law – rising in successive terraces of horror,"[44] and had widened the distance scholars needed between themselves and their literary texts into an often unbridgeable chasm. Beginning with Friedrich Nietzsche (himself a professor of Classical philology) and moving toward contemporary theorists like Jacques Derrida, the philosophical and then philological distinction between literary and scientific writing and knowledge has been under increasing attack by those who advocate – in the end – a reversal of the development Plato and the Greek philologists began, an academic discourse in which science and philosophy would again become more like poetry, just as poetry once upon a time was considered to convey knowledge. Most recently, radical voices, such as Bernard Cerquiglini, have encouraged medieval scholars to think of the typical philologist as a dinosaur of sorts, a person of pre-conceived and unchangeable ideas, a "Monsieur Procruste, Philologue"[45] who would attempt to normalise variants, dialectal traits, copying errors, deliberate scribal or authorial changes, only to establish the abstractive ideal of the modern critical edition. Following Cerquiglini, a small group of North American scholars, the so-called "New Philologists" or "New Medievalists," have suggested – although somewhat vaguely – that medievalists should "return to the medieval origins of philology, to its roots in manuscript culture"[46] and have published a number of works in which they condescendingly critique the efforts of nineteenth-century scholars whose unexamined positivism is said to have inhibited dialogue between medievalists and specialists in other fields. Instead, they want to be led in their own efforts by

> an *enthusiastic* sense of wonder at the discovery of how familiar the Middle Ages seem within the context of the contemporary discourses of cultural criticism, and thus a sense of relief that those who studied medieval texts are not as irrelevant to the present as many of our own teachers had hoped we would be.[47]
>
> (my emphasis)

Or, following Paul Zumthor, the "New Philologists" propose to recognise the place and effect of the subject in scholarly enterprises:

> Along the way, I will not apologise for speaking in the first person. This is not a stylistic device, but an intellectual necessity. . . . What counts is the possibility of identifying in an emblematic way the social function fulfilled by that individual (that is, by his work) as part of a given project, a given task, a given field of thought or research to which events (for a want of natural inclination) attached him for a fairly long time. In this way, the project, the task, or the field may be considered through the mediation of a person, that is, otherwise than in the library.[48]

Both quotes are indicative of the attempts by the practitioners of the "New Philology" to reunite the philological study of manuscripts with the poetic enthusiasm of the investigating subject who would no longer remain in the self-sought isolation of his museion/library, but make medieval texts and theories about the medieval Other more accessible and relevant to wider audiences. While it is problematic that the "New Philologists" condemn almost all of nineteenth and early twentieth-century (Old) philologists and, thus, have created a convenient "straw man, a fictitious creature that has never lived before and does not live now,"[49] who would deserve as thorough a process of historicising as the medieval texts themselves, their critique of some of the more fossilised philological methods might well be helpful in rethinking many of the elaborate scholarly practices by which medievalists habitually investigate and teach "dead" languages and cultures. Allen Frantzen, another scholar who has recently asked for a more conscious negotiation of the processes by which the most abstract and impersonal-sounding traditional methodologies in Medieval Studies ". . . incorporate and instantiate the beliefs and preferences of persons," explains:

> Recognising the theoretical bases on which those disciplines rest requires that we examine their history and relate them in new ways not only to the cultures they abstract for purposes of academic inquiry but to the persons who presided over those abstractions. The wish of contemporary critics to find a place from which to speak, therefore, is also a desire to identify traditional criticism as a place from which others have been speaking. As we trace a discipline to the scholars who presided over its foundation, we move from a scholarly system to the personal status of those who created it out of the fabric of their own history and social experience.[50]

If these recent voices and the numerous publications in the field of medievalism are evidence of a current, conscious reevaluation of the process by which the study of medieval languages and cultures evolved, an investigation of the career and work of Frederick James Furnivall as well his reception at different times and by different national traditions provides insight into some of the various elements influencing modern and postmodern attitudes toward medieval scholarship. Situated at the exact moment in history when German and other philologists radicalised and institutionalised at European and North American universities what Plato and the Greek philologists had initiated, Furnivall's keen interest in science-like methods and facts based on comparative methods made him a natural ally of philologists. At the same time, his refusal to join the ranks of an increasingly professionalised philology which demanded the full-time, disinterested pursuit of knowledge (and truth) for its own sake branded him as an amateur or privateer who dared esteem regular physical exercise (e.g. rowing) and political activism (e.g., the education of the working classes and women) at least as highly as some of his scholarly endeavors. It is this refusal to take a clear position in the more than 2000-year-old altercation between the cognitive enterprises of enthusiasm and philology which kept nineteenth-century German scholars from honoring him with the term "Philologe" and to envision him instead, "among the hosts of books and pamphlets and editions under his name," like "a soldier in battle with a legion of conquered foes around him."[51] And it is the same strict and scientistic philological categorising, which spread from the Valhallas of nineteenth-century German universities to research universities all over the world, which made Derek Pearsall, in the most recent essay on Furnivall, describe him as "hardly a scholar at all," but a "simple-minded *enthusiast*" (my emphasis).[52]

All things considered, Furnivall is astonishingly close to some of the positions of the "New Philology": he is mainly interested in authentic texts which should be made accessible and have relevance to a larger public; as one of the first men involved in philological work, he is inclusive and supportive of women and their academic work; he insists on the validity of the individual manuscript and is opposed to "doctored editions" based on what he would also have considered "Procrustean" emendations and conjectures; and, as anyone who has ever read his famous "Forewords" to EETS editions can attest, he certainly writes "at the intersection of the personal and the professional,"[53] showing an intuitive awareness of the importance of the investigating subject for the subject of investigation. In the area of editing, Furnivall has been said to have had little or no discrimination in judgement: "His idea of editing was to strew the text with final -e's to improve meter. . . which he did with an instinct based on experience rather than on collation, meanwhile encouraging readers to add more final -e's that they might think he had missed."[54] This accusation can be compared with Barbara Sargent-Baur's critique of the "New Philologists" whom she charges with championing the renewed study of manuscripts without having done extensive textual editing themselves:

> In spite of the importance they theoretically confer on manuscript study, their interpretations are. . . based on printed texts

edited by Old Philologists. That they often do not read accurately even these critical editions. . . I have demonstrated. . . .
The record to date suggests rather more *enthusiasm* on the[i]r
part for a "manuscript culture" than an ability to deal with
concrete specimens of it.[55] (my emphasis)

Sargent-Baur uses the term "enthusiasm" in exactly the way Plato, the
German philologists, and Derek Pearsall used it, namely as a means to
define their own area of cognitive expertise and its concomitant discursive
practices as more sophisticated, professional, and successful and to demar-
cate them against those who challenge them, intentionally or not, by
using a set of variant discursive practices to examine the same body of
cultural texts.

In the end, the distinction between Furnivall and his late nineteenth-
and early twentieth-century counterparts as well as between so-called
"Old" and "New" Philologists may be the same as the one Jacob Grimm
established between his own comparative philological practice and that of
his colleague, Karl Lachmann. In a speech Grimm wrote on the occasion
of Lachmann's death in 1851, he set up the defining boundaries between
philologists in the following binary manner:

All philological scholars who amount to anything can be cate-
gorised into those who investigate words for the sake of subjects
or subjects for the sake of words. Lachmann unmistakably
belonged among the latter group, and I do not overlook the
advantages of his position, even if I count myself among the
first.[56]

In the obituary for his brother, Wilhelm, Jacob Grimm had only vented
his own disdain for formal textual criticism and editorial work
(*Wortphilologie*) by the personal admission that "the production of critical
editions. . . gives me no pleasure."[57] In his speech on Lachmann, in much
less reticent a manner, he accuses his colleague of having concentrated too
exclusively on providing exact and secure texts "regardless of the texts'
implications or results."[58] Quite obviously, Jacob's general appreciation of
Lachmann's textual criticism was tempered by his belief that, more often
than not, the colleague's emendations and conjectures, based on abstract
aesthetic idea(l)s and preconceived numerical regularities (such as the
heptadic structure Lachmann imposed on the *Nibelungenlied*), violated
the value and authenticity of the original manuscript versions. According
to Jacob, Lachmann's philology is ". . . always robbing and deleting, it can

undo interpolations, but never reconstruct the original. . . . Who would be so anxious as to count all the battle days of the warriors in the Trojan war or the years of Kriemhild's life?"[59] Grimm's own, idiosyncratically adventurous, interdisciplinary and often wildly comparative *Sachphilologie*, for which the texts meant little but the ensuing associations and readings everything, rejected, just like Furnivall, the *horror vacui* of an all-too-limited and limiting, overly specialised and exclusive *Wortphilologie*.

With the help of medievalism, the conscious and critical investigation of the process by which the medieval period is remembered and studied, Furnivall's and Grimm's fascinating symbiosis of philology and enthusiasm should serve to redirect scholars' attention to look for alternative paths of approaching the current polarisations within the academic study of medieval culture: theory vs. literature, multiculturalism vs. canonicity, ideological critique vs. hermeneutics. While a return to nineteenth-century philological practices is not desirable, both scholars' close attention to linguistic, literary, and cultural detail as well as some of their Lachmannian colleagues' insistence on historical perspective, rigor, and exactitude might make for a healthy mélange of the supposedly mutually exclusive cognitive enterprises of philology and enthusiasm. Perhaps, as Peggy Knapp suggests, we could then " 'retheorize' the fascination with words and their relation to social formation philology signaled" for our future research and teaching.[60]

NOTES

1. Preliminary versions of this essay were presented at the 14th International Conference on Medievalism, at Montana State University in October 1999, and at the Meeting of the New Chaucer Society in London, in July 2000. Work on this essay was supported by an eight-week summer stipend from the Graduate College of the University of Northern Iowa. I am indebted to Carol Poster (Montana State University) and to the editor for many valuable suggestions on the topic.

2. Beatrice White, "Frederick James Furnivall," *Essays and Studies* n.s. 3 (1952): 64–76.

3. Alfred North Whitehead, *Process and Reality: An Essay in Cosmology* (New York: Macmillan, 1929), 63.

4. All quotes from Plato's texts are taken from Penelope Murray, ed., *Plato on Poetry* (Cambridge: Cambridge University Press, 1996).

5. Plato has Socrates also compare poets to Corybantes (*korubantiontes*, 533e8–534a1s), mythical attendants to the Phrygian mother Goddess, Cybele,

whose cult included wild orgiastic and frenzied dancing. See Penelope Murray, "Introduction," *Plato on Poetry*, 7: "Throughout Plato's work the mental state of the inspired poet is described in similar terms: the poet, when composing, is in frenzy and out of his mind; he creates by divine dispensation, but not with knowledge."

6. Heinz Schlaffer, *Poesie und Wissen: Die Entstehung des ästhetischen Bewusstseins und der philologischen Erkenntnis* (Frankfurt a.M.: Suhrkamp, 1990). In my analysis of "enthusiasm" in Classical Greek culture I am condensing Schlaffer's excellent discussion on pp. 11–25 of his study. On the history of the term "philology" in Greek and Latin texts see Heinrich Kuch's detailed monograph, *PHILOLOGOS: Untersuchung eines Wortes von seinem ersten Auftreten in der Tradition bis zur ersten lexikalischen Festlegung* (Berlin: Akademie Verlag, 1965), and Gabriël R.F.M. Nuchelmans, *Studien über philólogos, philología und philologeîn* (Zwolle: W.E.J. Tjeenk Willink, 1950).

7. Cited from the "Appendix" to *Plato on Poetry*, 235.

8. The *Zentrale Zeitschriftenbank*, the central database for all scholarly journals in Germany's research libraries, lists dozens of journals beginning with or containing *Museum* or *Archiv* in their titles. It is illustrative to keep in mind Michel Foucault's thoughts about the function(s) of the "archive" which, working alongside the "episteme," he describes as a set of discursive mechanisms which limit what may be researched and expressed, and in what form the texts may be known and remembered. See Foucault's *The History of Sexuality: An Introduction* (Harmondsworth, Middlesex: Penguin, 1978), vol. 1: 14ff., and especially his *L'Ordre du Discours: Leçon Inaugurale au Collège de France Prononcé le 2 decembre 1970* (Paris: Gallimard, 1971). Acceptance by the nineteenth-century journals defining themselves as philological archives or museums, e.g., played an important role in the canon formation of the old and new philologies.

9. When Isidore of Seville's *Etymologiae* teaches that horses shed tears at the occasion of their owner's death, he disguises as zoological fact what he must have read in book XI of the *Aeneid*. "When *auctores* come into play, Isidore makes no kind of differentiation between them. The Bible, Cicero, Horace, Martial, Pliny, Juvenal, and Lucan (the latter chiefly on snakes), all have for him exactly the same sort of authority. Yet his credulity has limits. He denies that weasels conceive by the mouth and bear by the ear. . . and rejects the many-headed hydra as *fabulosus*": C.S. Lewis, *The Discarded Image: An Introduction to Medieval and Renaissance Literature* (Cambridge: Cambridge University Press, 1964), 149.

10. On this process, see Schlaffer, *Poesie und Wissen*, 45–75.

11. John Munro, "Biography," in Munro, ed., *Frederick James Furnivall: A Volume of Personal Record* (London: Oxford University Press, 1906), xxiv. In addition to Munro's detailed text, the following publications provide ample information on Furnivall's biography: Derek Pearsall, "Frederick James Furnivall (1832–1910)," in Helen Damico, ed., *Medieval Scholarship: Biographical Studies on the Formation of a Discipline, vol. 2, Literature and Philology* (New York: Garland, 1998), 125–38; Donald C. Baker, "Frederick James Furnivall

(1825–1910)," in Paul G. Ruggiers, ed., *Editing Chaucer: The Great Tradition* (Norman, OK: Pilgrim, 1984), 157–69; William Benzie, *Dr. F.J. Furnivall: Victorian Scholar Adventurer* (Norman: Pilgrim, 1983); Derek Brewer, "Furnivall and the Old Chaucer Society," in *Chaucer Newsletter* 1 (1979): 2–6; Renate Haas, "The Social Functions of F.J. Furnivall's Medievalism," in Uwe Böker, Manfred Markus, and Rainer Schöwerling, eds., *The Living Middle Ages: Studies in Mediaeval English Literature and Its Tradition, A Festschrift for Karl Heinz Göller* (Stuttgart: Belser, 1989), 319–32; White, "Frederick James Furnivall."

12. Pearsall, "Frederick James Furnivall," 127.

13. For a complete bibliography of Furnivall's work as a medieval scholar, see Pearsall, "Furnivall," 136–8.

14. Pearsall, "Furnivall," 135.

15. Baker, "Furnivall," 169.

16. An excellent example of Furnivall's role as a gracious host is his personal concern about Alois Brandl's entirely unacceptable pronunciation of English. He encouraged Henry Sweet, the specialist in phonetics, to help out the young German colleague with private tutoring. See Alois Brandl's autobiography, *Zwischen Inn und Themse, Lebensbeobachtungen eines Anglisten: Alt-Tirol – England – Berlin* (Berlin: G. Grote'sche Verlagsbuchhandlung, 1936), 137–38.

17. Cambridge University Library, Bradshaw Papers, Correspondence, Add. 2591 (3), fol. 449.

18. Zupitza's remarks were made in the Early English Text Society Annual Report, September 1879, cited in Benzie, *Scholar Adventurer*, note 11 above, 154–5; for Wülcker's statement, see Benzie, 155, fn. 118.

19. See Benzie, *Scholar Adventurer*, 155–6.

20. Benzie, *Scholar Adventurer*, 156, fn. 121, adds Jakob Schipper's extensive treatment of the meters of the older periods in his *Englische Metrik in historischer und systematischer Entwicklung dargestellt* (1881–88) as another scholarly effort rendered possible by the publications of the EETS. Furnivall dedicated his edition of the *Parallel Print of the Minor Poems* to ten Brink; he was elected one of the few honorary members of the German "Shakspere Society" and received his honorary doctorate from the University of Berlin (1884).

21. Cf. also Ewald Flügel's statement about Furnivall's friendship with German scholars: "He would often speak of his German friends, ten Brink, Zupitza, and Koelbing" (Munro, *Furnivall*, 38). Because of his strong "Teutonic" bias, Furnivall was deeply shocked in January 1886, when the "Kruger telegram" became public, a message from Emperor Wilhelm II of Germany to President Paul Kruger, of the South African Republic (Transvaal), congratulating him on repelling Jameson's Raid, a British attack launched from the British-controlled Cape Colony. The telegram, meant to demonstrate to the British their diplomatic isolation and the necessity to bond with Germany, made Furnivall repeatedly state to German scholar Alois Brandl that he considered "the Germans as cousins only, but the Americans as brothers. This feeling ebbed away in course of time, and in 1909 he made his peace by a charming act of courtesy, when he

once more nominated a German to a vice-presidency in the Early English Text
Society." Cited in Munro, *Furnivall*, 14–15.

22. On the beginnings of this process of "philologisation" (ca. 1830–60),
see the detailed study of the careers and works of two nineteenth-century
German Anglicists by Renate Haas, *V.A. Huber, S. Imanuel und die
Formationsphase der deutschen Anglistik: Zur Philologisierung der Fremdsprache und
der sozialen Demokratie* (Frankfurt a.M.: Peter Lang, 1990). T.A. Shippey, who
has written one of the most insightful general surveys of the rise and fall of philological studies in the first chapter of *The Road to Middle-earth* (Boston:
Houghton Mifflin, 1983), comments on the developments in the late nineteenth
and the early twentieth centuries: "Further down the scale, the discoveries of
Grimm and his successors as far as Ferdinand de Saussure (now famous for
inventing 'structuralism' but before that a student of Ablaut) were communicated
increasingly to students as facts, systems divorced from the texts they had been
found in" (9). The interconnections between nationalism and philology in
Germany will be the subject of Richard Utz, *Chaucer and the Discourse of German
Philology* (forthcoming in 2001).

23. For case studies of these "arms races" see, e.g., the essays by Alain
Corbellari ("Joseph Bédier, Philologist and Writer," 269–85), Per Nykrog ("A
Warrior Scholar at the Collège de France: Joseph Bédier," 286–307) in R.
Howard Bloch and Stephen G. Nichols, eds., *Medievalism and the Modernist
Temper* (Baltimore, MD, and London: Johns Hopkins University Press, 1996),
and T.A. Shippey's "Introduction" to Shippey and Andreas Haarder, eds.,
*Beowulf: The Critical Heritage* (London and New York: Routledge, 1998), 1–74.
The influence of the Prussian and – after 1871 – the German government on the
expansive development and success of the German universities has been surveyed
by Fritz K. Ringer, *The Decline of the German Mandarins: The German Academic
Community, 1890–1933* (1969; repr. Hanover, NH, and London: Wesleyan
University Press, 1983), 14–80; a fine comparison between the German, British,
and U.S. institutions in the nineteenth century is Lenore O'Boyle's essay,
"Learning for its Own Sake: The German University as Nineteenth-Century
Model," *Comparative Studies in Society and History* 25 (1983): 3–25.

24. On the deterioration of the relationships between German and British
scholars, see Clare Simmons, "Anglo-Saxonism, the Future, and the Franco-
Prussian War," in Leslie Workman and Kathleen Verduin, eds., *Medievalism in
England II, Studies in Medievalism* 7 (1995): 131–42.

25. Using "lend a hand" may be a fairly neutral translation in this case; the
German original has "*zur Hand gehen*," which one might also translate as "to do
handiwork" (i.e., menial work as opposed to critical, intellectual, philological
work).

26. Arnold Schröer, "Aus der Frühzeit der englischen Philologie I.:
Persönliche Erinnerungen und Eindrücke," *Germanisch-Romanische Monatsschrift*
13 (1929): 32–51 (34). Unless otherwise indicated, all English translations from
German sources are mine (R.U.). For a large body of texts providing similar

examples of the German hegemonic view in philological studies, see John Koch's reviews of Chaucer publications from the 1880s to the 1930s in journals such as *Anglia: Zeitschrift für englische Philologie, Englische Studien*, and *Archiv für das Studium der neueren Sprachen und Literaturen*.

27. Schröer, "Aus der Frühzeit," 40.

28. Schröer, "Aus der Frühzeit," 45.

29. Schröer, "Aus der Frühzeit," 47.

30. See Walter Jackson Bate, "The Crisis in English Studies," in *Harvard Magazine* (September/October, 1982): 46–53. "[P]hilology. . . achieved a stranglehold on English studies from the 1880s to the 1940s. If you took a Ph.D. here in English as late as the 1930s, you were suddenly shoved – with grammars written in German – into Anglo-Saxon and Middle Scots, plus Old Norse (Icelandic), Gothic, Old French, and so on. I used to sympathise with the Japanese and Chinese students who had come here to study literature, struggling with a German grammar to translate Gothic into English! William Allan Neilson, the famous president of Smith College, had been a professor of English here for years. Forgivably, he stated that the Egyptians took only five weeks to make a mummy, but the Harvard English Department took five years" (49). On the negotiations of the German professionalisation of philology in Britain, see O'Boyle, "Learning for Its Own Sake," 13–17.

31. Munro, *Furnivall*, 10–14.

32. The uses of the term "enthusiasm" in descriptions of Furnivall's character, work, and behavior are legion: see, e.g., A.W. Pollard (Munro, *Furnivall*, 148), Benzie (*Scholar Adventurer*, 20, 53, 54, 88, 125, 178, 191); J.C. Castell and C.F.W. Mead (Munro, *Furnivall*, 21–22); George W. Prothero (*A Memoir of Henry Bradshaw, Fellow of King's College, Cambridge and University Librarian* (London: Kegan Paul & Trench, 1888), 213); Joseph M. Dent (Hugh R. Dent, *The House of Dent, 1888–1938* (London: Dent, 1938), 106–7); Furnivall about himself (see W. Robertson Nicoll and Thomas J. Wise, eds., *Literary Anecdotes of the Nineteenth Century*, 2 vols. (1895–96; repr. New York: AMS, 1967), 2:46); White, "Frederick James Furnivall," 66: "Furnivall had . . . the power of arousing *enthusiasm*." The habit of describing Furnivall as doing everything in an "enthusiastic" manner has trickled down into numerous late twentieth-century publications: see, e.g., Baker, "Furnivall," where the term (as noun, adjective, or adverb) has become something like an epithet: 157: ". . . for inevitably any treatment of his work must at least by indirection touch upon his personal qualities, his *enthusiasm*"; ". . . his personal qualities, his *enthusiasm*, his zest for work, his admiration for learning"; and "the Chaucer Society was formed with Furnivall's characteristic directness, suddenness, and *enthusiasm*"; 158, "one must not, as we will see, be led into the assumption that Furnivall was merely an ignorant *enthusiast*"; and "Furnivall fell upon accurate scholarship with *enthusiasm* and gratitude"; 160, "in the order of the Tales which Furnivall had *enthusiastically* embraced"; 167, "Skeat had adopted the 'Bradshaw shift,' which Furnivall had *enthusiastically* seized upon"; 169, "he is the giant upon whose shoulders we all

stand – *enthusiastic*, genial, enormously hard-working" (my emphases). The most recent case of a scholar to characterise Furnivall's work as based on "*enthusiasm*" is Pearsall's, "Furnivall," 133.

33. Munro, *Furnivall*, 43.

34. Of course, Dyboski's own understanding of "philology" as that of a scientific discipline based entirely on empirical-descriptive methods may have colored his reading of Furnivall's statement. On Dyboski and philology, see Karl Heinz Göller, "Roman Dyboski's Book on Tennysons *Sprache und Stil*," in Teresa Bela and Elzbieta Manczak-Wohlfeld, eds., *Professor Roman Dyboski: Founder of English Studies in Poland, Proceedings of the Commemorative Conference for Roman Dyboski (1883–1945), Kraków 1–2 June 1995* (Kraków: Universitas, 1998), 77–87.

35. Haas, "The Social Functions," 329.

36. Haas, "The Social Functions," 330.

37. Gunta Haenicke, *Zur Geschichte der Anglistik an deutschsprachigen Universitäten 1850–1925* (Augsburg: Institut für Anglistik, 1979), 127.

38. Commenting on Furnivall's collaboration with Zupitza, Alois Brandl (Munro, *Furnivall*, 14) states: "They were not always of one mind. Zupitza insisted on critical editions, and Furnivall would not hear of them – 'doctored editions' he called them. Zupitza was mainly concerned with accuracy of texts and rhyme-investigations, Furnivall went mainly for the human and sociological interest of the matter."

39. The term "wild philology" has been successfully employed by Ulrich Wyss, *Die wilde Philologie: Jacob Grimm und der Historismus* (Munich: Beck, 1979) to describe the philological practices of Jacob Grimm and to distinguish them from those of Wilhelm Grimm and Karl Lachmann. Jacob Grimm's comparative, broadly cultural and often politically-minded philology was superseded, during the process of academic institutionalisation of German (and later Romance, English, Slavic) philology, by the objectivist, exclusively academic practices of Lachmann and his followers.

40. See Benzie, *Scholar Adventurer*, 23–25, 31, 141–42, 147, and 231; in *Teena Rochfort-Smith: A Memoir* (1883), Furnivall also mentions that she did important work for the Shakspere Society, the Browning Society, and the EETS, including copying manuscripts in Sir Thomas Phillipps's collection at Cheltenham and *The Old-Spelling Shakspere*; Eleanor Marx, who had a strong interest in theatre and also became a member of the Browning Society, helped transcribe the manuscript of the Macro Plays which would be used for editions of *Mankind* by J.M. Manly (1897) and in Alois Brandl's *Quellen des weltlichen Dramas in England vor Shakespeare* (1898).

41. White, "Furnivall," 75.

42. Rickert's and Spurgeon's strong sense of gratitude is expressed in their contributions to the Furnivall Festschrift (Munro, *Furnivall*, 165–69 and 182–88). For the difficult and painfully slow process of women entering the field of English studies in Germany, see Renate Haas, "Women and the Development

of English Studies in Germany," in Günther Blaicher and Brigitte Glaser, eds., *Anglistentag 1993 Eichstädt: Proceedings* (Tübingen: Max Niemeyer, 1994), 528–40.

43. Shippey, *The Road to Middle-earth*, 10.

44. R.W. Chambers, *Man's Unconquerable Mind* (London: Jonathan Cape, 1939), 342–3.

45. Chapter heading, on p. 31 of Cerquiglini's book *Éloge de la variante: histoire critique de la philologie* (Paris: Seuil, 1989).

46. Stephen Nichols, "Introduction: Philology in a Manuscript Culture," *Speculum* 65 (1990): 1–10 (1).

47. Bloch and Nichols, "Introduction," in *Medievalism and the Modernist Temper*, 1–22 (3).

48. Paul Zumthor, *Speaking of the Middle Ages* (Lincoln, NE: University of Nebraska Press, 1986), 3–4; quoted from Bloch/Nichols, "Introduction", 5.

49. Barbara N. Sargent-Baur, "Philology Through the Looking Glass," in Keith Busby, ed., *Toward a Synthesis? Essays on the New Philology* (Amsterdam and Atlanta: Rodopi, 1993), 97–118, (99).

50. Allen J. Frantzen, "Prologue: Documents and Monuments: Difference and Interdisciplinarity in the Study of Medieval Culture," in Frantzen, ed., *Speaking Two Languages: Traditional Disciplines and Contemporary Theory in Medieval Studies* (Albany, NY: State University of New York Press, 1991), 1–33, (6). Frantzen's book *Desire For Origins: New Language, Old English, and Teaching the Tradition* (New Brunswick and London: Rutgers University Press, 1990), is a successful attempt at "tracing" and historicising scholarly practices in medieval studies.

51. This warlike and heroic image of Furnivall was invoked by Josef Schick (Munro, *Furnivall*, 170), a professor of English at the University of Munich, who would volunteer to participate in the trench warfare of World War I at 55 years of age.

52. Pearsall, "Furnivall," 133; on the same page, Pearsall compares a "meticulous and cautious" Henry Bradshaw with "the torrent of Furnivall's *enthusiasm*", in the first line of his essay, however, Pearsall does attribute to Furnivall the epithets of "English *philologist* and editor" (my emphases). For an original account of the relationship between the philological Bradshaw and the enthusiastic Furnivall, see Joseph A. Dane, "The Chaucerian Reception of Henry Bradshaw," *Archiv* 235 (1998): 48–64, esp. the section on "Bradshaw, Furnivall, and the Decorum of Time and Place," 53–6.

53. Bloch/Nichols, "Introduction," 8.

54. Pearsall, "Furnivall," 133.

55. Sargent-Baur, "Philology Through the Looking-Glass," 117, n. 28. For additional critical discussions of the New Philology/New Medievalism, see Karl Stackmann, "Neue Philologie," in Joachim Heinzle, ed., *Modernes Mittelalter: Neue Bilder einer populären Epoche* (Frankfurt a.M.: Insel, 1994), 398–427, and Richard Utz, "Resistance to (The New) Medievalism? Comparative Deliberations

on (National) Philology, *Mediävalismus*, and *Mittelalter-Rezeption* in Germany and North America," in Roger Dahood, ed., *The Future of the Middle Ages and the Renaissance: Problems, Trends, and Opportunities for Research* (Turnhout: Brepols, 1998), 151–70.

56. Jacob Grimm, *Kleinere Schriften*, vol. 1: *Reden und Abhandlungen* (Berlin: Dümmler, 1864), 150.

57. Jacob Grimm, *Reden und Abhandlungen*, 174.

58. Jacob Grimm, *Reden und Abhandlungen*, 151.

59. Jacob Grimm, *Reden und Abhandlungen*, 156. Furnivall was similarly negative about Carl Elze's attempts at "*Wortphilologie*," as Ewald Flügel (Munro, *Furnivall*, p. 38), remembers: "Speaking of Elze, he told me with a smile and a sigh . . . how their friendship had ended. Elze had sent him a bunch of his Conjectures on Elizabethan dramatists, atrocious jeux – scarcely d'esprit; and 'Furnivallo Furioso' . . . wrote him on a postcard . . . that if he, Elze, were an Englishman and would dare to perpetrate such nonsense, he would hang him on the next lamp post – a postcard to which no reply was received."

60. Peggy A. Knapp, "Recycling Philology," *ADE Bulletin* 106 (Winter 1993): 13–16 (13).

# Medievalism and a New Leaf by the Spanish Forger[1]

## John Block Friedman

Among the many forgers of antique or medieval objects in the last century, one of the most fascinating is the person who manufactured the numerous pseudo-medieval panel paintings, manuscript leaves, and even whole manuscripts found in many private and public collections, especially American university collections. Though known as the Spanish Forger through an early and erroneous connection with a fifteenth-century painter (who was actually English), Jorge Inglès,[2] in fact, no key to a nationality can be found in the forger's work, and a French origin is much more plausible than a Spanish one.[3] Indeed, some thirty-one of his works with known provenance out of those inventoried by William Voelkle were acquired by their owners in Paris, making that city the most likely center of his operations.[4] As he has long been known as the Spanish Forger, however, he will be called SF for consistency. And since he is customarily referred to as male – again on no evidence – I retain that gender for him.

Voelkle believes that this forger was responsible for at least 300 works of fake medieval art. Of these, 207 are single leaves, eighty-seven are panel paintings and eight are manuscripts. This vast oeuvre, amazingly, seems to have been produced between about 1909, when the first documents for purchase or acquisition of the SF's works – leaves in the collection of John Pierpont Morgan – begin to appear, and the late 1920s. He is not only an interesting and enigmatic character, but in his own way as much an exponent of medievalism as were the Pre-Raphaelites and similar artistic schools of a slightly earlier period.

The Spurlock Museum (formerly the World Heritage Museum) of the University of Illinois[5] possesses an illuminated leaf from an antiphonal, which is clearly the work of this artist, making it the 208th known leaf he painted[6] (figure 1). Unfortunately, the leaf in question escaped inclusion in William Voelkle's handlist of the SF's works published by the Pierpont Morgan Library in 1978. It is also not mentioned in the same author's catalogue of the exhibition of newly identified works by this artist held in 1987–1988 at the Patrick and Beatrice Haggerty Museum of Art at Marquette University in Milwaukee.[7] This leaf, which I call from its subject – the apparent drowning of a female saint – the Urbana Martyrdom, illustrates the SF's typical working method for his large scale pseudo-miniatures, which was to use authentic choirbook leaves, scraping off very evenly music and text from one half or three quarters of the existing text-box to provide a new and seemingly original space for his paintings. Such choir books provided a cheap and readily obtainable supply of leaf stock, which was already aged and which contained "authenticating" text and music.[8] These books were so large and heavy that frequently they were despoiled of their illuminated initials, leaving the denuded books to pass from bookseller to bookseller at ever lower prices. England, for example, in the early nineteenth century had a considerable duty on bound manuscripts and early books which was calculated on weight,[9] and thus large Continental service books were frequently reduced to their most decorated and hence most saleable leaves before importation.

The full page miniature added by the forger to the verso of the leaf in the Spurlock Museum shows a gold-haloed female saint, her hands bound before her, being led or forced into a fishpond before a king seated in a oratory or enclosure roofed with a late Gothic architectural canopy.[10] The king is flanked by a figure grouping of four courtiers or nobles. Another figure with a goad waits near the pond, perhaps to press the woman below the surface. The person leading her by a cord tied around her wrists has the characteristically unnatural tip-toeing stance, red hose and green jerkin, and long pointed shoes, of many figures in other leaves by the SF (some of them with colours reversed), such as the tormenters of Saint Lawrence in L3, L43, and L51 or the huntsman of L78.[11]

Like most of the SF's production, this martyrdom scene appears to have been created from disparate elements, some sacred and some secular. Voelkle's hand-list treats in detail the way that the SF reproduced pseudo-medieval scenes from models provided by the popularising illustrated volumes on medieval life and customs written by Paul Lacroix (1806–1884), which were published between 1869 and 1882 and translated into several languages.[12] The forger apparently took over from such a printed source a standard scene of a female figure – not necessarily a saint at all – presented to a king, as he had already painted such a presentation on another leaf, whose present location is now unknown.[13] With such a heterogeneous iconographic background, the saint in the Urbana Martyrdom understandably lacks a specific identifying attribute; indeed her only connection to any known saint is to Godelieva or Godelaine of Flanders (July 11), whose *vita* indicates she suffered drowning or some form of ritual cleansing.[14]

Though not appreciably different in quality or representativeness of method and subject from other leaves by the SF, the Urbana Martyrdom has the particular distinction of being painted on a page from a choir book not inventoried as a source for the SF's leaf stock,[15] as well as having a clearly documented provenance of dealer, sale date, price, and purchaser which moves the leaf uninterruptedly from near the time of its creation to the seller and then to the first institutional purchaser. Moreover, it is among the last if not actually the last work placed on the market by the SF before his apparent disappearance from the art world in the late 1920s. The purpose of the present discussion then is to describe and make better known this leaf in the SF's oeuvre, to situate it in the context of late nineteenth-century medievalism, and to suggest that one of the forger's production outlets can perhaps be localised to the Paris dealer who sold the Urbana Martyrdom to the University of Illinois. The SF's extensive production catered to several nineteenth-century tides of taste. Among these was the "rediscovery" of late Gothic manuscript painting in the mid century, especially scenes from courtly life in romances. Large scale miniatures depicting hawking, hunting, music making and dancing, courtship, feasting, tournaments, castle architecture and the like, such as those in the Manesse Manuscript,[16] the Très Riches Heures,[17] or the Grimani Breviary,[18] became extremely popular as subjects for reproduction in domestic decoration. As A.N.L Munby well expressed it, "illuminations to medieval patterns vied with tatting and Berlin woolwork as a fitting pursuit for young ladies and cheap methods of reproduction in colour, such as chromolithography, made illuminated manuscripts familiar to a much wider public."[19] William Morris, who stimulated the developing interest in Gothic manuscripts among connoisseurs by making several illuminated books, also disseminated his designs to wallpaper and textiles, making medieval images more available to the popular consciousness.

By mid-century in England and France, especially, there was a great interest in medieval book making – especially illuminators' materials and techniques, gilding, and practical calligraphy and illumination of manuscripts – sparked by such scholars as Merry Philadelphia Merrifield in her superb *Original Treatises Dating from the XIIth to the XVIIIth Centuries on the Arts of Painting* (1849), A. Lecoy de la Marche's *L'art d'enlumineur, manuel technique du XIVe siècle* (1887), and working gilders and scribes like William Graily Hewitt, and Edward Johnston, who wrote a practical work called *Writing and Illuminating and Lettering* published in 1906. Album-like collections as well, such as *The Illuminated Books of the Middle Ages* and *The Art of Illumination and Missal Painting* (1849), by Henry Noel Humphreys (1810–1879), which had chromolithographic plates, and Auguste de Bastard d'Estang's costly *Peintures et Ornements des Manuscrits* made illuminations accessible in England and France (Humphreys's *Art of Illumination* had colouring book-like outlines of letters and pictures with which the student could practise). Eventually these currents contributed to the rise in England of periodicals like *The Illuminator* and connoisseur groups like the Burlington and Roxburghe Clubs and the Society for Scribes and Illuminators.[20]

Sometimes this interest in practical calligraphy and illumination could combine with religious enthusiasm. For example, there is a handsomely illuminated book of hours of York use in the Municipal Library at Boulogne-sur-Mer, MS 93.[21] One of its miniatures was at some time cut out and then later repaired by an aristocratic amateur, certainly while it was in the French municipal library, most likely as a pious act of restoration and exercise in illumination by an English Catholic living in this sea-side town. The initial, showing Christ before Pilate, was replaced with a piece of parchment on which was recreated both the historiated initial and the damaged letters at the beginning of each line. At the upper left margin can be seen the words "Lady Strange restituit, 1847."[22] Though the manuscript was made in York about 1410, and shows no French influence, Lady Strange turned to the late fifteenth-century Tours-Bourges styles of Jean Colombe and Jean Fouquet for her models, which was also the general geographic area of inspiration for the SF's sources for many of his forgeries.

Though the early history of manuscript collecting shows it to have been an aristocratic pastime, again by mid-century it reached a wider audience. It was common for Manchester merchants and American tycoons to own manuscripts. And dealers quickly catered to those who could not afford complete codices, yet wished instead to create and display as "conversation pieces" albums of illuminated initials cut from manuscripts, by breaking up books and selling framed individual leaves at relatively modest prices. Indeed, even well-to-do collectors shared the taste for albums and cuttings which was later to fuel the market for the SF's work. For example, the late Victorian aesthete John Ruskin (1819–1900), from the 1850s onward enthusiastically purchased illuminated manuscripts; in the course of his life he owned some eighty-seven. He observed that "a well-illuminated missal is a fairy cathedral full of painted windows."[23] Yet he was also not above describing in his diary in December of 1853 how he "cut some leaves from large missal," and on the first day of the new year "put two pages of missal in frame," while on January 3, 1854 he notes how he "cut missal up in evening – hard work."[24] One of his surviving "albums" consists of twenty cuttings from a French horae pasted round a center piece – another cutting of a page by a follower of Jean Bourdichon.[25] The Carmelite Missal cuttings now in the British Library and so well studied by Margaret Rickert give us further insights into the minds and tastes of somewhat less cultivated "album" makers than Ruskin, but ones who shared the same attitude towards illuminated medieval books.[26]

It is also probable that the SF's activities reflect the fondness in Catholic European households for devotional chromolithographs of saints and other sacred subjects such as those produced in the mid-century by the famous Parisian lithographic printing firm of Bouasse-Lebel, and he may have been by training and profession part of the industry which provided them for shops offering religious goods.[27] Indeed, a substantial portion of his output involved romanticised and haloed female figures exactly like the mysterious "saint" being martyred in the Urbana leaf. This new process of colour reproduction was bringing medieval art and colour into many homes for the first time. Though the use of large limestone slabs on which separate grease pencilled drawings coated with red, blue, and yellow inks could be juxtaposed in a multi-colour printing process was known in the late eighteenth century, it was perfected by an Alsatian, Gottfried Engelmann in 1837, who developed a system of frame registration which insured a perfect match in colour imposition and which enabled the printer to create a broad range of intermediate tones. A separate stone with black ink was used for outlines or contours.[28] By 1839 the process was common in books and became enormously popular in the late Victorian period, first in France, then in Germany, England, and later, in America with firms like Prang and Currier & Ives. By 1882, however, as the cheaper and less labour-intensive photographic half-tone process replaced it, chromolithography with its "hand painted" look seems to have remained popular chiefly amomg Parisian poster artists and in the religious market, where it lingered into the 1920s in mass produced copies of sacred art from the Middle Ages and Renaissance. In the author's possession is a chromolithograph of Saint Veronica, obtained in Quebec, which shows that saint displaying the sudarium and Holy Face (figure 2);[29] it employs much the same odd mix of medievalism and pre-Raphaelite touches which we see in the SF's work,[30] and could have been made any time from the 1880s to the 1920s.

As the iconographic subjects of many of his forgeries have ties to chromolithographs in Lacroix's books, it is likely that the SF began to draw on them – and indeed to be influenced by the style of their illustrations – perhaps a decade or so after the books had been widely disseminated and had created a taste for a certain sort of medievalism reflected in the Saint Veronica picture just discussed. He seems also to have studied reproductions of actual medieval miniatures from French, Flemish, Italian, and Spanish manuscript books, most particularly the Très Riches Heures and the Grimani Breviary, as well as the work of Memling. Once the SF's taste and style were established and a stock of images built up, he could have continued to copy scenes from the Lacroix volumes and religious chromolithographs available in magazines and for sale in religious shops up through the late 1920s.

The Urbana Martyrdom is painted on a piece of medium quality parchment measuring 490 millimeters in height by 360 in width and taken from an antiphonal, a book containing the music and texts of the daily offices as sung in the choir. Because of their size and weight such books often rested on a stand while in use. The verso of the page on which the scene is painted contains the original music in a good grade of fifteenth-century French, or Flemish, liturgical *textura quadrata*, with six-line blue pen work capitals (figure 3). Ascenders are clubbed and there are numerous hairlines and finishing strokes. The letter A has its lower compartment made of a distinctive lozenge or diamond. All told, the script exhibits the broken forms of northern Gothic rather than the smooth curves of the Italian *textura rotunda* script in the other choir books known to have been used by the SF, and indicates the existence of a hitherto unknown source of his leaf stock. Measuring 240 millimeters by 390, the writing space on this side of the leaf was established by dry point double rulings whose grooves can still be seen. The texts were written on rulings also made with dry point, and these rulings for the lines of text seem to have been located by a pair of very faint horizontal pricking marks in the parchment, which intersect the vertical ruling lines at the outer edges of the text box. The staves for the notes were done with red ink by means of a rustrum whose teeth were about 10 mm apart.

In order to place the miniature within the confines of the page, the forger scraped the parchment completely from the head line of the old music at the top all the way to the bottom. He retained, however, the faint double rulings at the edges of his original, which are perceptibly narrower than the bar borders of the painting. How this parchment surface was manipulated to produce the Urbana Martyrdom can be determined through ultraviolet examination of the miniature and through micrometer measurement. When the Urbana Martyrdom is studied under an ultraviolet lamp, it can be seen that the top of the page at the point of the old headline has been scraped to remove the horizontal headline all across the page as far as the vertical side ruling lines now incorporated into the borders. This is evident to the unaided eye as a faint blur on the parchment at top right but the area has a strong fluorescence when examined under ultraviolet light. Ultraviolet also brings out what appears to be the remains of an original ruling line more or less on an axis with the lance butt of the figure at lower right. Also, faint traces of ruling-line runover can be seen protruding beyond the border near this figure. Pricking or slitting for this line is concealed in the border bar.

The overall thickness of the parchment is about .02.5–.03 mm except at the top line downward heavily scraped to make a fresh writing surface of about .02 mm in thickness. Thus, there is a fairly noticeable dip or hollow on the page where the miniature was placed. Undoubtedly, the scraping process, however carefully done, gave a furry surface to the parchment which would not have been suitable for painting, and it appears that the forger used gesso as a size for his new painting, which contributes to the somewhat flat or chalky tone of the colours.

Further examination of the leaf under the ultraviolet lamp shows a number of rulings still visible through the underpainting and pigment of the miniature, which fluoresce vividly, like chain lines on laid paper.[31] These are caused by the fact that the rulings on the verso were made with a dry point stylus. They fluoresce as a series of horizontal lines under the picture showing that they were once higher than the surface on which the picture was painted and were scraped down, thinning the parchment along their ridges at the points where they show up as the grooves from the back side. This phenomenon also appears in Voelkle's inventory M3.10 and M3.11, as well as L7 and L8. The dry point tooled marginal double ruling lines, which also came through from the music side, have been cleverly concealed by highlighting them with white lead and thus hiding them in the borders. It is possible too, that the forger rolled his leaf into a tight cylinder after painting it and then flattened the cylinder slightly. This caused a series of lines across the page which seem to have come from rolling and squeezing but in fact also serve to conceal to some degree the old lines, now showing up in very thin areas of the parchment.

The music and text on the Urbana Martyrdom's recto consists of two antiphons, the first for lauds and the second for vespers of the octave of Pentecost, a mid week feast which today would be called Whit Tuesday of

Whitsun Week. These two antiphons are indicated by the rubrics "feria iii ad b[enedictus]" ("Ego sum ostium, dicit dominus: Per me si quis introierit, salvabitur, et pascua inveniet, alleluia") and "ad ma[gnificat]" an[tiphona] ("Pacem relinquo vobis, pacem meam do vobis: non quomodo mundus dat, ego do vobis, Alleluia: Psalmus").[32] Such a feast is not of major liturgical significance and would normally be marked in a service book only by a coloured initial and rubric.

Thus, neither in theme, in size, nor in placement does the full page miniature fit the liturgical framework of the verso. Nor do the themes of the antiphon for lauds, Christ's lesson to the Pharisees from John 10.9, and for vespers, also from John 14.27, correspond at all to the subject of the miniature, a martyrdom. Moreover, it seems improbable from a liturgical standpoint that a full page miniature would occur within a sequence of offices for a Tuesday rather than the Sunday in the octave of Pentecost.[33] So too, by the fifteenth century, the period to which the miniature belongs by its style, the sanctorale and temporale were physically distinct in service books, often forming two volumes. Thus, it is highly unlikely that a representation of a saint's martyrdom naturally belonging to the sanctorale would be used to illustrate the temporale or cycle of the days and weeks for the offices for the feast of Pentecost. Finally, antiphonals, placed at a distance from the singers, were not generally ornamented by full-page miniatures in the way that books intended for close inspection and private devotion, such as horae, would have been. For these codicological and liturgical reasons alone, the leaf should have aroused the suspicions of knowledgeable purchasers or dealers.

As noted earlier, the Urbana Martyrdom does not fit with other of the forger's works classed in seven groups A–G according to similar leaf stock, since the script is not a liturgical rotunda, suggesting that he used a different antiphonal, which should be called H, as a source of vellum stock. From its size, it is probable that the SF had painted the Urbana Martyrdom to be one of a pair of leaves or large set of leaves to appeal to collectors who wished to frame them, where "the members of such a set are generally thematically related and the same size, have the same border, and are on the same manuscript stock."[34] Such a companion leaf or leaves is as yet unknown.

The Urbana Martyrdom does have connections, however, with several specific works by the SF. It belongs, through its use of heraldic bearings, with a Presentation in the Temple, L 20 2, now in the Dartmouth College Library, with a Virgin and Child in the Mark Lansburgh Collection, L 21 and with a manuscript, M 5, of Juvenal's *Satires*, whose location is now unknown. At bottom and middle left of the

Urbana Martyrdom's floral borders, hanging from ribbons on the arabesque vines, are shields with heraldic bearings. None of the blazons of the shields correspond to those of known fifteenth-century families. The Dartmouth Presentation (figure 4) shows shovel-shaped shields identical in size and proportions to those of the Urbana leaf also hanging from ribbons, but from the branches of a tree, rather than from arabesques, while the leaf with the Virgin and Child offers similar shovel-shaped shields with the same diagonal band of diamonds as a charge (figure 5).[35] Miniatures 1 and 2 from this "Juvenal" (figures 6 7) employ these shields but they do not hang from ribbons. These are the only known uses of such shields, and suggest that the SF must have returned to this motif several times during his career, since the first two miniatures came from the same collector, who obtained them in Switzerland before 1925, while the manuscript was in the hands of a Leipzig book dealer, C.G. Boerner and was published in his catalogue in 1913.[36]

Now that we have seen something of the Urbana Martyrdom's iconography and general appearance, we can move to the question of its presence at the University of Illinois, for its acquisition history fortunately is recoverable from records still held in the Spurlock Museum's archives. The Museum sought to develop a collection of objects suitable for teaching and illustrating European culture. To that end, the Curator of the European Section, Neil C. Brooks, travelled in France, especially Paris, during the summers of 1926 and 1928. On the first visit, in June, 1926, he bought four works of art for 755 dollars from the firm of A. Semail-Pares, at 17, Rue Bonaparte, Paris, VI, a business described on its letterhead simply as "*antiquaire*" in the singular. These give some idea of the range of the wares offered by the firm. The items were a Flemish triptych dated 1558 of oil on wood panel depicting the Madonna and Saints Beatrice and Lucia, a fourteenth century English oak panel, a framed piece of petit point work, and a French ivory carving of the Dormition of the Virgin; there is nothing suspect about the antiquity of these pieces.[37]

On 10 July, 1928, on a return trip to Paris he made another purchase from the same dealer for 7500 francs or 300 dollars, a sum explained in the bill presented to the Accounting Office of the University as payment for a "large miniature, School of Burgundy, late 15th century." Oddly, the bill from A. Semail-Pares, calling the work an "*enlumineure gouachée de XVeme siècle*," notes the price at 4000 francs. Thus the Urbana Martyrdom was not especially expensive – costing about the same amount as the triptych – and did not seem to be considered as appreciably more important than the items bought in 1926. Once at the Museum, the page was handsomely framed and catalogued as a genuine

Burgundian work. By the late 1970s, however, it had aroused the curiosity and suspicions of several art history students and faculty members. Though I had studied the leaf for many years, my interest became more focused when I realised that it ought properly to be seen in the context of the medievalism and calligraphy movements of the mid- to later nineteenth century.

That A. Semail-Pares may have been an outlet for the forger's work, and that the SF may even have been a sort of house artist supported by that firm and other dealers is suggested by an ambiguous and circumstantial but interesting piece of evidence which I shall offer shortly.

The firm of A. Semail-Pares went out of business in 1991–1992, though it had been dormant for a long time before closing its doors, and thus nothing can now be determined about how the shop came to have the leaf. In the post-war period, the business seems to have been run by Jacques Semail at a different Paris location, 10 Rue du Cherche Midi; he was presumably a son or close relative of the original dealer. He appears to have lived only a year or so after closing his business. A search by the profession of *antiquaire* from 1914 to 1921 in the Paris *annuaires* now held in microfilm in the Bibliothèque Ségur shows no listing for either business or owner. The firm appears in 1925, a year before Brooks first made purchases there from its apparently already substantial stock, and just about the time when the majority of leaves with a French provenance were acquired by their owners.

In the *annuaire* of Paris streets for that year we find A. Semail-Pares, *antiquaire*, on Rue Bonaparte and again in 1928. By 1930 the firm seems to have enlarged, as we find the same listing by profession: *antiquaire*, and street: Rue Bonaparte for A. Semail-Pares, but now an E. Pares "*marchand*" and "*antiquaire*" also appears at the fashionable address of 171 Boulevard St. Germain. Both A. and E. Pares listings occur through 1931, but by 1934, E. Pares has disappeared, and, by 1935, A. Semail no longer retains the compound Pares and has moved to 10, Rue du Cherche-Midi where the business remained under this name until 1947. In this year a G. not E. Pares is shown at 12, Rue du Cherche Midi with a different 'phone number, while A. Semail remains at 10, Rue du Cherche Midi. By 1958, still listed as an *antiquaire*, A. Semail is at 10, Rue du Cherche Midi and G. Pares has disappeared and there is no further mention of 12, Rue du Cherche Midi. Thus, there were at least two forms of the name, one with compound and one without, and persons with both forms of the name were dealers in antiquities. We see, then, that this firm remained in business for some sixty-seven years, seemingly without any other ties with the production of the SF. All that can be said from a study of the receipts in the University of Illinois Archives is that Brooks bought from the dealer on two occasions and that no suspicion prevented him from spending a very substantial amount of money on A. Semail-Pares' wares. And of course the dealer could have come by the leaf in any number of legitimate ways and could actually have regarded it as genuine.

In recent years, however, many new works have been identified as by the SF and one of these has some interesting possible connections with the antiquities dealers using the names Semail and Pares. In the last decade a betrothal scene – one of the SF's favorite subjects – painted on panel board surrounded by a carved "medieval" ivory frame has been recognised as the work of the SF and is now called P 47 (figure 8).[38] The picture was last known to be in the collection of the journalist Lady Jeanne Campbell Cram (Mrs John Sargeant Cram) of New York City.[39] P 47 shows a woman and her retinue about to walk on to the gangplank of a ship. At lower right is a figure in jerkin and hose whose appearance and stance exactly duplicates that of the figure leading the saint to the pool in the Urbana Martyrdom. The Cram panel's composition appears to be a secular adaptation of Hans Memling's painting for the Shrine of Saint Ursula (1489) now in the Hospital of St. John in Bruges, where the saint arriving at Cologne is walking off of rather than on to the ship.[40] The Cram panel was originally purchased in Paris in the 1920s and resold through a Sothebys' auction in 1950.

Directly under the right foot of the figure in the foreground is the name P. Parres (figure 9). It is partly obscured by the semi-circular pieces of the frame intended to hold in the panel at the corners. This name raises a number of puzzling problems. The script is a bold modern printing which would be historically out of place on the panel. It could have been added at some point much later in the panel's history, but to what end? While it may not be possible to resolve these issues, the name Parres, though containing one extra letter, on yet another work made by the SF leads one inevitably to a connection with the A. Semail-Pares who sold the Urbana Martyrdom.

To return to the seller of the leaf, the orthography of the firm's name yields few clues about its principal. Semail is a Turkish name and Pares is an uncommon name in France. For example, the current Paris and environs telephone directory yields only seventeen listings for Pares and six for Parres. The names sounds Sephardic; Pares and Parres are probable variants of Portuguese Peres (e.g. Shimon Peres), Spanish or Catalan Pe'rez, or possibly Paris as a city name. For example, in the registers of Sephardic Jewish marriages in Amsterdam from 1598 to 1811 we find a reference to a Moses Pares who served as a witness for a marriage in Amsterdam in 1784.[41] Though A. Semail-Pares as a name is genderless, a possible scenario for the owner's name might go something like this. A Turkish woman A. Semail marries a Sephardic Jew named Pares living in Turkey and adopts his name as a compound. Large numbers of Sephardic Jews emigrated to the Ottoman empire just before and after the Expulsion of the Jews from Spain in 1492 and after the Expulsion during the reign of Bajazet II.[42] Though they had been reasonably well assimilated into late Ottoman society, the break up of the empire at the end of World War I and particularly the rise of the nationalist Young Turk movement under Kemal in late 1918 meant that the somewhat privileged position of the ethnic minorities in Turkey changed radically.[43] Thus, a Turkish woman with a Jewish husband might have felt that emigration from Turkey in the early 1920s was advantageous and such a scenario would help to explain the appearance of the dealership in the *annuaires* beginning in 1925. Moreover, since the largest educational initiative among Turkish Jews was French inspired and led – the Alliance Israélite Universelle, which had founded schools in Turkey from 1867 onward[44] and had as one of its primary goals the development of competence in the French language among its students,[45] – Paris would seem a good choice for Turkish Jewish immigration.

However they arrived in Paris, it is possible that perhaps E. Pares "*marchand*" and "*antiquaire*" was the husband of A. Semail and that he eventually went into business on his own. Later, either through death or divorce E. Pares disappears and A. Semail returned to her original name. The G. Pares who lives near by could perhaps have been a child or a relative of E. If we assume that the firm of A. Semail-Pares acquired the Urbana Martyrdom directly from the SF to act as his agent, or acquired it from another dealer who may have represented the forger, we have found only one piece of the puzzle. If we add yet another dealer or agent, who knew the SF but was familiar with A. Semail-Pares only in the general way of business and was not clear about the exact spelling of the firm's name, it is possible that such a dealer acquired the then unframed Lady Jeanne Campbell Cram panel (P 47) and knowing of the Pares connection with the SF, wrote P. Parres on the panel for identification of the item in a lot, intending, though misspelling, the initial and surname of one of the owners of the Rue Bonaparte shop and not the name of the artist who painted the panel. So too, the framer himself, with a similarly vague knowledge of the owners of A. Semail-Pares, could have written this name as a form of identification on the panel while it was on his premises. When the panel was still unframed, the location of a signature on it would not seem critical. After the panel acquired the present fake ivory frame, which does not hide the name, the intention may have been to remove the name P. Parres. Admittedly, such a chain of association places A. Semail-Pares and the Urbana Martyrdom with P 47 only in a rather general way but it does serve to tie two works by the SF in different media to a dealer who would then sell the works to collectors.

It could be said, of course, that the Urbana Martyrdom is a fairly crude forgery and its cloying style and mix of incongruous liturgical, hagiographic, and decorative motifs should not have failed to warn an honest dealer or a knowledgeable collector. Nonetheless, they apparently fooled several, in part because at the time the SF worked, many potential buyers still saw the "Middle Ages" in the chalky colours of Gobelins tapestry and the sweet expressions of Pre-Raphaelite painters like D.G. Rossetti and Edward Burne-Jones.

If one thinks of the various kinds of copyists, noted by Charles Sterling,[46] as those who merely imitate – for example the photographic student reproducers of works of art one used to see in the Louvre on Sundays – the plain forgers, who attempt to reproduce for profit a valuable work while adding nothing of their own to it, and finally the most interesting imitator, the artist who creates a work like his original in mood and attitude, trying to imitate the mindset of the original artist as much as his colours and brushstrokes, it is clear that the SF combined a desire for gain with a desire to create the vanished world of Burgundian gaiety, public ritual and splendor so apparent in the Très Riches Heures and the Grimani Breviary as well as in the later horae calendar paintings of Simon Bening with their many scenes of feasting, venery (where aristocratic hunters and peasant watchers are contrasted), and of courtship in the pleasure gardens, public squares, and canal boats of Bruges and Ghent.[47]

However much the forger may try to recreate the past, he is a creature of his own age, as the medievalism of this painting so strikingly reveals. His historical past was that of the books of costume, albums, religious chromolithography, and "coffee table" books of his youth. Still, one can only speculate about the energy of an artist who could create some three hundred works of this type and complexity, and hope that some day the secret of the Spanish Forger's true identity and the nature of his art dealer connections will come to light.

## NOTES

1. I am grateful to Dr Barbara Bohen, the former Director of the World Heritage Museum, now Spurlock Museum, at the University of Illinois at Urbana- Champaign, for allowing me to study and photograph the Urbana Martyrdom, and to the interim Director and staff for information on acquisition history and for permission to reproduce the leaf; to Claudie Faure of the CNRS, Paris for her help in obtaining old Paris telephone book information; to Lynn Tarte Ramey of the University of Montevallo for information about A. Semail-Pares; and to Steven Bowman, Lillian Friedman, Deborah Gatewood, Karen Gould of Austin, Texas, Maureen Kofkee, Richard Newhauser, Patricia A. Teter of the Provenance Index, J. Paul Getty Museum, Holly Stec, William Voelkle of the Pierpont Morgan Library, and Estelle Wolfers for advice and information during the research for and preparation of this paper. The Librarians of Kent State University Salem Lilith Kunkle and Cynthia Rottenborn were extremely helpful in obtaining Interlibrary Loan materials for me. Versions of the present study were presented at the Saint Louis Manuscript Conference and at the International Medieval Congress at Western Michigan University, Kalamazoo, MI.

2. This name was assigned to him by Belle da Costa Greene, from 1906, Librarian of the Pierpont Morgan Library; she also began to assemble a catalogue of his works.

3. See for example, Janet Backhouse, "The Spanish Forger," *British Museum Quarterly* 33.1–2 (1968): 65–71 and her "A Miniature Masterpiece by the Spanish Forger," *Quarto: Abbott Hall Art Gallery Quarterly Bulletin* 9 (Jan. 1975): 8–15. Charles Sterling, "Les émules des Primitifs," *La Revue de l'art* 21 (1973): 80–93 has argued for the forger's Italian origins. This article contains, in my opinion, the best stylistic analysis of the SF's work and formative influences. Overlooking how the majority of the SF's leaves of known provenance are associated with France, and focussing chiefly on the panel paintings, Sterling claimed that the artist had seen, before it was sold to an American collector in 1911, the Adoration of the Shepherds by Stefano Folchetti, active 1492–1513, in the province of the Marches – something not easily done by a non-Italian – and that this and other of Folchetti's works had had a profound influence on his imagery (91). There is, certainly, a strong resemblance between the SF's poses and figure groupings and those of Folchetti's Adoration. See Pietro Zampetti, *Paintings from the Marches, Gentile to Raphael* (London: Phaidon, 1971), 191, 198.

4. William Voelkle, *The Spanish Forger* (New York: Pierpont Morgan Library, 1978). This work expands on the catalogue of the SF's works compiled by Otto Kurz, *Fakes: A Handbook for Collectors and Students* (New York: Dover, 1967), pp. 90–91. Voelkle divides the SF's output into panels, manuscripts, and leaves referred to as P, M, or L followed by a number. I retain this division.

5. The name changes of this museum require some comment. Originally it was called The European Culture Museum and Classical Museum, was founded

in 1911 (growing out of a yet earlier Museum of Classical Archaeology) and directed by Albert Olmstead, Arthur S. Pease, and Neil C. Brooks. In 1917 the Oriental and Archaeology Museum was added. The Oriental and Classical Museums were combined in 1929 and the resulting institution was again combined with the European Culture Museum in 1954. In 1971 it was renamed the World Heritage Museum and it is now called the Spurlock Museum. For a fuller account, see John B. Friedman, "Resources for Scholars: Medieval Manuscripts in Two Illinois Libraries," *The Library Quarterly* 57.1 (1987): 71. As the leaf I discuss here is clearly not medieval, it is not mentioned in my census of the University of Illinois medieval manuscripts.

    6. Spurlock Museum accession number 1928.11.0001.

    7. Though he had written to the then World Heritage Museum for a copy of the leaf in 1986, he never received it and so could not include or describe it in the Marquette exhibition (letter of May 9, 1992). See *The Spanish Forger, Master of Deception: December 10, 1987–February 8, 1988, The Patrick and Beatrice Haggerty Museum of Art, Marquette University* (Milwaukee: The Museum, 1987).

    8. Owing to the complexities of trying to set them in type, antiphonals continued to be produced in manuscript form long after the age of print and in Spain until at least the eighteenth-century.

    9. See A.N.L. Munby, *The Formation of the Phillipps Library*, Phillipps Studies III (Cambridge: Cambridge University Press, 1954–1956), 33–35.

    10. This canopy is very similar to those in M 6, two leaves from a manuscript whose present location is unknown.

    11. All aspects of this stock figure in the SF's oeuvre, pointed shoes, green hose and red jerkin with knotted sash at waist are taken from the identical figure standing at the head of Saint Lawrence in a chromolithograph in Charles Léopold Louandre, *Les arts somptuaires* (Paris: Hangard-Maugé, 1857–1858), vol. 1. See Voelkle, *The Spanish Forger: Master of Deception*, 11.

    12. The works of this author most important for the present discussion are *Moeurs, usages et costumes au Moyen Age et à l'époque de la Renaissance* (Paris: Firmin Didot frères, 1871); *Vie militaire et religieuse au Moyen Age et à l'époque de la Renaissance* (Paris: Firmin Didot frères, 1873); *Les Arts au Moyen Age et à l'époque de la Renaissance* (Paris: Firmin Didot frères, 1873); *Sciences et lettres au Moyen Age et à l'époque de la Renaissance* (Paris: Firmin Didot & cie, 1877); and *Louis XII et Anne de Bretagne* (Paris: Firmin Didot & cie, 1882).

    13. Voelkle, *The Spanish Forger*, L 84, 60, fig. 255.

    14. Godelieva of Flanders, born 1040 at Lonfort in the diocese of Tournai near Boulogne, was martyred in 1070 – through the machinations of her husband Berthou and a diabolical mother-in-law – by strangling. Apparently she was also cleansed before or just after her death in a pool or well. See Frederick George Holweck, *A Biographical Dictionary of the Saints* (rpt. Detroit: Omnigraphics, 1990), 439.

    15. The complete stock-to-leaf breakdown appears in *The Spanish Forger*, 75. William Voelkle has indicated to me in a letter of March 15, 2000 that the

script of the leaf used by the Spanish Forger in the preparation of the Urbana Martyrdom is unlike that of any of the leaves from the choir books, lettered A–G in Voelkle's catalogue, used to supply parchment for the Forger's other works.

16. The SF seems to have seen the colour reproductions from the Manesse manuscript published in 1897 by Otto Kaemmel in *Spamers Illustrierte Weltgeschichte* (Leipzig: O. Spamer, 1893–1898).

17. Léopold Delisle, "Les Livres des heures du duc de Berry," in the *Gazette des Beaux Arts* 29 (1884): 97–110. Later, Paul Durrieu, *Les Très riches heures de Jean de France, duc de Berry* (Paris: Plon-Nourrit, 1904) had published miniatures from Chantilly, MS 65.

18. The facsimile of the Grimani Breviary (Venice: Ferd. Ongania, 1906) is another probable influence for the SF's formative years.

19. A.N.L. Munby, *Connoisseurs and Medieval Miniatures 1750–1850* (Oxford: Clarendon, 1972), 1.

20. See the extremely informative article by Janet Backhouse, "Pioneers of Modern Calligraphy and Illumination," *The British Museum Quarterly* 33. 1 (1968): 71–79.

21. See John B. Friedman, *Northern English Books, Owners, and Makers in the Late Middle Ages* (Syracuse: Syracuse University Press, 1995) for fuller discussion, 122–31.

22. Caleb Wing did a number of retouchings in the 1850s of water damaged manuscripts once in the Jarman Collection and now in the British Library; he even added a landscape to a horae and did a copy of a Flight into Egypt miniature. See Janet Backhouse, "A Victorian Connoisseur and his Manuscripts: The Tale of Mr. Jarman and Mr. Wing," *British Museum Quarterly* 32 (1968): 76–92. Equally fascinating are the activities of an apparently London based "restorer" who overpainted the present Annunciation miniature, placed it at Lauds instead of Matins and made many other changes to conceal gaps in a fifteenth-century book of hours now in the Harry Ransom Research Center of the University of Texas, HRC MS 2. See on this matter Karen Gould, "The Recovery of a Fifteenth-Century Flemish Book of Hours," *Scriptorium* 43 (1989): 76–100.

23. *Praeterita* III, c. 18, in E.T. Cook and Alexander D.O. Wedderburn, eds., *The Works of John Ruskin* (London: G. Allen and New York: Longmans, Green and Co., 1903–1912), vol. 35, 491. See also James S. Dearden, "John Ruskin, the Collector: With a Catalogue of the Illuminated and Other Manuscripts formerly in his Collection," *The Library* 5th ser. 21.2 (June 1966): 124–54.

24. Joan Evans and John Howard Whitehouse, eds., *The Diaries of John Ruskin* (Oxford: Clarendon, 1956–1959), vol. 2.

25. This "collage" is reproduced by Dearden (146) as item 52, plate ix, and is now in the Ruskin Galleries, Bembridge.

26. Rickert, *The Reconstructed Carmelite Missal* (London: Faber and Faber, 1952).

27. Voelkle, in *The Spanish Forger: Master of Deception*, 14 has suggested

that the SF "was a chromolithographer who was put out of work when chromolithography was replaced by photographic reproductions" in book and picture manufacture. Another candidate sometimes suggested for the SF was F. Kellerhoven, who did the chromolithographs for the Lacroix volumes mentioned above, but he is certainly too early.

28. See Phillip Dennis Cate and Sinclair Hamilton Hitchings, *The Color Revolution: Color Lithography in France, 1890–1900* (Santa Barbara, CA and Salt Lake City: Peregrine, 1978), 2, 4; George Ashdown Audsley, *Art of Chromolithography* (New York, C. Scribner's sons, 1883); Joan M. Friedman, *Color Printing in England, 1486–1870: An Exhibition, Yale Center for British Art, New Haven, 20 April to 25 June, 1978* (New Haven: The Center, 1978); and Peter C. Marzio, *Democratic Art:: Pictures for a 19th-Century America: Chromolithography, 1840–1900* (Boston: D.R. Godine; Fort Worth: Amon Carter Museum of Western Art, 1979). A fine selection of popular chromolithography giving an idea of the sentimentalising possibilities for this medium is offered by Carol Belanger Grafton, ed., *Full-Color Victorian Vignettes and Illustrations* (New York: Dover, 1983).

29. See A. Chastel, "La Véronique," *Revue archéologique* 40–41 (1978): 71–82, and Flora Lewis, "The Veronica, Image Legend and Viewer," in W.H. Omrod, ed., *England in the Thirteenth Century: Proceedings of the 1984 Harlaxton Symposium* (Woodbridge: Boydell, 1986): 100–106.

30. This chromolithograph which measures $400 \times 355$ mm, is of unknown provenance. It bears the cartouched initial of its maker "M" and is number 243 of what one might presume was a series of similar saints one could choose from a stock in stores selling religious objects. The title of the scene, St. Veronica, appears in the major languages across the bottom to fit the work for contemplation by virtually any household. A probable source for the composition is the fifteenth-century Master of Saint Veronica's panel painting of the saint and sudarium now in the Pinothek in Munich. See Charles Sterling, *Les peintres primitifs* (n.p.: Fernand Nathan, 1949), plate 29.

31. A series of experimental photographs of the leaf under ultraviolet light was made by John B. Friedman and Maureen Kofkee at the University of Illinois in 1994–1995 through the kindness of the then Director of the World Heritage Museum, Dr Barbara Bohen.

32. See *Breviarium Romanum* (London: Burns Oates & Washbourne, 1946), Verna, 600–602, and *The Liber Usualis . . . edited by the Benedictines of Solesmes* (Tournai: Desclée, 1953), 891–2.

33. On these liturgical matters see the helpful study by Andrew Hughes, *Medieval Manuscripts for Mass and Office: A Guide to their Organization and Terminology* (Toronto and Buffalo, New York: University of Toronto Press, rpt. 1995).

34. Voelkle, *The Spanish Forger*, 14.

35. See Robert C. McGrath, "The Case of the 'Spanish Forger'," *Dartmouth College Library Bulletin* 7 NS 1 (October, 1966): 7–12 and *Illuminated Manuscripts in the Dartmouth College Library* (Hanover: Dartmouth College Library, 1972), no. 70, 34–35.

36. Voelkle, *The Spanish Forger*, 40.

37. The accession numbers are 1926.03.0001–4.

38. Voelkle has noted that the SF "himself was no stranger to forgery workshops . . . indicated by the fake ivory tabernacle to which he, before 1908, contributed the paintings on the wings," *The Spanish Forger: Master of Deception*, 17. This tabernacle has now been lost but is reproduced as figure 54, P 31 in *The Spanish Forger*.

39. I am indebted for a photograph of P47 and for information about the panel to William Voelkle.

40. See Sterling, *Les peintres primitifs*, plate 83, and more recently, Dirk de Vos, *Hans Memling: the Complete Works* (Ghent: Ludion, 1994), 41–56. The Memling subject grouping, ship, female costume with train, and architecture was used by the SF in P 6, 19, 26, 31 32, 33, and 34 in Voelkle's inventory.

41. See Dave Verdooner and Harmen Snel, eds., *Trouwen in Mokum: Jewish Marriage in Amsterdam 1598–1811* ('s Gravenhage: Warray, 1992), Vol. 2, Index 2, 131; Index 4, 269; Index 8, 517 and Index 6, 478. I owe this reference to the kindness of Estelle Wolfers.

42. See Abraham Galant, *Histoire des Juifs d'Istanbul depuis la prise de cette ville, en 1453 par Mehmed II jusqu'à nos jours* (Istanbul: Hüsnütabiat, 1941–1942); the same author's *Histoire des Juifs de Turquie* (Istanbul: Isis, 1985); and Joseph R. Hacker, "Ottoman Policy towards the Jews and Jewish Attitudes towards the Ottomans during the Fifteenth Century," in Benjamin Braude and Bernard Lewis, eds., *Christians and Jews in the Ottoman Empire: The Functioning of a Plural Society* (New York: Holmes & Meier, 1984), 117–26.

43. See E.E. Ramsaur, *The Young Turks: Prelude to the Revolution of 1908* (New York: Russell & Russell, 1970), and Bernard Lewis, *The Emergence of Modern Turkey* (London: Oxford UP, 1968).

44. See Paul Dumont, "Jewish Communities in Turkey during the Last Decades of the Nineteenth Century in the light of the Archives of the Alliance Israélite Universelle," in Braude and Lewis, eds., *Christians and Jews*, 209–42.

45. Dumont, "Jewish Communities in Turkey," 226.

46. Stirling, "Les émules des Primitifs," 80.

47. See, for example, Bridget Ann Henisch, *The Medieval Calendar Year* (University Park, PA: Pennsylvania State UP, 1999), 156–7 and fig. 6–16. It is not clear if the SF was familiar with the works of the Housebook Master, who often portrayed a somewhat nostalgically rendered aristocratic world of youth and play.

* Too late for inclusion here is the exhibition Manuscript Illumination in the Modern Age held at the Block Museum of Art at Northwestern University in January of 2001. This exhibition makes clear the pro-Monarchist context for the Spanish Forger's "medievalizing," as well as the English and American taste for "medieval" cuttings and whole leaves as a sign of belief in the Middle Ages' supposed "virtues of sincerity, honesty and morality." The Spanish Forger is discussed by Sandra Hindman et al., *Manuscript Illumination in the Modern Age: Recovery and Reconstruction* (Evanston, Il, 2001), pp. 155–164.

Fig. 1  Martrydom of female saint and fictitious shields. Leaf by the Spanish
Forger, c.1925. Spurlock Museum of the University of Illinois at
Urbana-Champaign 490 × 360 mm.

Fig. 2 Artist unknown, chromolithograph of Saint Veronica c.1890–1920. 400 × 355 mm. Collection John Friedman and Kristen Figg.

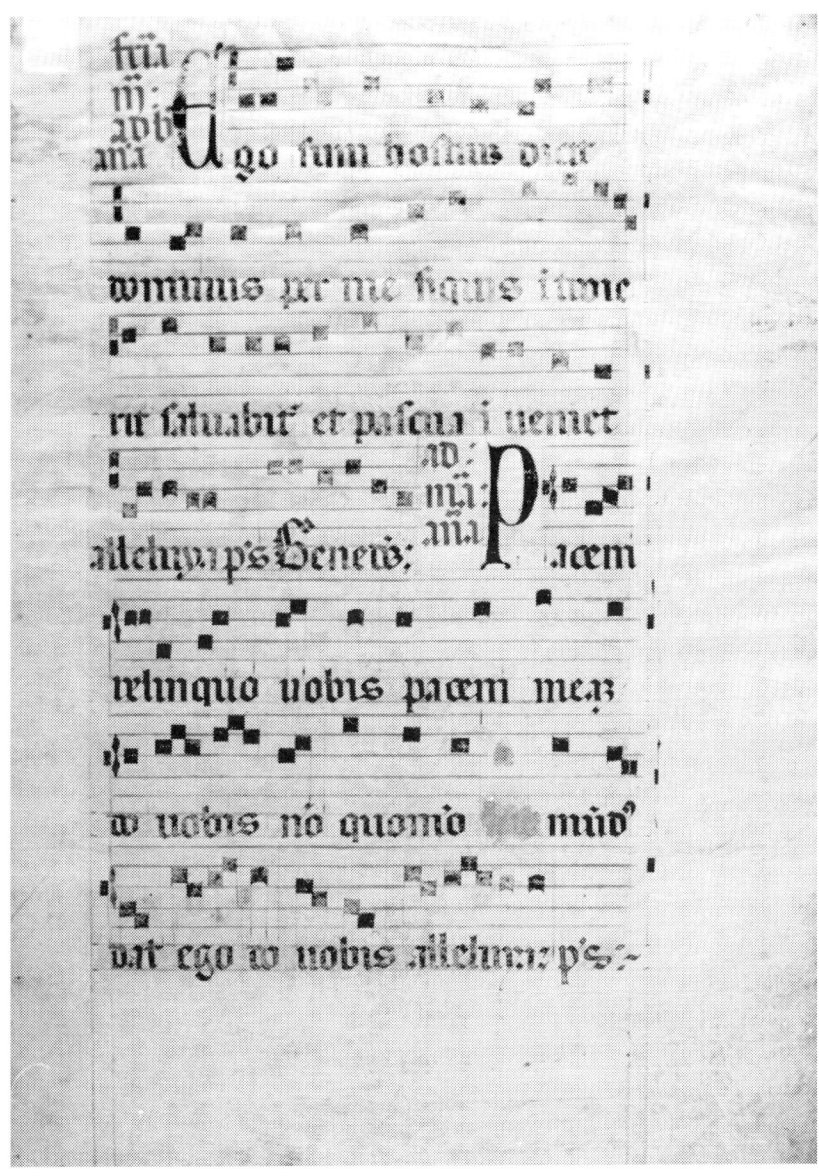

Fig. 3  Verso of Urbana Martrydom, antiphonal page for octave of Pentecost.
Fifteenth-century, northern Gothic textura script. Spurlock Museum of the
University of Illinois at Urbana-Champaign.

Fig. 4 Presentation of Christ and fictitious heraldic shields. Leaf by the Spanish Forger, c.1900. Dartmouth College Library MS 70. 547 × 375 mm.

Fig. 5 Virgin and Child in Heaven, with fictitious heraldic shields. Leaf by the Spanish Forger, c.1920. Mark Lansburgh collection, Tesuque. 550 × 378 mm.

Figs. 6–7  Fictitious heraldic shields and miniatures by the Spanish Forger in "Juvenal" manuscript c.1900, formerly in collection of C.G. Boerner, Leipzig.

Fig. 8  Betrothal scene. Panel painting by the Spanish Forger, c.1920.
Collection Lady Jeanne Campbell Cram, New York.

Fig. 9  Detail of signature Parres, from Cram panel.

# Touring the Medieval:
# Tourism, Heritage and Medievalism, in Northumbria

## Steve Watson

English Heritage, the statutory agency which manages state-owned heritage sites in England, has begun to animate them with jousting tournaments, re-enactments and entertainments of various kinds. Site and spectacle thus combine to create the "sights" and "attractions" so much associated with contemporary heritage production. At Scarborough Castle recently the author witnessed just such an event in which "King Arthur" broke off from a speech he was making to point out that a World War Two Spitfire was flying overhead. The "medieval" was suspended briefly while an abbreviated Battle of Britain was sampled. King Arthur then returned rather gravely to the matter of Lancelot and his faithless queen. Afterwards the actor joked that the flypast had been planned in advance: "it all adds to the attraction" someone remarked.[1]

The same stories of Arthur were recounted at several other English Heritage properties in Northumbria during the summer of 1999. At Richmond Castle, however, which is also owned by English Heritage, there is a genuine local tradition that Arthur and his knights sleep in a secret vault beneath the ramparts. There they had lain since they were almost awakened by one Potter Thompson who, in the middle ages, had stumbled upon a cleft in the rocks which had led him to their chamber.[2] No reference was made to this story, and so it is that the heritage industry brushes away the genuine, the locally significant, the valuable object of the tourist and replaces it with verisimilitude, in much the same way that George Street, the medievalist architect, demolished original medieval walls and replaced them with his own quotations from the gothic. Patrick

Wright has described this tendency in terms of an abstracted view of history:

> History is presented as a gloss, as the light touch of a dab hand, an impression of pastness which can be caught at a glance. This moonlight impression of history can actually submerge the differences between the figures or presences through which it declares itself, leaving only a multiple invocation of the same sense of "the historical."[3]

Historic sites cast as tourist attractions often have very little to do with their contemporary locale. They are in separate space, touristic space, sacrilised[4] for that purpose, institutionalised, branded as a heritage product, an artefact not of the past but of modernity, where history has been quietly terminated, preserved to death and buried under a neatly manicured lawn. The relationship of the medieval with modernity is a major concern in this essay and the role of the tourist in modulating this relationship will be explored as it has developed, along with changing concepts of the medieval itself, over the last three centuries. The contemporary tourist may no longer be "modern" however and under the conditions of postmodernity may have the potential to explore new relationships between the medieval and the present.

The literature on heritage is characteristically critical of tourist-orientated practices, particularly in respect of commodification, alleged ideological function, and the dissonance revealed when different groups offer conflicting accounts of the same events or lay claim to the same territory (see especially Hewison, Walsh, Tunbridge and Ashworth, and Dubin, for some recent American examples of contested museum displays[5]). The extent and vehemence of this critique is such that Lowenthal has identified an "anti-heritage animus" within the academy.[6] Beyond this critique operational activity remains largely untheorised except for the various discourses surrounding interpretation and other aspects of heritage management practice. There is scope, therefore, for a more rigorous understanding of the way the past is received in touristic space and the role that tourism plays in developing an appreciation of the past. That the medieval is a major resource for tourism is surely worthy of investigation, and the reasons for its significance as such may help in understanding the relationship between the two.

Northumbria, as an Anglo-Saxon kingdom, is itself an artefact of the early medieval and reference to it here is justified by the wealth of its built and cultural heritage and the extent to which this has been appropriated by the tourist industry. More than this it is a region well known to the author, mindful though he is of the wonders of the East Anglia, Mercia, Scotland, Cumbria and the South. Boundaries change and so do names, but for the purposes of the present study Northumbria is defined as the region of the Saxon Kingdom of the same name and the Earldom which followed it. Examples are drawn therefore from the traditional (pre-1974) counties of Northumberland, Durham, the Ridings of Yorkshire and the City of York.

The built remains of the medieval period in Northumbria are extensive. They are scattered about the countryside in churches, castles, earthworks of various kinds, houses, deserted villages and field systems. The churches often contain medieval art, which occasionally, as in the case of Saxon and Viking sculpture, predates the building in which it is contained. The medieval is preserved in place names, field and parish boundaries, patterns of land holding as well as oral traditions, local myths and legends and even the way that people speak. In urban settings it might, in the form of a church steeple, poke through layers of surrounding industrial modernity, or it might, as at York and Chester, dominate the townscape with major buildings and patterns of streets that have hardly changed in a thousand years. Medievalism as well as the medieval is significant in the built environment as John Simons has observed from his study window in Southport. The church tower that dominated his view looked medieval although it was built in the 1860s.[7] Given the amount of medieval material that remains and the cultural value attached to it, its significance as resource for tourism is hardly surprising. A number of sites have thus become *sights* and attractions of international significance with thousands of visitors from around the world every year.[8] The questions remain however: what do tourists seek from these sights? What are they offered, and why, apparently is this form of consumption so important?

Much of the tourism in the UK is thus supported by the "Heritage Industry." Heritage in this sense has been described as a commodified version of the received past that depends upon natural, built and artefactual resources in order to market tourist destinations for economic gain.[9] Understandings of the past are thus, inevitably, constructed and promulgated by contemporary cultural practices embodied not only in the activities of historians and archivists but also in those of museum curators and the managers of commercial attractions. Tourism, furthermore, depends to a large extent on the perception of distinctions of various kinds, most obviously between work and leisure, but more significantly, perhaps, between home and destination. It relies, in short, on cultural differentiation. As Jennifer Craik has put it:

Tourists revel in the otherness of destinations, people and activities because they offer the illusion or fantasy of otherness, of difference of counterpoint to the everyday. At the same time the advantages, comforts and benefits of home are reinforced through the exposure to difference.[10]

The sociologist Dean MacCannell developed a general theory of tourism in which sightseeing provides access to differentiations which construct and represent modernity. The tourist thus becomes unwittingly involved in the processes by which modernity is differentiated from other modalities. Such distinctions form the entertainments of the heritage industry:

These displaced forms, embedded in modern society, are the spoils of the victory of the modern over the non-modern world, They establish in consciousness the definition and boundary of modernity by rendering concrete and immediate that which modernity is not.[11]

Sometimes the past is dangerous and the present safe. Alternatively, the present may feel dangerous and uncertain and the past a pleasant and nostalgic resort from unwelcome change.[12] There is a sense then in which the past is "toured," in much the same way as any spatial destination, with similar differentiations between *then* and *now* as exist between *here* and *there*, and with a similar and often common organisational infrastructure to facilitate the tour.[13]

This is particularly important in the case of the medieval. Simons has argued convincingly that the medieval has been an active cultural force since the fifteenth century,[14] but its relationship with industrial modernity is peculiar in that it has provided an almost polar definition of it, a legitimation of its social and political structures and, conversely, a resort from the stresses of the rapid social change with which it is associated. There are very good reasons, therefore, in social and cultural terms, for touring the medieval. Similar dynamics may be relevant to a number of defined periods in history, but that the medieval has a unique contrapuntal relationship to industrial modernity is evidenced in its periodic appropriation, reinvention and representation. The medieval is not simply a past which is toured in some kind of original and pure form. What is toured now is a cultural palimpsest of original material and versions of it produced later, disembedded from its chronological context and dispersed through subsequent periods. As Simons has said:

. . . the process of medievalism is a permanent and transhistorical feature of British culture and the middle ages are a permanent presence in the national consciousness as this manifests itself in the material production and practice of its life.[15]

Touring the medieval therefore, involves not only an engagement with the material of the epoch itself, but with *medievalism* as a distinct cultural dynamic. A popular perception of the medieval at the close of the twentieth century is thus conditioned by a wide variety of images and sources which might include school-taught history, Hollywood films, television, literature, heritage industry representations, destination marketing initiatives, re-enactments at historic sites and fragments of myth in its various forms. The figures of Robin Hood and King Arthur figure largely in this imagery and it is even possible that the post-Tolkien fantasy culture replete with dungeons and dragons has become tangled up with it in the popular imagination.

The primary constituents of the medieval toured are the buildings and artefacts which are to varying extents framed as visitor attractions. In the United Kingdom there is a considerable artefactual resource dating from the Saxon immigrations through to the early sixteenth century – a span of some thousand years. Even modest local museum collections will contain something from one or more of the periods concerned, and the archaeological record will encompass a variety of sites from early settle-ments to the great religious buildings of the fifteenth century. Much is also recorded in the landscape and in place names, the latter, especially for the Saxon and Viking periods from which it is possible to identify the progressive phases of settlement and dispersion. Most of the built medi-eval takes the form of churches, fortifications of various kinds, the greater churches and cathedrals, and monastic remains. Individual houses and groups of houses also survive, but these are comparatively rare. There are twenty-six medieval Cathedrals in England and those of York and Durham are among the finest buildings of their type in Northern Europe. While there is little in Northumbria to compare with the parish churches of East Anglia, the Cotswolds and the South-West, the remains of the great medieval monasteries litter the countryside. The dissolution of 1537 bequeathed a great many in a pleasingly ruined state, of which the abbeys at Fountains and Rievaulx, have long been tourist attractions. Castles of various forms are a major part of the *real* cultural capital of the medieval period. They vary in status from little more than sites marked by bumps in the ground to complete, though often heavily restored buildings, dating from the late eleventh century onwards. Bamburgh, Alnwick, Dunstanburgh and Warkworth are the most important in Northumberland, where although there are a great many smaller castles few are open to tourists. Durham, Barnard and Raby castles are major attractions in Country Durham, and in Yorkshire the ruined castles of Richmond, Helmsley, Pickering, Middleham, Scarborough and York dominate any tour of the medieval.

While this represents the stock of genuine medieval buildings, the medievalist dynamic is represented largely by the restorations of churches and castles and by new building, especially of churches in the eighteenth and nineteenth centuries. Here is found the dynamic at full strength, in the recasting of the medieval within the parameters of a contemporary aesthetic sensibility, a reference to the medieval in the light of how it was now perceived in terms of religious, cultural or political idealisations. As with other cultural productions, the medieval in the built environment is not merely composed of those relics which have survived from the original, but every reinvention of it which has taken place since and tourism as cultural practice cannot fail to act upon the results of this process in the construction of tourism sights and touristic space. Reciprocally, tourism itself has fed the process through sight sacrilisation and the concept of attraction, as well as the less pure activities of the heritage industry.

As an expression of the medievalist dynamic the "gothic revival" found perhaps its greatest expression in Horace Walpole's Strawberry Hill. Alnwick Castle in Northumberland, however, provides a more illuminating example for reasons that will become apparent later. This massive castle was the power base of the famous Percy family, later the Dukes of Northumberland. At the time of the first Duke in the mid-eighteenth century a painting by Canaletto shows that the castle was in a ruinous condition. After some minor work by Paine, Robert Adam was employed to conduct a major restoration resulting in what Pevsner et al. called "the most complete and fanciful decorations he ever designed" and they quote a guide book of 1822 in which the work is described as "the gayest and most elegant style of gothic architecture."[16] Although it started early in Northumberland,[17] the use of gothic in the eighteenth century was clearly an affront to the prevailing taste and the classical influence of Palladio was hard to gainsay. It was also an affront to the more serious reading of it which followed: a feeling expressed most vehemently in Vallance's criticisms of Hawksmoor's work at All Souls College Oxford, which he dismisses as "a puerile caricature of the kind that only brings the noble name of gothic into contempt."[18]

The antiquarianism born in the seventeenth century (Aubrey made the first attempt to taxonomise medieval architectural styles in his *Chronologia Architectonica* of c.1670), began to inform a new quest for authenticity. Thus shorn of its picturesque aesthetic the medieval was recast at the turn of the nineteenth century into a powerful symbol of nationhood and imperialism. As Peter Mandler has observed:

> . . . moving into the nineteenth century, we find ourselves in the midst of a great revolution not so much in elite as in popular culture. It is here that the two elements necessary to the making of a national heritage should be sought: the growth of a cultural nation and that nation's identification with the past. Very soon after they were built, the picturesque houses and castles were to be buried under a deluge of criticism as inauthentic, barbarous, unfeeling.[19]

The Fourth Duke obliterated Adam's work at Alnwick in the 1850s, when Salvin was commissioned to restore a more authentically medieval baronial style and something very similar happened at Ford Castle a few miles up the road. John Hussey Delaval had gothicised the medieval stronghold in the 1760s, but in 1828 this work was described as a "melancholy instance of the frippery and degrading taste of George II's time."[20] Ford had to wait until the 1860s to be recast in a medieval more appropriate to nineteenth century sensibilities. Similar instances could be catalogued and they demonstrate the ways in which the medievalist dynamic produced two very different idealisations within a very short period of time: first as an aesthetic expression and second, a grand statement of nationhood and enduring social values.

The need for authenticity drew on the antiquarian movement of the late eighteenth and early nineteenth century within which interest in understanding medieval architecture was growing. The early work of Grose, Carte and Milner was followed by a flood of accounts, histories, observations and local and regional gazetteers.[21] Thomas Rickman created the basic typology of gothic styles in 1817 with his *Attempt to Discriminate the Styles of English Architecture, from the Conquest to the Reformation; Preceded by a Sketch of the Grecian and Roman Orders, with Notices of Nearly Five Hundred Buildings*. By 1881 the book had run to seven editions and introduced such terms as "Early English," "Decorated" (or "Middle pointed") and "Perpendicular" in to the lexicon of the architectural historian. Revealingly, English architecture is equated with gothic and the category is described as one of the two principal modes of design, the other being "antique" or what would now be referred to as classical.[22] In 1825 Britton produced a corpus of detailed elevational drawings of medieval buildings of all types, and his seminal *Cathedral Antiquities of England* in 14 volumes was to have a lasting influence on the development of the gothic taste in the nineteenth century.[23] The medievalist dynamic expressed through the Oxford movement and an associated desire to link the church with its early history provided the basis for a growing interest in antiquarianism within the church. The ecclesiological activities of the Oxford Architectural Society and Cambridge's Camden Society, created a doctrine through which the gothic was portrayed not only as Christian architecture, but as English Christian architecture[24] in the service of particular vision of the liturgy.[25]

By the 1830s the gothic style was well and truly rehabilitated. This coincided with the beginning of a period of church building that rivalled the fifteenth century, both in its alteration of what already existed and in new building to provide for the spiritual needs of the recently urbanised and suburbanised industrial population. The great architect of this expansion was Augustus Pugin, who, significantly, was equally concerned with what his designs represented in terms of religious doctrine. His polemical works of the 1830s and 1840s including *The True Principles of Pointed or Christian Architecture* (1841), were an attempt to combine a philosophy of visual taste with the values of Catholicism.[26] He was immensely influential in forming a concept of the medieval with a moral purpose in the midst of an expanding industrial modernity and like others he was also at pains to point out that the gothic was an essentially English form and that classicism more properly belonged in southern Europe. Others followed in Pugin's footsteps, either as faithful medieval copyists, such as Gilbert Scott, or as ardent tractarians such as Butterfield, Street and Pearson, realising in stone and brick the "High Church" ideals of the Cambridge Camden Society. The doctrinaire attitude of the latter led to a commitment to rebuilding rather than to preserving the original.[27] George Street produced some archetypal Victorian gothic buildings but was not averse to demolishing an original for the sake of his own medieval vision. Thus was lost a large original perpendicular window at Hedon in the East Riding, and his pre-occupation with the replacement of medieval windows is particularly noticable at Pickhill in North Yorkshire. There is nothing in Northumbria, however to compare with his wholesale attack on St Lawrence's at Castle Rising in Norfolk.[28]

The work of Pugin also gave license to many regional architects to produce ambitious designs fuelled by the desire for an authentic retelling of the medieval. Thus northern towns are endowed with the work of

Ignatious Bonomi, John and Benjamin Green and, in particular, J.P. Pritchett of Darlington who specialised in providing ambitious buildings in the Early English style for the Congregational Movement. Superb examples of his work remain in Darlington, Halifax, Pudsey, Ilkley, York and Whitby, replete with geometric and plate tracery, rose windows, crocketed pinnacles and spires, elaborate yet robust.[29] The movement that created these buildings disappeared in the 1970s and many that survive find use as commercial premises such as at Darlington, where Pritchett is now the architect of a carpet warehouse.[30]

Although the significance of this in relation to industrial modernity has already been stated, the point should be emphasised, however, as Brett has done, that this high point of medievalism occurred during the dramatic mid-period in the development of industrial modernity and was functional to it in providing both legitimation and a comforting resort.[31] The point has been made before, notably by Chandler,[32] but what followed was an assertion of medievalism with a completely different ideological perspective and agenda. With the Pre-Raphaelites, Ruskin, and later, William Morris and the arts and crafts movement, the medieval was no longer a legitimation either for the liturgy or for the social structure. It became a resort, in the sense of an ideological alternative to the industrial-urban nature of nineteenth-century modernity. The latter was an aberration, but one that could be countered through political agitation and a commitment to the simple qualities of medieval life as it was expressed in the rural, the celebration of simplicity and, as much as anything, in the practice of traditional craft and design.[33] In architecture this movement gave impetus to a fresher, freer version of the medieval seen in abundance with the work of Ferguson at Bamburgh Castle, Lutyens at Lindisfarne Castle and the truly amazing St Andrews church at Roker, by Prior and Wells: a version of gothic to herald the twentieth century. An earlier manifestation is St Martins at Scarborough, designed by George Frederick Bodley, the first patron of Morris's firm.[34] The pulpit is of particular interest, with painted panels by Rosetti, Ford Madox Brown and Morris.

Another contrast with the earlier medievalists was in the attitude to restoration. The Society for the Preservation of Ancient Buildings was founded by William Morris in 1877 and an early item on its agenda was an open challenge to the church authorities over the damage caused by restoration. Morris roundly condemned the Gothic revival as a licence for architects to "correct" old buildings and attacked both the Church of England and George Gilbert Scott, one of its principal architects.[36] These were early skirmishes in a long running campaign to establish the preservation and conservation of old buildings within the national consciousness, a campaign which is active to the present day.

The role of the state was established in landmark legislation such as the Ancient Monuments Protection Acts of 1882 and 1900. The Royal Commissioners on Ancient Monuments thus provided an inventory of buildings worthy of preservation. The present statutory framework owes much to the Ancient Monuments Consolidation and Amendment Act of 1913 which established powers of protection, through preservation orders and the bringing into public ownership and public access of a vast estate of largely medieval ruins. These are the castles, abbeys and other remains now owned and presented by English Heritage and which form a major part of the stock in trade of the heritage industry. English Heritage thus plays a key role in defining the medieval monument as a tourist resource, though what its early progenitors would make of some of its more ebullient activities is difficult to imagine.

At the beginning of the twenty-first century the medieval and the productions of medievalism present the tourist with a jumbled mixture of images, a combination of original, restored and later material in the built environment as well as the narratives of the heritage and entertainment industries. An English Heritage site, a townscape with Victorian churches, a *gothick* mansion, *Braveheart* on video or at the cinema, a novel by Ellis Peters based on a twelfth-century monk in Shrewsbury and produced for TV (in Eastern Europe). All of these present mutually reinforcing signifiers of the medieval so that it becomes, almost, a *brand image*, the value of which is based on its significance in contemporary culture.

The material of medievalism has thus emerged from a complex series of historical episodes where in each of these its meaning has been conditioned by its contrapuntal relationship with existing social processes and particularly those associated with industrial modernity. But how has that meaning been received? What has been described above is what is available for the tourist to consume. If MacCannell is right, the act of sightseeing and the differentiations to which it provides access are the means by which society is understood. What then are the implications for touring the medieval?

The gothic revival coincided with a number of cultural trends, not least of which were the developing aesthetics of the sublime and the picturesque, and the beginnings of rural and country house, tourism. With William Gilpin's tours in the 1780s, the medieval ruin became part of the ensemble of components which as Gilpin had it would "look well in a picture." Gilpin also, ironically, asserted his appreciation of Oliver

Cromwell "that picturesque genius [who] omitted no opportunity of adorning the counties through which he passed with noble ruins."[37] The decayed magificence represented by ruins was a major part of their attraction. Tintern Abbey in the South and Fountains in the North provided and early source of touristic fascination. By the 1790s both were major sights. It was the emotional response that they elicited rather than any engagement with history that was, however, the chief characteristic of this sensibility. As Mandler states:

> True, the cult of sensibility invited the traveller to view the relics of the past in order to elicit certain feelings, but these were not feelings of identification or sympathy. On the contrary, relics were meant to transmit moral messages about the transgressions of our ancestors: they were images of superstition, of shattered ambition, of hubris punished.[38]

This coincidence of aesthetics with an early form of sightseeing worked on both the original and the appropriated medieval. The three hundred or so visitors at Strawberry Hill in the years between 1780 and 1800 were, though a tiny minority of the population, the vanguard of what was to become the heritage industry.[39] Thus, what people began to tour at Strawberry Hill, Alnwick and other destinations was not only the medieval, but an idealisation of it realised through the works of the designer, the architect and the cultivated patron. In short, they were touring *medievalism*.

The activities of aesthetes such as Gilpin at once established and modified the medieval according to contemporary taste. The picturesque thus sacrilised the landscape of which medieval relics were an intrinsic part. This process continued until medieval relics became an adornment to the parks surrounding neo-classical country houses, an excellent example being Fountains Abbey in Yorkshire which was suitably trimmed and dressed for the purpose. Aesthetic considerations aside, the gothic revival also, according to Mandler, presented a symbolism of sturdy resistance to the ideas of revolution fomenting on the continent. The "great hulking castles built" by Thomas Smirke for Lords Lowther and Summers represented a less than benevolent expression of power.[40]

The change of taste that occurred in the nineteenth century was dramatic, widespread and strongly expressed. Sir Stephen Glynne toured medieval churches in Yorkshire in the 1820s and noticed some "new" churches in the Bradford area:

I was shocked to see here, and in many other places in the neighbourhood, new churches built of very good stone, but in the most depraved taste, being very faulty and inelegant attempts at imitation of Gothic architecture.[41]

Unburdened of these thoughts he turns his attention to the "pictur-esque" ruins of Kirkstall Abbey, and the City of York. Glynne was an early representative of the antiquarian tourist, a species of grand tourist who made rural England the object of his travels. Travel writers of the middle and later nineteenth century built on this tradition and thus was declared the medieval as an emblem of taste and as an object of tourism. Walter White wrote his *Month in Yorkshire* in 1858 and it is worth recording his notes on tourism as he discovered it at Fountains Abbey:

> Carriage after carriage laden with sight-seers rattled past as I walked to Studley, a distance of nearly three miles. Even at the toll bar on the way you can buy guide-books as well as ginger beer.[41]

Later in the century Edmund Bogg made an epic journey from the Ouse at York to the Vale of Eden in Westmorland, recounting on his travels the majesty of the medieval relics which he encountered, including Fountains Abbey, where he attempts a communion with the medieval past:

> Standing on the footpath overlooking the Abbey, listening to the purling waters of the tiny Skell rippling under ruined and ivy-clad arches, still clinging to us the same sweet music as it sang to the monks of old, on whose ruined home we now gaze and ponder in astonishment, and marvel on this architectural magnificence, the palatial dwelling house of the priesthood of feudal ages. Under the shadow of an enormous yew, we think of the glorious past of this Abbey; under its boughs monks have walked and mused as they gently paced the cloister court. Could its dark branches whisper, many a scene of monkish days would be recorded.[42]

Bogg's romanticism, though produced at the end of the nineteenth century, belongs to an earlier generation (he hardly mentions rail travel) and a new wave of antiquarian tourists with a mission to catalogue and analyse rather than merely to adumbrate soon came to the fore. Fallow's *Memorials of Old Yorkshire* is typical of this trend. Thus the village

churches of Yorkshire are listed along with the Norman doorways of
Yorkshire churches, the bells of the same, the castles of Yorkshire and
Yorkshire folklore. Photography is used extensively and every effort is
made to avoid the romantic hyperbole of earlier generations of travel
writers.[43]

William Tomlinson[44] represents the trend in Northumberland and
whilst clearly influenced by the aesthetic of the sublime,[45] his main
purpose is to catalogue and reveal, which he does in great detail and with
reference to fold-out maps on a scale of four miles to the inch. The
County is divided into ten sections within each of which is plotted a
series of tours: Bamburgh to Budle; Bamburgh to Dunstanburgh;
Alnwick to Edlingham etc. Details of the geology, botany, medieval relics,
historical references and local legends are recounted along the way as well
as the opening hours and admission prices of the various attractions.
Architectural and historical accounts are accurate and encyclopaedic, and
lists are appended of all the medieval churches with their dedication and
predominant architectural styles according to the Rickman taxonomy, the
principal castles and towers, ruined churches and chapels and the remains
of monastic houses. This was medievalism for the tourist (the principal
hotels and inns are also listed), and the medievalist buildings of the nineteenth century are also included as objects of the tour. Interest in
recording medieval relics was sustained by the county archaeological societies which sprang up during the nineteenth century. Representative of
this are the Yorkshire Archaeological Society, founded in 1863, the
Thoresby Society, founded in 1889 and the Society of Antiquaries of
Newcastle-upon-Tyne, founded in 1813. Part of the activities of such
societies would be day trips by train and coach to some location to tour
its ancient buildings, and reflect upon their historical associations. The
proceedings of the Society of Antiquaries of Newcastle-upon-Tyne
contain many accounts of such excursions from the nineteenth century.[46]

The late nineteenth and early to mid-twentieth centuries saw a transformation of tourism from the essentially elitist activity represented above
to "mass" participation. Better pay, paid holidays and cheaper and easier
transport were the key factors. The rapid expansion of rail network was,
of course, the most significant development and new seaside resorts such
as Scarborough were established largely as a consequence of this. But the
rail network also made the medieval accessible in ways that it had not
been previously. The sacrilisation of medieval and medievalist buildings
in the nineteenth century is marked by the production, on a large scale, of
lithographic prints sold singly or used to illustrate guide books. An
impressive example is R.W. Billings's book on the medieval antiquities of

County Durham, in which his own fine engravings were the very first representations of many of the buildings illustrated.[47] A much wider medievalism was thus brought to a much wider public. Even the smallest ruin found its way into print, so that nowadays nineteenth-century lithographs may be had for a few pounds from an antiquarian bookseller. The essentially visual quality of tourist activity has been analysed by Urry,[48] and the mechanical reproduction of such images played an important part in the development of the tourist imagination through the century. Improvements in technology moved ultimately to those perennial necessities of the tourist, the camera and the picture postcard.[49]

The development of motor transport in the twentieth century went hand in hand with the access created to many medieval sites by public ownership. This coincidence of travel technology and access was a major impetus in the transformation of many from *sites* to *sights*, from objects of antiquarian interest to mass tourist attractions. Gordon Home offered the following guidance to tourists in Yorkshire, in 1922:

> In order to make it easy to reach any of the places described, I have indicated the nearest railway station . . . This information is of no interest to the motorist, for his means of locomotion will take him right to castle, abbey, village or moor . . .[50]

Twelve years (and a lot of traffic) later Riley, writing another guide for tourists, was expressing present-day concerns about the environmental impacts of the car in these same locations:

> All the roads upon the line of our route are possible to motorists and I have made sure by going over the whole course ourselves in a "petrol engine" that was too well-bred to roar and wail [but] if he belongs to the order of speed merchants the Pennines are not for him.[51]

According to Urry, the transformation to mass tourism was characterised by a change in the "gaze" of the tourist from being predominantly romantic and individualistic to something which was more organised and rationalised. When Thomas Cook took his first train full of temperance tourists from Leicester to Loughborough in 1844 he thus began a movement which was to make mass tourism one of the key phenomena of industrial modernity.[52]

The heritage industry has experienced tremendous growth over the last twenty years, as a corollary of the growth in tourism[53] and as part of a cultural movement in which an interest in the past and especially the *things* of the past has been a characteristic. The past has been fashionable in a way that the future once was, and the period since 1980 has seen a particularly vigorous increase in public interest.[54] The National Heritage Act 1983 established English Heritage (The Historic Monuments Commission) with the principal aims of conserving England's historic sites, monuments, buildings and areas, promoting access and enjoyment and raising understanding and awareness of the heritage. It is responsible for 409 sites which it inherited from the Department of the Environment.

English Heritage, according to Wright, set out

> . . . to go beyond the gauntly authentic stone and the baize-like lawns ("Keep off the Grass") traditional and the Department of the Environment's semi academic stewardship of the nation's ruins. Respectful but commercially-minded reanimation is to be the way forward in this new world of theme-parks and mass tourism.[55]

Receiving around 10.5 million visits per annum English Heritage has made the medieval a mass tourist resource. A 23% growth in visits to historic properties is recorded for the period 1975 to 1994. Similar sources provide indicative data on the extent of church and cathedral visiting. Of those historic properties offering free admission all twenty-six recording more than 200,00 visitors annually are cathedrals or greater churches including some such as Liverpool and Truro which are medievalist rather than medieval per se. At least 28 churches attracted more than 50,000 visitors each. Figures for churches generally are difficult to come by and they vary dramatically according to the level recognition a particular church has as a tourist sight. A survey carried out by the English Tourist Board in 1996 suggests around 27,000 visitors at Beverley St Mary and 19,000 at Escomb. In Northumbria, York Minster attracts over 2 million visitors a year and is second only to Westminster Abbey on the national scale. Durham Cathedral records half a million visitors annually and Beverley Minster over 100,000. The English Heritage castles at such as Dunstanburgh Warkworth and Scarborough each attract over 50,000 visitors annually. Figures for privately owned attractions such as Alnwick and Bamburgh castles are similar, if not higher. Bamburgh has recorded over 100,000.[56]

Never has the medieval been more significant as a resource for tourism. But do the analyses of its cultural context presented earlier still hold true? If, for example, the medieval is a defining category in the construction of modernity, how then does it stand in relation to postmodernity which is widely believed to be the condition which has replaced it?

Postmodernity would not appear to require the contrapuntal support of the medieval, so perhaps under these new conditions, if indeed they do prevail, the medieval is finally toured for its own sake, with the tourist engaging more genuinely in history. This seems unlikely given the commitment of English Heritage to the kinds of animation and events mentioned at the beginning and the whole "theme park" approach that conditions contemporary approaches to heritage management.[57] It seems more likely that the medieval becomes just another surface impression among many more derived from the past, something to be consumed without distinction from any other commodity. Under the condition of postmodernity individuals are said to define themselves not so much by what they produce as what they consume and their consumption is characterised by an almost unlimited choice expressed characteristically by shopping malls – the cathedrals of postmodernity. The notion of lifestyle and the micro-segmentation of markets support this process. Mass markets hardly exist anymore, they have been transformed into a series of *niches* responding to lifestyle/lifestage market segments each one defined through market research and serviced through carefully targeted marketing. Consumption and choice have spawned an eclecticism which is also one of the defining features of postmodernity and which enables all manner of objects to be represented and consumed together in a chaotic mixture, the mixture itself being of more interest than its constituent parts. Here we return to Richmond Castle and Scarborough and Spitfires and forgotten, sleeping knights. Peter Fowler remarks upon the odd mixture of heritage attractions encountered typically on a journey through Northern England:

> Driving along he motorway recently, I passed a large white-on-brown sign. It exhorted me, in one and the same breath. . . to visit the Derbyshire Dales, Gulliver's Kingdom and the Heights of Abraham. . . by carrying these three messages, this particular sign might be taken to imply that all three potential destinations were of similar validity. In that sense it well serves my purpose here for it illustrates the "anything goes," "it's all grist to the mill" attitude which seems to have infiltrated the working practices, even the rationale, of much that is made available as heritage for public consumption.[58]

Collage, pastiche and playful irony become characteristic features of culture and representation. Taken a step further in the work of sociologists theorists such as Jean Baudrillard[59] and Umberto Eco,[60] representation becomes duplication and simulation, the only reality, hyper-reality. There is no longer any depth, any reality behind representation, only other representations. Image and reality merge. Theme parks and museums are particular exponents of such simulcra and the hyper-real. The Jorvik Viking Centre and the Beamish Open Air Museum are thus perceived as attempts to represent the past by duplicating reality, but in the process they create their own reality, which is then re-represented elsewhere as tenth-century York or nineteenth-century Durham.

Heritage in general, and the medieval in particular come to be defined by those who consume them in subtle reciprocity with those who market them as products and representations. The actual relics of the past are almost irrelevant and certainly unnecessary at the point of consumption, only representations are important. What is significant, according to Jameson, is the intensity of the cultural activity concerned with what he calls the "nostalgia mode" which has "insensibly colonised" the present. Using the medium of film as his example he demonstrates how the past becomes no more than a stylistic referent, with no place for genuine historicity. From this develops a

> complex and interesting new formal inventiveness; it being understood that the nostalgia film was never a matter of some old-fashioned "representation" of historical content, but instead approached the "past" through stylistic connotation, conveying "pastness" by the glossy qualities of the image, and the "1930s-ness" or "1950s-ness" by the attributes of fashion . . .[61]

The past is thus created in the depthlessness of its own representation, the links with relics and therefore with the need for effective interpretation having been shorn away. By extension into other areas of production it is created through reciprocal acts of marketing and consumption, as a series of representative ideals and stereotypes.

Hewison articulates a similar perspective and would have no difficulty in explaining a juxtaposition of Spitfires and Arthurian knights:

> . . . this pastiched and collaged past, once it has received the high gloss of presentation from the new breed of "heritage managers", succeeds in presenting a curiously unified image, where change, conflict, clashes of interest, are neutralised

within a single seamless and depthless surface, which merely reflects our contemporary anxieties. If there is any allusion to the historical perspective in this image it is usually the pastoral perspective surveyed from the terrace of a country house.[62]

Thus the process which creates the conditions for a chain of shops selling reproduction medieval jewellery and decorative items (many of them manufactured in the third world) also allows English Heritage to provide medievalist entertainments in its ruined castles. Sieges that never took place are "re-enacted," events that appeal more to received notions of medieval England than to history, which is of no interest anyway to the postmodernists. The York Viking Festival can end with a firework display! Such celebrations are truly the stuff of the heritage industry. The conditions are thus created for the National Trust to own and present Fountains Abbey *and* the birthplace of Paul McCartney and the consumer of culture may be astonished in equal measure by Durham Cathedral and by Disneyland Paris. It seems clear that if postmodernity is accepted as the prevailing social and cultural condition (and this is by no means necessary) then the medieval is reduced in status to one of many depthless forms which may be consumed without significance. Touring the medieval is a meaningless activity for *touring* is the essential thing, it matters not what.

There is perhaps some possibility of redemption for the tourist and for others who would seek access to the medieval beyond that which the heritage industry offers. It depends on the extent to which heritage operators and others can rehabilitate the notion that the present is a continuation of the past and not differentiated from it as it is under both modern and postmodern cultural conditions.

Wright has identified the various ways in which the alignment of past and present have been conditioned in the service of prevailing hegemonic goals, and each of these represents some kind of disjuncture, a way of presenting the past as frozen over and realised only in bourgeois interpretations of history and society.[63] Walsh, meanwhile, provides the conceptual orientation:

> As people have been distanced from the processes which affect their daily lives, the past has been promoted as something which is completed, and no longer contingent upon our experiences in the world.
>
> . . . the past became something which emerged as yet another form of institutionalised discourse, often articulated through

the museum and the academy. The past was gradually isolated and obscured, and was promoted as that which was no longer important to and contingent upon people's daily experiences. Rationalised in the removed and rarefied discourse of the professions, the past was sequestered from those to whom it belonged.

This process has been one which has steadily intensified to the point where, during the later twentieth century, the past has emerged as a reservoir of shallow surfaces which can be exploited in the heritage centre or the biscuit tin.[64]

This briefly encapsulates much of what the contemporary heritage industry is about, a selective institutionalised version of the past which physically separates it from people's lives and, under the condition of modernity, neutralises it as anything other than a signification that modernity exists in contrast to that which is being toured. Under postmodernity the heritage industry condenses the representation of the past into the shallow, evanescent surfaces of contemporary cultural practice.

This need not, however, be the case and Raphael Samuel[65] has explored the ways in which the conservation movement has often represented a movement from below, encapsulating oppositional values rather than promulgating some hegemonic project of the ruling classes. Such activity on a local scale, reconnecting people with their past (and the medieval figures largely in this) may yet provide a positive way of addressing the issues generated at the interface of tourism, the medieval and the heritage industry. Macdonald has identified an instance of local expression, using the methods of heritage industry to reveal a local understanding of the past,[66] and Jim Russell has developed a model of heritage integration with community development based on Australian experience.[67]

Is it possible that the medieval, on its journey through time, might fetch up again as something valued, as it has done so many times in the past? Could it be that the medieval in its abundance and diversity provides opportunities to tour the past outside the bright and visually enriched spaces created by the global heritage tourism industry? Appropriating the medieval for the twenty-first century means recognising and realising the "real" cultural capital that such relics represent, and connecting it with the communities with whom it resides. The village church, the ruined castle, Saxon cross or deserted village can all add value and meaning to a particular location, and can help to create a *sense* of place. The tourist might even be freed from the appropriations of the heritage industry altogether and engage with a new medieval, locally relevant and locally realised, a counterpoint now, not to industrial modernity but to global postmodernity.

There may yet be room in all of this for King Arthur to wave at passing Spitfires in front of a passive audience oblivious to the anachronism. They are both, after all, the stuff of legend and have their place in any pageant of the National past. But next time an actor points a sword to the sky at Scarborough Castle it could be for a higher purpose than the promotion of the heritage industry. It may be something that celebrates the place, rather than vacuously exploiting it, played out by people who understand its significance and for the benefit of tourists who are willing to be actively engaged by the story. It might even find precedence over the artifice of a commercially constructed mythology.

## NOTES

1. These events were part of the English Heritage Events programme for the summer of 1999. The events at Scarborough took place over the weekend of August 14–15. A Spitfire and a Hurricane appeared on the afternoon of the 15th and though much in evidence the reason for their presence remains a mystery.

2. W. Riley, *The Yorkshire Pennines of the North West* (London: Herbert Jenkins Limited, 1934), 101; and W. White, *A Month in Yorkshire* (Leeds: M.T.D. Rigg Publications, 1991 [facsimile of 1858 edition]), 299. The version recorded in the latter has the potter guided to the chamber by a mysterious figure and presented with a sword and a horn. Either way the hapless potter began to draw Arthur's sword from its scabbard, but as he did so Arthur and the knights around him began to stir and wake. Taking fright he replaced the sword in its scabbard and ran out into the daylight. Regaining his composure he determined to return to the chamber but was never again able to find the cleft in the rocks.

3. Patrick Wright, *On Living in an Old Country* (London: Verso, 1985), 69.

4. The term as it is used here and at other points is borrowed from MacCannell who uses it to describe the stages through which tourist "sights" are constructed as cultural productions, see Dean MacCannell, *The Tourist: A New Theory of the Leisure Class* (Berkeley: University of California, 1999), 43–46.

5. See especially Robert Hewison, *The Heritage Industry* (London: Methuen, 1987). This has become the classic "anti-heritage" account, a touchstone in the developing critique of heritage and its uses; Kevin Walsh, *The Representation of the Past: Museums and Heritage in the Post-modern World* (London: Routledge, 1992); J.E. Tunbridge and G.J. Ashworth, *Dissonant Heritage* (London: John Wiley & Sons, 1995), and Steven C. Dubin, *Displays of Power:*

*Memory and Amnesia in the American Museum* (New York and London: New York University Press, 1999).

6. David Lowenthal, *The Heritage Crusade and the Spoils of History* (Cambridge: Cambridge University Press, 1998), ch. 4.

7. John Simons, "Christopher Middleton and Elizabethan Medievalism," in Richard Utz and Tom Shippey, eds., *Medievalism in the Modern World: Essays in Honour of Leslie J. Workman*, The Making of the Middle Ages vol. 1 (Turnhout: Brepols, 1999), 19.

8. Fountains Abbey and Durham Cathedral are "World Heritage Sites" and York Minster is hardly less significant.

9. E.A.J. Carr, "Tourism and Heritage," in G.J. Ashworth and P.J. Larkham, eds., *Building a New Heritage: Tourism, Culture and Identity in the New Europe* (London: Routledge, 1994), ch. 4.

10. Jennifer Craik, "The Culture of Tourism," in Chris Rojek and John Urry, eds., *Touring Cultures: Transformations of Travel and Theory* (London: Routledge, 1997), 114.

11. MacCannell, *The Tourist*, 8–9 and 78–79 where he develops the idea of modernity defined and elevated by cultural and historical otherness in his discussion of the function of the museum and other attractions in modern culture.

12. David Lowenthal, *The Past is a Foreign Country* (Cambridge: Cambridge University Press, 1985), 4–13.

13. David Brett, *The Construction of Heritage* (Cork: Cork University Press, 1996), 14–15, 34.

14. Simons, "Christopher Middleton," 44.

15. Simons, "Christopher Middleton," 44.

16. Nikolaus Pevsner et al., *The Buildings of England: Northumberland* (London: Penguin, 1992), 136.

17. Pevsner et al., *Buildings*, 75–76.

18. Quoted in David Watkins, *The Rise of Architectural History* (Architectural Press, 1983), 128.

19. Peter Mandler, *The Fall and Rise of the Stately Home* (New Haven and London: Yale University Press, 1997), 17.

20. John F. Dodds, *Bastions and Belligerents, Medieval Strongholds in Northumberland* (Newcastle-upon-Tyne: Keepdate Publishing, 1999), 86.

21. B.F.L. Clarke, *Church Builders of the Nineteenth Century* (London: SPCK, 1938), 17.

22. Thomas Rickman, *An Attempt to Discriminate the Styles of Architecture in England from the Conquest to the Reformation . . .* (London: Longman, Rees, Orme, Green and Longman, 1835), B.

23. Watkin, *The Rise of Architectural History*, 60–61.

24. Clarke, *Church Builders*, 73.

25. J. Stevens Curl, *Victorian Churches* (London: Batsford/English Heritage, 1995, 25–29.

26. Curl, *Churches*, 30–46. See also Clarke, *Church Builders*, ch. 4.

27. Michael Hunter, ed., *Preserving the Past: The Rise of Heritage in Modern Britain* (Stroud: Alan Sutton, 1996), 6.

28. See Chris Miele "The First Conservation Militants: William Morris and the Society for the Protection of Ancient Buildings," in Hunter, *Preserving the Past*, 18.

29. For a splendid pictorial account of Pritchett's early work see J. Horsfall Turner, *Yorkshire Notes and Queries*, vol. 2, 17 October 1889: 122.

30. This is the Congregational Church which was latterly Northgate United Reformed Church built in 1862–2.

31. Brett, *Construction of Heritage*, 15–16

32. Alice Chandler, *A Dream of Order: The Medieval Ideal in Nineteenth Century Literature* (London: Routlege and Kegan Paul), 1971.

33. Martin J. Weiner, *English Culture and the Decline of the Industrial Spirit* (London: Pelican, 1985), 118–21.

34. Nikolaus Pevsner, *The Buildings of England, Yorkshire: The North Riding* (London: Penguin, 1966), 322.

35. For a detailed account see Miele, "The First Conservation Militants," 21–27.

36. Cited in Brett, *Construction of Heritage*, 42.

37. Mandler, *Fall and Rise of the Country House*, 13.

38. Mandler, *Fall and Rise*, 10.

39. Mandler, *Fall and Rise*, 16–17.

40. This is from an undated manuscript in the possession of the author. Glynne's tours were eventualy reported in various volumes of the *Journal of the Yorkshire Archaeological Society*.

41. White, *A Month in Yorkshire*, 302.

42. Edmund Bogg, *From Eden Vale to the Plains of York* (Leeds: Edmund Bogg, 1894), 320.

43. T.M. Fallow, ed., *Memorials of Old Yorkshire* (London: George Allen & Sons, 1909).

44. W.W. Tomlinson, *Comprehensive Guide to Northumberland* (London and Newcastle-upon-Tyne: Walter Scott Publishing Company), 1895.

45. See especially his description his description of Bamburgh Castle "For rugged strength and barbaric grandeur it is the King of Northumbrian castles," 427–8.

46. Typical of these is the trip taken by members of the Society of Antiquaries of Newcastle-Upon-Tyne, on September 2, 1905. They assembled after a short journey by train at Chester-le-Street in County Durham, there to tour the important medieval church of St Mary and St Cuthbert (with its recently installed screen and refurbished chancel), and the nearby Lumley Castle, thirteenth century with a little eighteenth century gothic. See *Proceedings of the Society of Antiquaries of Newcastle-upon-Tyne*, 3rd series, vol. 2, no. 11, 1905.

47. R.W. Billings, *Illustrations of the Architectural Antiquities of the County*

*of Durham: Ecclesiastical, Castellated and Domestic* (Durham: George Andrews and the Author, 1846).

48. John Urry, *The Tourist Gaze: Leisure and Travel in Contemporary Societies* (London: Sage, 1990).

49. See Carol Crawshaw and John Urry, "Tourism and the Photographic Eye," in Rojek and Urry, eds., *Touring Cultures*, ch. 9.

50. George Home, *Through Yorkshire, the County of Broad Acres* (London: J.M. Dent & Sons, 1922), v.

51. Riley, *The Yorkshire Pennines of the North West*, 17.

52. Urry, *Tourist Gaze*.

53. Urry, *Tourist Gaze*, 128–31, where Urry explores the idea of the "aura" having been replaced by "nostalgia" as being a conditioning response to the artefacts of the past. See also Peter Vergo, ed., *The New Museology* (London: Reaktion Books, 1989), for a classic account of the transformation of museums into visitor attractions.

54. See Raphael Samuel, *Theatres of Memory* (London: Verso, 1994), for a detailed analysis of the pervasiveness of interest in all things old from the heritage site to interior decorating and "retro-chic."

55. Wright, *On Living in an Old Country*, 150.

56. All of this data is recorded in *English Heritage Monitor*, published jointly by English Heritage and English Tourist Council. The material quoted here is from the 1998 edition.

57. Chris Rojek, *Ways of Escape* (London: Routledge, 1993), 161–65, and Lumley, *New Museology*, ch. 4.

58. Peter Fowler, "Heritage: A Post-Modernist Perspective," in David Uzzell, ed., *Heritage Interpretation, Volume 1, The Natural and Built Environment* (London: Belhaven Press, 1989), 57.

59. Jean Baudrillard, *Simulations* (New York: Semiotext, 1983).

60. Umberto Eco, *Travels in Hyper-Reality* (London: Picador, 1986).

61. Frederic Jameson, *Postmodernism or the Cultural Logic of Late Capitalism* (London: Verso), 19.

62. Robert Hewison, "Heritage: an Interpretation," in Uzzell, ed., *Heritage Interpretation*, 22.

63. Wright, *On Living in an Old Country*, 55, 78 and *passim*. See also R. Hewison, *The Heritage Industry*, 141, where a similar point is made, that the production of heritage depends on the idea that "history is over."

64. Walsh, *The Representation of the Past*, 2–3.

65. Samuel, *Theatres of Memory*.

66. Sharon Macdonald, "A People's Story: Heritage, Identity and Authenticity," in Rojek and Urry, *Touring Cultures*, ch. 8.

67. Jim Russell, "Towards a More Inclusive, Vital Model of Heritage: an Australian Perspective," *International Journal of Heritage Studies*, 3/2, 1997: 71–80.

# Notes on Contributors

GERALDINE BARNES teaches in the Department of English at the University of Sydney. She is the author of *Counsel and Strategy in Middle English Romance* (1993) and articles on the development of English romance which have appeared in *Arthurian Literature, Medieval Scandinavia: an Encyclopedia*, and *Arkiv for Nordisk Filologi*. Her most recent book is *Viking America: the First Millennium* (D.S. Brewer, Cambridge, 2001). She is currently investigating the widespread popularity of 1990s crime fiction novels with medieval settings.

BETSY BOWDEN teaches at Rutgers University, Camden. Her books include *Chaucer Aloud* (1987), *Eighteenth Century Modernizations from the Canterbury Tales* (1994), and *Performed Literature: Words and Music by Bob Dylan* (1982, to be reprinted by the University Press of America). She is working currently on presentations of the Wife of Bath in the eighteenth century, and on medieval Latin pedagogy.

ROLF H. BREMMER JR is a senior lecturer at the University of Leiden, where he teaches Old and Middle English. His publications include a *Companion to Old English Poetry*, co-edited with Henk Aertsen (1994), an edited collection on *Aspects of Old Frisian Philology* (1990), and the recent collection *Franciscus Junius F.F. and his Circle* (1998), as well as articles on subjects as diverse as kinship and widowhood. He is currently preparing a handbook of Old Frisian.

JOHN B. FRIEDMAN is Professor Emeritus of English from the University of Illinois, Urbana-Champaign. His books include *Orpheus in the Middle Ages* (1970) and *The Monstrous Races in Medieval Art and Thought* (1981), both about to be reprinted; an edition of *John de Foxton's Liber Cosmographiae* (1988); and *Northern English Books, Owners and Makers in the Late Middle Ages* (1995). He recently co-edited with Kristen Figg the Garland Encyclopedia of *Trade, Travel and Exploration in the Middle Ages* (2000), and is currently working on articles on Chaucer and alchemy, and on a fifteenth-century book of armchair travel.

JUDITH JOHNSTON teaches English at the University of Western Australia. She is the author of *Anna Jameson; Victorian, feminist, woman of letters* (1997), and with Margaret Harris published *The Journals of George*

*Eliot* (1998). She is currently completing a book on Victorian journalism, *Gender Divides*, with her colleagues Hilary Fraser and Stephanie Green. She is also exploring nineteenth-century women's translations with a view to advancing the understanding of the complex role played by British women in the appropriation of varying cultures.

RICHARD UTZ is currently Associate Professor of English at the University of Northern Iowa. He is the author of *Literarischer Nominalismus im Spätmittelalter* (1990), the editor of *Literary Nominalism and the Rereading of Late Medieval Texts* (1995), and co-editor (with H. Keiper and C. Bode) of *Nominalism and Literary Discourse* (1997) and (with Tom Shippey) of *Medievalism in the Modern World* (1998). He also co-edits the journals *Disputatio* and *Prolepsis*. His study on *Chaucer and the Discourse of German Philology* will appear in 2001.

SOPHIE VAN ROMBURGH studied English Language and Literature at Leiden University, where she also taught Old English. She is currently finishing her Ph.D. there, an annotated edition of the correspondence of Franciscus Junius, to be published under the title *For My Worthy Freind*. She now teaches Old and Middle English at Nijmegen University. Her fields of interest include the humanist scholarship of the Germanic languages, etymology, Old English and Anglo-Saxon culture.

STEPHEN WATSON is Principal Lecturer in Tourism Management at the Scarborough campus of the University of Hull. He specialises in the study of heritage and cultural tourism, with an emphasis on the processes by which destinations develop as tourist attractions. His research has dealt recently with the changing nature of local perceptions of touristic space, and has appeared in *International Journal of Heritage Studies*, *The Journal of the English Tourist Council*, and in the collections *Tourism 2000: Reflections on Tourism in the New Millennium* and *European Heritage: Europe at the Crossroads*, both published in 2000.

WERNER WUNDERLICH read German studies, history and political science at the University of Heidelberg, taking his doctorate in 1972, and presenting his *Habilitationsschrift* at the University of Hanover in 1978. He has been Visiting Professor at the University of Wisconsin-Madison and Pennsylvania State University, and since 1986 has been professor of German Language and Literature at the University of St. Gall in Switzerland. He works on medieval German literature, on the history of its reception, and also on media studies and on Mozart.